Great Concepts in Philosophy

Great Concepts in Philosophy

A HISTORICAL INTRODUCTION

First Edition

Edited by Jeremy Proulx

Bassim Hamadeh, CEO and Publisher
Angela Schultz, Acquisitions Editor
Michelle Piehl, Project Editor
Casey Hands, Associate Production Editor
Emely Villavicencio, Senior Graphic Designer
Stephanie Kohl, Licensing Coordinator
Gustavo Youngberg, Interior Designer
Natalie Piccotti, Senior Marketing Manager
Kassie Graves, Vice President of Editorial
Jamie Giganti, Director of Academic Publishing

Contents

What is Philosophy?

T HERE ARE AS many answers to this question as there are philosophers. The question is so general that it is almost impossible to answer it in a way that is both general enough to satisfy all those who call themselves philosophers and substantial enough to be meaningful. To get a sense of what philosophy is, one simply has to read some philosophical texts and struggle with some of the great concepts that philosophers have given us to better understand our world. This textbook is designed to do just that: introduce you to philosophy through a set of classic philosophical texts, thinkers, and concepts. The book is organized historically, and it covers philosophy all the way from the earliest Greek and Chinese thinkers to today.

This historical approach to philosophy has the advantage of providing some deeper context to the philosophers we will read. Philosophers almost always have interesting and insightful arguments to offer, but it is also almost impossible to understand where they are coming from without understanding a little about their historical context, what they are reacting to, the climate in which they are writing, and who and what their influences are. In this way, empathy is an extremely important soft skill in philosophy, one that studying philosophy can help you to cultivate. Why, for instance, does Plato say that all learning is recollection? How does this claim fit into his more general theory of knowledge? How does Plato support this claim? It is easy to be critical and simply discard a claim like this as silly. Learning is recollection? When I learn, I'm really just remembering things I've forgotten? It sounds a little crazy, right? But, it is only once we take the time to empathize with Plato's claim and perform the necessary analysis that we can even begin to ask more critical questions about what Plato is trying to say and whether Plato's argument establishes his conclusion. Through reading and thinking about the texts collected here, I hope that you take the opportunity to develop this important skill of empathy. And, I hope you can arrive at an understanding of what philosophy is by learning a little about what it has been and how it has evolved as a tirelessly vibrant tradition for 2,500 years. So, what is it that characterizes philosophy?

WHAT IS A PHILOSOPHICAL TEXT?

Perhaps the only way to get a sense of what characterizes philosophy is to read philosophical texts. The vocation of the philosopher, after all, consists in writing philosophical arguments in a clear and concise manner and analyzing and articulating ideas. All of this can only be achieved through the written word.

Philosophical texts are generally extended arguments about some basic question. Philosophers of science think about things such as the nature of science, of scientific reasoning, biological processes and relations, etc. Philosophers of economics think about the nature of economies, economic motivation, etc. Moral philosophers think about the nature of the good, of justice, moral motivation, etc. Philosophers of art think about the nature of art and the definition of good and bad art. Some philosophers write about philosophy itself. More generally, philosophers pursue basic questions about the nature of humanity, of knowledge and belief, of human responsibility, what constitutes justice, how meaning in life is generated, and about human existence in general. We are not used to hearing people ask these kinds of questions, so one of the things that makes philosophy challenging, at least at first, is that one needs to get used to thinking about these kinds of basic questions. Once you get past this basic strangeness, reading philosophy is just like reading anything else.

So, understanding a philosophical text means understanding the rather unusual question the philosopher is addressing. For instance, it's a little weird to read Parmenides (see chapter 1) arguing that *being* just is. I mean, what could be more obvious? But, some of this strangeness can be dispelled by seeing that the question Parmenides is addressing is one of how finite human beings can have access to a truth beyond the constant fluctuations of things that our senses reveal to us. It may likewise be rather odd to read Hobbes's notion of the human being as a kind of machine (see chapter 7) until we learn that Hobbes is making these claims in the context of his materialist theory of the universe. It's also very difficult to understand what Nietzsche (chapter 12) is talking about at all until we understand that he is addressing a problem he finds in the basic assumptions about knowledge and truth.

ARGUMENTS IN PHILOSOPHICAL TEXTS

But, even once you get used to the sheer strangeness of philosophy, it can still be an awfully difficult thing to read. I recall from my first year or so of studying philosophy that I felt like I understood absolutely nothing, and I realize now that even though I once felt like I understood things, I actually understood almost nothing. Philosophy can be very difficult to read and very few people learn to read it well, including philosophers themselves. But, it can be made easier by paying attention to the simple fact that a philosophical text is always forwarding some kind of an argument for a position on a certain subject. If you can figure out what a philosopher is arguing for, then you can work backwards to determine what kinds of reasons he or she is offering in support of his or her position.

We tend to understand arguments as confrontational, like when we argue with another person. But this is not how we use the word in philosophy. An argument consists in a set of reasons (premises) offered in support of a particular claim (conclusion). In this sense, we make arguments all the time; arguments are fundamental to our thinking and reasoning in general (e.g., "Someone was driving my car. How do I know? My seat has been moved from its position and I never move my seat, so someone must have been driving my car." This is a set of reasons that supports my claim that someone has been driving my car.)

Arguments can take all sorts of different forms; indeed, it is arguable that there are no strict formal requirements for arguments at all. Arguments can be literary, aesthetic, historical, formal, and mathematical, but no matter the form, philosophy always makes arguments. People new to reading philosophy often miss the fact that an essential part of philosophy is making arguments (good or bad, all philosophers make arguments). Philosophers don't just give their opinions about things. A philosopher certainly has opinions, but he or she is always supported by arguments. A key to reading philosophy is thus to keep track of the argument being offered, the conclusion it's attempting to establish, and the reasons offered for it. So, if you like to argue, this is the place for you!

CONCEPTS IN PHILOSOPHY

Concepts are central to philosophy because they give us a way to understand our reality. A concept in philosophy is almost never unambiguous; that is, important concepts in philosophical texts tend to not be the kinds of things that admit clear definition. This is because philosophical concepts are not perfectly tied to facts. Indeed, there are many cases where our interpretation of facts depends on our concepts. For instance, until Copernicus (1473–1543), everyone took the concept of a geocentric universe (the universe revolves around the Earth) to represent a fact about the universe. After Copernicus (and, later, Galileo), the concept of a heliocentric universe (the universe revolves around the sun) was taken to represent a fact about the structure of the universe. Today, we have carved up the universe into more specific parts and identify the sun as the center of our solar system.

Concepts themselves are not reality; that is, concepts are indispensable for our understanding of the world, but they are themselves not mere reflections of the world, and they are especially not the world itself. In fact, the philosopher Alfred North Whitehead (1861–1947) has a name for the mistake of confusing concepts for reality: the fallacy of misplaced concreteness. But, what philosophical concepts can do is help us to see the world in a completely new way. Mengzi, for instance, as we shall see in chapter 4, invents the notion of the *four beginnings* to help us understand the function of cultivation and ritual in the context of Confucian philosophy and practice. Another example is from chapter 7, where we will see that Hobbes invents the concept of *leviathan* (his word for the state) in order to help us understand the natural origin of political power, the logic of how it develops, and its legitimate domain. Philosophers use complex webs of concepts to help them describe the world.

Indeed, two twentieth-century philosophers Gilles Deleuze (1925–1995) and Felix Guattari (1930–1992) go so far as to define philosophy itself as "the art of forming, inventing, and fabricating concepts."[1] What they mean by this is that philosophy itself is a creative exercise; that is, philosophy is the practice of creating concepts in order to understand the world in new and different ways. Philosophers don't just reflect on human life and culture. And philosophers especially

---

1   Hugh Tomlinson and Graham Burchill, trans., *What Is Philosophy?* (New York: Verso, 1994), 2.

don't ponder the world in some detached way, from up on high in the ivory tower. Philosophers might do their work in the intellectual safety net provided by universities and modern academia, but what they do is invent concepts through which we can understand the world around us. All the works collected in this book develop some new concept or help us to understand an old concept in a new way. So, in addition to following the argument of a philosophical text, paying attention to the concepts a philosopher uses to describe his or her views is one more way that you can strive to understand a philosophical text.

You will notice that this text is organized around highlighting the concepts philosophers invent to help us understand the world. The idea is that understanding a few basic concepts can go a long way to helping you understand a philosopher's complex arguments. As you read, you will notice that the introduction to each chapter contains a list of important concepts. This list is meant to help orient your reading, both of the introductory material and of the primary texts themselves. Even if you are not fully understanding what you are reading, you can go back to the list of important concepts, try to locate them in the text, and then explain them in your own words. Try to do at least this for each chapter we cover in this book and you will be well on your way to understanding the exciting tradition of philosophy.

PART ONE

Philosophy from Antiquity to the Middle Ages

PHILOSOPHY AS WE know it in the West began in Greece during classical antiquity a little over 2,500 years ago. While philosophy in the ancient world is dominated by the period of classical philosophy (470–320 BCE) during which Plato (chapter 2) and Aristotle (chapter 3) were writing, classical antiquity ran for about one thousand years, from around 600 BCE until about 400 CE and embraced a wide range of schools of thought from the earliest pre-Socratic philosophers all the way to stoicism, epicureanism, and ancient skepticism. Other nonwestern philosophical traditions were also active at this time. In Chinese intellectual history, Confucius (551–479 BCE) lived during the spring and autumn period, corresponding to the Western 771–476 BCE. In Part 1 of this text, we will explore the work of eight ancient philosophers: Parmenides and Zeno, Socrates and Plato, Aristotle, Mengzi and Xunzi, and Epictetus. We will also explore some philosophy from the Middle Ages in order to get a sense of how philosophy developed under the influence of Christianity. In this Introduction, I will attempt to provide some historical context for philosophy as it emerged as a unique intellectual discipline in the West.

MYTH AND PHILOSOPHY

Ancient philosophy began in a cultural context in which myth played a central role in structuring the view of the world, of man, and of our moral obligations. Today, we might look back on ancient myths and regard them as naïve since the view of the world it portrays is nonscientific and noncritical. Mythical thought does not seem concerned with truth, opting instead for a fantastical view in which gods rule over the natural world. Hesiod is one of the earliest poets we know of. It is likely that whoever Hesiod was, the poems collected under that name were recordings of poems and stories that were passed around through an oral tradition of storytelling. Here is a passage from Hesiod's *Theogony*:

> First came the Chasm; and then broad-breasted Earth, secure seat for
> ever of all the immortals who occupy the peak of snowy Olympus; the
> misty Tartara in a remote recess of the broad-pathed earth; and Eros, the
> most handsome among the immortal Gods, dissolver of flesh, who over-
> comes the reason and purpose in the breasts of all Gods and men.[1]

Here, the basic forces of the universe are identified with personified gods. Eros is a handsome person; the gods all live on a snowy mountain peak. The gods for the ancients are very much of *this world*. But notice how the gods are understood as basic concepts and how we are given a conceptual framework for understanding the origin of the world. Earth comes from a *chasm*; eros (*love, sex, passion*) is basic and fundamental and can overcome *reason*. Again, from our own twenty-first-century context we might be tempted to dismiss this account of the natural world—it's storytelling, *not* science, and it thus offers us no reason to accept its account of things.

Now, it is of course true that mythical thinking does not attempt to provide arguments for its claims. Mythmakers employ intuitive, imaginative faculties in addressing the problems of how to understand the world and the human place within it. Mythmakers are, in this way, not at all concerned with truth in the way we generally understand it as some kind of correspondence between what we think about things and the ways things actually are. Indeed, mythmakers create entire worlds of meaning and significance without worrying one bit about truth. But, this does not mean that mythical thinking is without value, especially from a historical perspective. And myth should not be faulted for not caring about truth. Just because something is not true, does not mean that it is without value. Isaac Asimov's famous *Foundation Series*, a classic work of science fiction, is a complete fabrication, but it is widely regarded as one of the deepest and most significant texts of its genre, and I would defy anyone to dismiss the relevance of just about any great work of literature for anyone who wants to understand a little more about humanity and the human condition.

The very first philosophers, people such as Thales, Anaximander, and Anaximenes, did not provide arguments, just more or less compelling stories, and we still call them philosophers. In this way, it's hard to dismiss myth as naïve storytelling. They were indeed telling stories, but they were doing so in such a way as to better understand their world. There is a rational content to myth in so far as it goes beyond sense experience and mere imagery to speculate about the origin of the world. Myth offers us a picture of the cosmos and of the origin of the universe—it offers us a view of the place of Heaven, of Earth, of the gods and of humankind.

---

1   Hesiod, *Theogony*, trans. M. L. West. (Oxford: Oxford University Press 1988) 6.

THE EARLIEST PHILOSOPHERS

In the West, philosophy proper is generally thought to begin with the *Milesians*, philosophers living in an area called Miletus. No longer are their efforts merely mythical, symbolic, or imaginative; rather, they pursue a rational-critical investigation of the natural world. Miletus was in what is modern Turkey, which meant that philosophers there where uniquely located to take advantage of knowledge from the East. Thales, the first Greek philosopher, is said to have introduced geometry to Greece after learning the methods on a trip through Egypt. Another early Greek philosopher, Anaximander, employed Babylonian methods to construct a sundial. Coupled with these imported empirical methods, the Milesian philosophers began the philosophic-scientific task of constructing a rational system of the universe.

The first philosopher, Thales, earns this title generally because he employed empirical methods of investigation to come to a reasoned conclusion about how nature as a whole functions, of how change, growth, development and decay are possible. Thales is known today for his idea that water is the most basic element of life. From a purely empirical perspective, it's not hard to see where Thales is coming from. He lived, after all, in Miletus, a city on an island off the Western Coast of modern-day Turkey, in the Aegean Sea. Thales was surrounded by water. And, if you think about it for a moment, it's not hard to see how one could reach the conclusion that water is fundamental everywhere. Dig down far enough and you'll hit the water table. Snap the branch of a plant and water oozes out. Water falls from the sky and all land is surrounded by it. We can live much longer without food than we can without water. So, while Thales's ideas might seems strange to us now, his thinking was not just fanciful speculation.

One of the reasons why these early thinkers are called philosophers is that they were searching for answers to questions about single principles, universal pattern's, etc. From what we have, it's impossible to tell whether Thales dealt with this problem. But, another philosopher, Anaximander, proposed a highly complex solution.

Anaximander thought that the whole universe could be explained by something he called the *apeiron*, a kind of unifying principle that contains all the basic constituents of matter and the principles of physical process. This early philosophical concept allowed Anaximander to think about the *aperion* as a boundless mass of matter; it's vital, alive with boundless energy, and pulsating with an eternal motion. Within this basic mass of matter is the primal opposition of hot and cold, revolving in eternal motion. The cold condensed into the center of the earth; the hot expanded out into the periphery and became fire, becoming circles of fire around the earth, the stars, moon, and sun. In this way, the primal opposition develops into the plurality of nature, or into all the different things we see in the world around us.

Again, this might seem a little silly to us today. Indeed, the idea that Earth has a cold, condensed center is completely false. But, just because it turned out to be false does not mean that it was a bad idea, and we have to remember that the Milesians were not working with any complex instrumentation or history of scientific knowledge. Indeed, any high school science student knows vastly more about the world than the Milesians ever did. If we put ourselves in Anaximander's shoes, we can perhaps understand what he had in mind—cold things freeze and congeal together; hot things boil, burn, and scatter around. In this way, we can see that just by carefully observing the world (without all the instrumentation we have today) Anaximander could have come up with such things. And, in fact, without a concept like *aperion*, abstract thinking about such things is not even possible. So, silly as it might seem to us, Anaximander's thinking is one of the earliest steps toward exploring the world with conceptual paradigms that go beyond what we can see to invent explanations about how the world around us is possible.

The *apeiron* is the alpha and omega of all things; everything comes from and everything returns to it. The whole universe is a precarious balance of opposites in perpetual strife—hot destroys cold; cold destroys hot. Anaximander calls the balance that obtains in the universe justice. There must always be an equality in what each opposite takes from the whole—and imbalance in this distribution is an injustice. For Anaximander, finding the ultimate balance is not possible in the present world. Ultimate balance—ultimate justice—is only possible in the final return to the *apeiron*.

This is another idea we will see repeated in Plato. Perfect justice, perfect balance, perfect beauty, perfect knowledge, indeed perfection in general is not possible in the present world. This is the purpose of philosophy; namely, to help us see past the imperfection of the world around us to another world that is in fact perfect, the world of Ideas—Plato's answer to Anaximander's *aperion*.

In another section of this part of the text, we will explore how two classical Chinese philosophers interrogate this tension between human intellectual effort (philosophy) and what is given by nature. Two Confucian thinkers, Mengzi and Xunzi, both agree with Plato that the path to improving human life consists in engaging in a practice of intellectual and moral discipline. Plato and others in the West called this practice philosophy while Mengzi and Xunzi thought of it as ritual practice. The debate between Mengzi and Xunzi amounts to a basic disagreement about just what it is that ritual practice achieves. Mengzi thinks that it helps to develop the naturally good tendencies of humanity, while Xunzi thinks that it steers people away from their natural tendency to choose bad actions over good. In both cases, however, ritual practice is meant to help us promote harmony and balance (compare Anaximander and the notion of justice) in human relations and in ourselves.

CHAPTER 1

The Eleatics, Parmenides, and Zeno

P ARMENIDES AND ZENO are important members of the so-called "Eleatic school" of early Greek philosophy. This school originated in the city of Elea sometime during the fifth century BCE. Very little is known of this school, and no complete original texts survive. We rely on the accounts of various philosophers and historians for their transmission of the original texts.

Parmenides and Zeno are pre-Socratic philosophers, a term used to name philosophers living and working before Socrates. Just the fact that philosophers before Socrates are referred to as pre-Socratic should give you some idea of just how influential Socrates was for the development of philosophy as we know it today. Nevertheless, the style of argument, and indeed the very idea of using reason and logic to learn the truth about the world, is something that remains influential today and that Parmenides and Zeno were pivotal in developing.

Important Concepts: Argument; BEING.

PARMENIDES

Parmenides is famous for having authored a large-scale metaphysical poem in hexameter verse. This style of poetry was the standard medium for epic poetry during classical antiquity. You might be familiar with this from classics of Greek literature such as the *Iliad* and the *Odyssey,* both well-known epic poems that document the Trojan War and the voyage home after the war of one of its great heroes, Odysseus. Parmenides's epic poem, partially excerpted in this chapter, uses this classical artistic medium to do something that had not really been done before. While poems such as the *Odyssey* unfold a narrative, Parmenides uses poetry to make a philosophical argument. This is one of the central developments of ancient philosophy. And, notice the role that *the concept of an argument* plays. Without the explicit idea that the purpose of a text is to not to tell a story, but rather to make an argument, something like Parmenides's use of the style of hexameter verse would not have even been conceivable. People, of course, made arguments before Parmenides, but when Parmenides isolates the concept of an argument and puts poetry to work for the purpose of making an argument, he does something totally new: From within the stylistic constraints of his time, Parmenides invents logic and deductive reasoning. For this reason alone, Parmenides has an important place in intellectual history, especially in the history of philosophy. Nothing is more important to philosophers than logic and reason.

In the earliest developments of philosophical thought, logic and reason were seen as a kind of spiritual discipline, a way to save us from the habits of our worldly existence. Logic is, in this way, seen as a tool for bringing our minds back from illusion to reality. For Parmenides, the illusion is the common sense, habitual way in which we regard the world as changing, as moving along from one state to another. Our senses tell us that the world is constantly changing: Open your eyes and you see things moving around, changing shape and place; listen and you hear audible fluctuations in things; even biting into an apple reveals a complex and changing parade of flavor as the fruit rolls around different parts of your tongue, and your sense of smell picks up the fragrance of the juice. But, all this variation and change is, according to Parmenides, nothing but the story we get from our senses, so it is not really that this is an illusion; rather, it is that our senses can only give us so much, and they can certainly not lead us to truth. The truth—that *BEING is* and that BEING is just a single thing that never changes, that BEING, in short, is absolutely One—is the truth that we need philosophical argumentation to be able to adequately understand. So, how does Parmenides use philosophy and *argument* to develop his concept of BEING?

In the passage that follows, Parmenides constructs a complex derivation to develop his claim that existence simply exists, that what is does not come into being or cease to exist. A derivation is a form of deductive reasoning; it's a kind of argument. Recall the concept of argument. A derivation is a form of argument that proceeds systematically from premises (statements or claims) to derive a conclusion that is entailed by (follows from) those premises. A simple argument such as, "John reads philosophy and all people who read philosophy are good company, so John is good company" is a simple derivation of the conclusion "John is good company" from the premises "John reads philosophy" and "all people who read philosophy are good company." So long as the premises are true, the conclusion must be true because it is logically entailed by the premises.

Parmenides's derivation is, of course, much more complex, but the basic form is the same. In the first part of fragment 8, for instance, he argues in the following way:

1. To speak of something coming into existence or passing away is to speak of a time when that thing did not exist since.
2. We can neither talk about nor think about what does not exist.
3. Therefore, nothing comes into existence and nothing passes away.
4. Therefore, existence is; it is now, "all at once, a continuous one."

The claim here is not that things do not come into existence and pass away; that is, the claim is not that there is no change. Rather, the claim is that when we speak and think about things, we are thinking about things *as existing*. We cannot think and speak about things that do not exist. We can of course *speculate* about such things, but this is just imagination—we imagine our lives being different than they are; we imagine something existing and some other thing not existing. These things do not exist. Parmenides's claim, then, is just this: BEING IS—we cannot think of being (what exists) in any other way. This idea of *BEING is another important concept Parmenides gives to philosophy*. The concept is useful because it helps us to focus on what actually exists and to distinguish that from speculative fancy.

Notice that while the conclusion "nothing comes into existence and nothing passes away" is a controversial one, the supporting premises are not so difficult to swallow. Of course, it is the case that once we start talking about something coming into existence, we are committed to speaking about a time when that thing did not exist. If I say that I built a deck, then I am committed to the claim that the deck to which I am referring was not there before. But, in speaking and thinking this way, I am not really thinking of something that does not exist; rather, I am thinking of a time when a thing that does exist (a deck) did not exist at all. Even children get this when they ask about where they were before they were born. There is no real way to answer the child's question in a rigorously true manner. I told my three-year old son that he was in our hearts before he was born, which my son interpreted literally and then asked whether there was a slide from Mommy's heart to her tummy. This adorable image is a nice bit of poetry, but the fact that we only have recourse to the poetic imagination in such cases is evidence that we cannot speak clearly and distinctly about what does not exist. And again, notice that in this example of a child imagining a time when he did not exist, we are not speaking about what does not exist; that is, we are speaking about an existing thing and imagining a time when it did not exist. Before it existed, we could not speak of it at all. We can imagine and speak about a time *before* we existed and about a time *after* we exist, but we cannot even speak about *our own* non-existence since there is nothing to speak about. Existence simply *is* and we can only speak about what exists. Let us turn to the text.

Fragments of Parmenides

Parmenides

Fragments 2 and 3

Come now, I will tell thee—and do thou hearken to my saying and carry it away—
the only two ways of search that can be thought of.
The first, namely, that It is, and that it is impossible for it not to be,
is the way of belief, for truth is its companion.
The other, namely, that It is not, and that it must needs not be,—
that, I tell thee, is a path that none can learn of at all.
For thou canst not know what is not—that is impossible—
nor utter it; ...

... for it is the same thing that can be thought and that can be.[4]

Parmenides, Selections from *Fragments of Parmenides*, trans. John Burnet, 1920.

Fragment 8

... One path only
is left for us to speak of, namely, that It is. In this path are very many tokens
that what is is uncreated and indestructible;
for it is complete,[9] immovable, and without end.
Nor was it ever, nor will it be; for now it is, all at once,
a continuous one. For what kind of origin for it wilt thou look for?
In what way and from what source could it have drawn its increase? I shall not let thee say nor think
that it came from what is not; for it can neither be thought nor uttered
that anything is not. And, if it came from nothing, what need
could have made it arise later rather than sooner?
Therefore must it either be altogether or be not at all.
Nor will the force of truth suffer aught to arise
besides itself from that which is not. Wherefore,
justice doth not loose her fetters and let anything come into being or pass away,
but holds it fast. Our judgment thereon depends on this:
"Is it or is it not?" Surely it is adjudged, as it needs must be,
that we are to set aside the one way as unthinkable and nameless (for it is no true way),
and that the other path is real and true.
How, then, can what is be going to be in the future? Or how could it come into being?
If it came into being, it is not; nor is it if it is going to be in the future.
Thus is becoming extinguished and passing away not to be heard of.

Nor is it divisible, since it is all alike,
and there is no more[10] of it in one place than in another, to hinder it from holding together,
nor less of it, but everything is full of what is.
Wherefore it is wholly continuous; for what is, is in contact with what is.

Moreover, it is immovable in the bonds of mighty chains,
without beginning and without end; since coming into being and passing away
have been driven afar, and true belief has cast them away.
It is the same, and it rests in the self-same place, abiding in itself.
And thus it remaineth constant in its place; for hard necessity
keeps it in the bonds of the limit that holds it fast on every side.
Wherefore it is not permitted to what is to be infinite;

for it is in need of nothing; while, if it were infinite, it would stand in need of everything.

The thing that can be thought and that for the sake of which the thought exists is the same;
for you cannot find thought without something that is, as to which it is uttered.

And there is not, and never shall be,
anything besides what is, since fate has chained it
so as to be whole and immovable. Wherefore all these things are but names
which mortals have given, believing them to be true—
coming into being and passing away, being and not being,
change of place and alteration of bright colour.

Since, then, it has a furthest limit, it is complete
on every side, like the mass of a rounded sphere,
equally poised from the centre in every direction; for it cannot be greater
or smaller in one place than in another.
For there is no nothing that could keep it from reaching
out equally, nor can aught that is be
more here and less there than what is, since it is all inviolable.
For the point from which it is equal in every direction tends equally to the limits.

ZENO

It is often assumed that Zeno was a student of Parmenides, but the truth is that we don't know much about either figure. What we do know is that Zeno provided some ingenious arguments that challenge views contrary to Parmenides's view that all that exists is One. In support of Parmenides, Zeno offers the following argument:

> *If there are many, they must be just as many as they are, neither more nor less. But if they are as many as they are, they must be limited. If there are many things, the things that are are unlimited, since between things that are there are always others, and still others between those. Therefore the things that are are unlimited. (Simplicius, Commentary on Aristotle's Physics 140.29–33)*[1]

Zeno here employs a form of argument called *reductio ad absurdum* to show that the view that many things exist is directly contradictory. The form of Zeno's argument looks like this:

1.   Suppose there are many things.

---

1   Cited in S. Marc Cohen, Patricia Curd, and C. D. C. Reeve, eds., *Readings in Ancient Greek Philosophy*, fourth edition. (Indianapolis: Hackett, 2011), p. 49.

2. If this supposition is correct, then there must be exactly as many things as there are; that is, there must be some definite number of things.
3. Therefore, things are limited.
4. If there are many things, there are always more things between things, and then more things between those, etc. In other words, there are always more things to discover, wherever we look.
5. Therefore, things are unlimited.
6. But, (3) and (5) are contradictory.
7. Therefore, the supposition in (1) is false.

Many of Zeno's arguments share this basic *reduction* format of showing that a particular view must be false since it leads to absurdity. In this case, Zeno assumes that there is a multiplicity of things and then goes on to derive a contradiction from this assumption. What this shows is that existence is not divisible, that, in support of Parmenides, there are not many things, but rather only One. We shall see another famous version of a *reductio* argument in chapter 8 when we look at St. Anselm's *ontological argument* for God's existence.

Parmenides and Zeno mark the very beginning of the study of logic and reasoning. This focus on careful argumentation and on providing good reasons for one's beliefs continues with Socrates and Plato, and it is something that characterizes philosophical inquiry in general, wherever and whenever in history we find it.

CHAPTER 2

Socrates and Plato

I F YOU'VE HEARD of any philosopher at all, you've probably heard of Plato (427–347 BCE). He is (still today) one of the most widely read and well-known philosophers of all time. He is also, as I hope you will come to appreciate, a remarkable stylist and beautiful writer. His philosophical works are structured as dialogues between two or more people, an approach which not only makes for great philosophy, but also for exciting reading. In Plato's dialogues, we don't just read abstract arguments; we witness philosophy itself in practice. The English word "philosophy" comes from a compound of two Greek words *philia* (friendship or love) and *sophia* (wisdom), so "philosophy" quite literally means "love of wisdom." Plato is responsible for having defined this *concept of philosophy itself: The philosopher is a lover or a friend of wisdom; to do philosophy is to pursue wisdom and knowledge in a loving, amicable, and respectful way.* Plato's dialogues give us a picture of his view of what it means to do philosophy and to be a philosopher; it's a view that has been and continues to be highly influential for philosophy as an intellectual discipline, and it's a view that continues to inform our own views about the ideal of intellectual and scientific inquiry.

Important Concepts: Philosophy; rationalism; Socratic irony; Sophist; justice.

SOCRATES AND HIS SIGNIFICANCE FOR PHILOSOPHY

In the last chapter, we saw that Parmenides and Zeno developed one of the core methods of philosophy (logic and deductive reasoning) from within the stylistic constraints of the medium of hexameter verse. This was a major step in the development of Western philosophy out of its mythic and narrative origins. Socrates represents another major step.

As we learned in the introduction to this section on philosophy in classical antiquity, most philosophers before Plato were engaged in something that we today might call "natural science." These philosophers (such as Anaximander) were interested in explaining the world around them, in particular with the problem of how change and development in the natural world can be explained. This approach to philosophy as a kind of natural science did not disappear with Socrates and Plato, but under their influence, philosophy took on a distinctly different flavor.

Socrates (469–399 BCE) was Plato's teacher, or at least his intellectual inspiration. We don't know a whole lot about Socrates since he did not leave behind any writing. Indeed, we're not even sure if he was a real person. But, Plato writes an awful lot about him, and we see him appear in several other Ancient sources. The character, real or not, is always the same: He's praised for being wise, almost transcendent in his wisdom. But, as Plato points out, he also claimed to know nothing at all.

It's not important whether or not he lived. What's more important is why this odd historical figure is credited with being the father of philosophy as we understand it today. He represents a transition from the first ancient Greek philosophers to classical Greek philosophy. As we've seen, he's so influential that philosophy before Socrates is referred to as pre-Socratic philosophy.

So, what does Socrates do differently? Socrates thought that philosophy was not just a tool for analyzing and understanding the world, but also for making a difference in the world. With Socrates, the West was introduced to the idea that philosophy is not just about exploring what is, but rather about making the world a better place. *This is part of what the very concept of philosophy implies: Loving wisdom, just like loving another person, means accepting it into your life and allowing it to change you for the better.* Many philosophers, including myself, still take themselves to be involved in this kind of a task, but this is not just an idea peculiar to philosophy. So pervasive is this equation of wisdom and knowledge with the good life that it's still difficult for us think differently. Would you be in a university if you didn't think that the knowledge you will obtain will somehow make your life better? Would our society in general place such an emphasis on education in the absence of the assumption that knowledge can make a difference in society and in individual life? Learning about Socrates and the whole tradition of philosophy that begins with him is important, then, not just for learning about philosophy; it's also important for learning about one of the most basic assumptions of the West, and of the modern world in general, the assumption that learning can make our lives better.

According to Plato, Socrates claimed that he was called to philosophy by the Delphic Oracle. The Delphic Oracle was the most revered place in the ancient world. People would have traveled from thousands of miles around to visit the oracle. As the story goes, a friend of Socrates visited the oracle and asked it who was the wisest. The oracle responded that is was Socrates.

Over the entrance to the oracle were inscribed the words "know yourself." As if to say that we must all be prepared to pursue and accept the truth the oracle offers, "know yourself" is a kind of invitation to philosophy. Know yourself: Be prepared to accept the truth about yourself, the truth that what you think you know might be an illusion, the truth about human knowledge, the human situation, and the purposes of human life. The oracle at Delphi bids you to take a good honest look at yourself, consider who you are, what makes you into who you are, and where your ideas come from in the first place. This is the call to philosophy; it's the call to knowledge, the call examine yourself and the origin of your ideas.

The oracle's proclamation that Socrates was the wisest person took him by surprise. Socrates always claimed to have no knowledge at all. Socrates's gift—what Socrates knew—is that we simple, embodied, finite human creatures can never really "know" anything at all. Our senses are only equipped to furnish us with appearances—things appear a certain way to our senses. True knowledge, however, as Plato teaches us, is eternal. And we are finite. This means that since philosophy is a call to knowledge and true knowledge is beyond our capacities as finite beings, philosophy is a never-ending task that will always leave us—as long as we are alive—in search of greater knowledge. The only hope we have is to use our minds to help us see past the limitations of our senses.

For this reason, Plato is referred to in the history of philosophy as a rationalist. Rationalism is the idea that when it comes to knowledge, there are certain things that the mind must contribute, that cannot be apprehended by the senses. Plato thinks that our senses, our bodies, all the finite parts of us that make us human, are an impediment to knowledge. To really know the truth of something, we can't just look; rather, we need to reason our way to truth; we need, that is, to use the human power of reason to see truth with our minds.

And this is precisely why Socrates is the wisest—he's the only one who knows that he knows nothing, who knows the limits of human knowledge, and who knows that the only way to truth is to question what is apparent. Socrates knows that he knows nothing; that is, he knows that he is a finite human creature with limited knowledge who nevertheless seeks an eternal, everlasting truth.

Does this sound ironic? It should. It is. There's even a name for it: *Socratic irony*. In the reading that follows, we will see the way in which Socrates probes his interlocutor for knowledge about a particular subject—in this case, Socrates probes Thrasymachus for knowledge about the nature of justice. Socrates does this everywhere, in all of Plato's dialogues; it's the *Socratic method*, the practice of asking questions, engaging in dialogue, and attempting to ferret out the truth about something. We will also see that Socrates and his interlocutor never arrive at any final truth. What justice is remains an open question. Socrates seems to know that this will be the result of his questioning. *Socratic irony means that Socrates treats his interlocutors as if they have knowledge when he knows full well they don't.* You'll notice that they never arrive at a final definition of justice, something Socrates seems to know would happen. *Socratic irony also means that Socrates disparages his own wisdom (insisting he knows nothing at all) and in the process displays his wisdom, the wisdom that he knows nothing, that none of us know anything, and that knowledge in the universal sense is not easy to come by, but is, nevertheless, something we must spend our lives striving for.*

The reading that follows is a selection from Plato's most well-known philosophical work, the *Republic.* In it, Plato meticulously develops a series of arguments defending a version of an ideal society. In this text, we are introduced to the idea of a philosopher king, a person who undergoes extensive academic training in his youth and then takes up various roles in society before being qualified to rule. The *Republic* is a highly stratified society in which people are organized to perform various social functions. Anything that does not serve the interests of social harmony is eliminated from Plato's ideal society. Even poets and artists are banned from the *Republic* since they don't serve the interests of truth and so can be dangerously influential on public attitudes.

Plato's Disagreement with Thrasymachus the Sophist

It is easy to pass judgment on Plato's rather extreme views about how a society should be structured. From our perspective, Plato seems to disregard the importance of modern values such as democracy, individual rights, self-expression, and personal freedom, but we should bear in mind that Plato was concerned with the problem of finding some common principles that would be true and beneficial for everyone. Extreme as it may sound to us today, Plato's dismissal of poets and artists from the *Republic* has its motivation in a desire to make every member of society accountable to the truth. Plato is thus not far from concerns we have today about what has been called our "post-truth" world. When we stop holding people accountable to the truth, we begin to lose sight of the basic value of reason and its role in social and political discourse. The importance of truth to Plato's vision of philosophy is central to his disagreement with *the sophists*.

The sophists were a group of teachers who sold their services to politicians and others interested in making compelling arguments and speeches. The major sophists (Protagoras, Gorgias, Prodicus, Hippias Antiphon, Thrasymachus) were famous, drawing large crowds and collecting large sums of money for their services. While there is considerable scholarly debate about just what the views of the sophists were, it is pretty clear that they were not concerned with truth in the same way that Plato (and Socrates) were. Antiphon for instance, claims that justice is simply a matter of obeying the laws of the city in which one is a citizen.[1] There's nothing deeper than this. And when it comes to carrying out justice, "[v]ictory," says Antiphon, "comes through speech."[2] This seems a little arbitrary, but it makes more sense when we consider how the ancient Greek legal system functioned. Courts of law depended heavily on the ability of the respective litigants to present their cases in a clear and compelling manner, and juries were massive, consisting of hundreds, even thousands of people, and they wielded vast power since they made final decisions. In the classical Greek world, it was very much the case that "victory comes through speech," that whoever makes the best speech wins. Plato thinks this is dangerous not because he thinks that rhetoric has no place in justice, but because it seems to throw out any notion of more universal principles of justice to which all people can be held, regardless of their ability to present their case in a more or less compelling way.

Thrasymachus's definition of justice (highlighted in the reading that follows) is a classic example of sophistry, a classic statement of the kind of thing Plato fears so much in the sophists. Thrasymachus argues that justice is the interest of the stronger. Never mind truth; justice is just what the strongest person says it is. In this sense—and Thrasymachus seems to recognize this—the definition is more of a critique of the whole notion of justice. If justice is just the interest of the most powerful members of society, of society's rulers, then what does justice really mean?

The preceding is precisely Socrates's question. Isn't what Thrasymachus says just a travesty of justice? Socrates thus focuses his efforts on revealing the inconsistency in Thrasymachus's view. Socrates first proceeds to show that justice cannot possibly be the interest of the stronger since rulers, like all people, can be mistaken about their interests; a ruler might, that is, create laws that turn out to be not in his interest. In this way, justice is both what is of interest to the stronger and what is not of interest, a clear contradiction. Socrates does not stop there.

---

1   As cited in S. Marc Cohen, Patricia Curd, and C. D. C. Reeve, eds., *Readings in Ancient Greek Philosophy*, fourth edition Indianapolis: Hackett, 2011), p. 114.

2   Ibid., p. 115.

If justice is the interest of the ruler, we would expect the ruler to be concerned with his own interests, but is this really the case for a just ruler? As an analogy, Socrates asks us to consider different kinds of craft. Horsemanship, for instance, is interested in horses, and healing considers the interests of the body, of the patient. All crafts consider the interests of their respective subjects, and so a ruler, by definition, considers the interests of his subjects, the weaker. Justice, then, turns out to be the interest of the weaker.

One might quite fairly ask whether this effectively captures what Thrasymachus is saying. I mean, is he really suggesting that justice is merely the whim of a ruler? Or is it rather that Thrasymachus is simply pointing out that since rulers get to make the rules, justice is relative to the system established by the ruler. From the perspective of a sophist who thinks that justice reaches no further than following the established laws of the state, there is nothing particularly controversial about this idea, but Plato is doing something highly innovative. At the time, justice was considered in very simple terms of reward and punishment. But, if justice is just about rewarding the righteous and punishing the wicked, then leading a just life is all about gaining as much reward as possible.

And that, many would probably agree, is a somewhat hollow account of justice. Surely, justice is about more than merely gaining reward for oneself. In the remainder of the dialogue, Socrates and Thrasymachus debate whether justice or injustice is more advantageous. Thrasymachus argues that it is normally better to be unjust, while Socrates argues that justice is always, in the end, the path that leads to greater reward. This dialogue is thus a fascinating exchange about something that we all face in our own lives. To what degree does following the rules and living a generally just life guarantee that one will be rewarded? I suspect that different people will answer this question quite differently depending on their own personal context. Think about how you would answer it.

The Republic

BOOK I

Plato

SOCRATES—GLAUCON

I WENT down yesterday to the Piraeus with Glaucon the son of Ariston, that I might offer up my prayers to the goddess; and also because I wanted to see in what manner they would celebrate the festival, which was a new thing. I was delighted with the procession of the inhabitants; but that of the Thracians was equally, if not more, beautiful. When we had finished our prayers and viewed the spectacle, we turned in the direction of the city; and at that instant Polemarchus the son of Cephalus chanced to catch sight of us from a distance as we were starting on our way

Plato, from *The Republic*, trans. Benjamin Jowett, 1888.

home, and told his servant to run and bid us wait for him. The servant took hold of me by the cloak behind, and said: Polemarchus desires you to wait.

I turned round, and asked him where his master was.

There he is, said the youth, coming after you, if you will only wait.

Certainly we will, said Glaucon; and in a few minutes Polemarchus appeared, and with him Adeimantus, Glaucon's brother, Niceratus the son of Nicias, and several others who had been at the procession.

SOCRATES - POLEMARCHUS - GLAUCON - ADEIMANTUS

Polemarchus said to me: I perceive, Socrates, that you and our companion are already on your way to the city.

You are not far wrong, I said.

But do you see, he rejoined, how many we are?

Of course.

And are you stronger than all these? for if not, you will have to remain where you are.

May there not be the alternative, I said, that we may persuade you to let us go?

But can you persuade us, if we refuse to listen to you? he said.

Certainly not, replied Glaucon.

Then we are not going to listen; of that you may be assured.

Adeimantus added: Has no one told you of the torch-race on horseback in honour of the goddess which will take place in the evening?

With horses! I replied: That is a novelty. Will horsemen carry torches and pass them one to another during the race?

Yes, said Polemarchus, and not only so, but a festival will he celebrated at night, which you certainly ought to see. Let us rise soon after supper and see this festival; there will be a gathering of young men, and we will have a good talk. Stay then, and do not be perverse.

Glaucon said: I suppose, since you insist, that we must.

Very good, I replied.

GLAUCON - CEPHALUS – SOCRATES

Accordingly we went with Polemarchus to his house; and there we found his brothers Lysias and Euthydemus, and with them Thrasymachus the Chalcedonian, Charmantides the Paeanian, and Cleitophon the son of Aristonymus. There too was Cephalus the father of Polemarchus, whom I had not seen for a long time, and I thought him very much aged. He was seated on a cushioned chair, and had a garland on his head, for he had been sacrificing in the court; and there were some other chairs in the room arranged in a semicircle, upon which we sat down by him. He saluted me eagerly, and then he said:—

You don't come to see me, Socrates, as often as you ought: If I were still able to go and see you I would not ask you to come to me. But at my age I can hardly get to the city, and therefore you should come oftener to the Piraeus. For let me tell you, that the more the pleasures of the body fade away, the greater to me is the pleasure and charm of conversation. Do not then deny my request, but make our house your resort and keep company with these young men; we are old friends, and you will be quite at home with us.

I replied: There is nothing which for my part I like better, Cephalus, than conversing with aged men; for I regard them as travellers who have gone a journey which I too may have to go, and of whom I ought to enquire, whether the way is smooth and easy, or rugged and difficult. And this is a question which I should like to ask of you who have arrived at that time which the poets call the 'threshold of old age'—Is life harder towards the end, or what report do you give of it?

I will tell you, Socrates, he said, what my own feeling is. Men of my age flock together; we are birds of a feather, as the old proverb says; and at our meetings the tale of my acquaintance commonly is—I cannot eat, I cannot drink; the pleasures of youth and love are fled away: there was a good time once, but now that is gone, and life is no longer life. Some complain of the slights which are put upon them by relations, and they will tell you sadly of how many evils their old age is the cause. But to me, Socrates, these complainers seem to blame that which is not really in fault. For if old age were the cause, I too being old, and every other old man, would have felt as they do. But this is not my own experience, nor that of others whom I have known. How well I remember the aged poet Sophocles, when in answer to the question, How does love suit with age, Sophocles,—are you still the man you were? Peace, he replied; most gladly have I escaped the thing of which you speak; I feel as if I had escaped from a mad and furious master. His words have often occurred to my mind since, and they seem as good to me now as at the time when he uttered them. For certainly old age has a great sense of calm and freedom; when the passions relax their hold, then, as Sophocles says, we are freed from the grasp not of one mad master only, but of many. The truth is, Socrates, that these regrets, and also the complaints about relations, are to be attributed to the same cause, which is not old age, but men's characters and tempers; for he who is of a calm and happy nature will hardly feel the pressure of age, but to him who is of an opposite disposition youth and age are equally a burden.

I listened in admiration, and wanting to draw him out, that he might go on—Yes, Cephalus, I said: but I rather suspect that people in general are not convinced by you when you speak thus; they think that old age sits lightly upon you, not because of your happy disposition, but because you are rich, and wealth is well known to be a great comforter.

You are right, he replied; they are not convinced: and there is something in what they say; not, however, so much as they imagine. I might answer them as Themistocles answered the Seriphian who was abusing him and saying that he was famous, not for his own merits but because he was an Athenian: 'If you had been a native of my country or I of yours, neither of us would have been famous.' And to those who are not rich and are impatient of old age, the same reply may be made; for to the good poor man old age cannot be a light burden, nor can a bad rich man ever have peace with himself.

May I ask, Cephalus, whether your fortune was for the most part inherited or acquired by you?

Acquired! Socrates; do you want to know how much I acquired? In the art of making money I have been midway between my father and grandfather: for my grandfather, whose name I bear, doubled and trebled the value of his patrimony, that which he inherited being much what I possess now; but my father Lysanias reduced the property below what it is at present: and I shall be satisfied if I leave to these my sons not less but a little more than I received.

That was why I asked you the question, I replied, because I see that you are indifferent about money, which is a characteristic rather of those who have inherited their fortunes than of those who have acquired them; the makers of fortunes have a second love of money as a creation of their own, resembling the affection of authors for their own poems, or of parents for their children, besides that natural love of it for the sake of use and profit which is common to them and all men. And hence they are very bad company, for they can talk about nothing but the praises of wealth. That is true, he said.

Yes, that is very true, but may I ask another question? What do you consider to be the greatest blessing which you have reaped from your wealth?

One, he said, of which I could not expect easily to convince others. For let me tell you, Socrates, that when a man thinks himself to be near death, fears and cares enter into his mind which he never had before; the tales of a world below and the punishment which is exacted there of deeds done here were once a laughing matter to him, but now he is tormented with the thought that they may be true: either from the weakness of age, or because he is now drawing nearer to that other place, he has a clearer view of these things; suspicions and alarms crowd thickly upon him, and he begins to reflect and consider what wrongs he has done to others. And when he finds that the sum of his transgressions is great he will many a time like a child start up in his sleep for fear, and he is filled with dark forebodings. But to him who is conscious of no sin, sweet hope, as Pindar charmingly says, is the kind nurse of his age:

Hope, he says, cherishes the soul of him who lives in justice and holiness and is the nurse of his age and the companion of his journey;—hope which is mightiest to sway the restless soul of man.

How admirable are his words! And the great blessing of riches, I do not say to every man, but to a good man, is, that he has had no occasion to deceive or to defraud others, either intentionally or unintentionally; and when he departs to the world below he is not in any apprehension about offerings due to the gods or debts which he owes to men. Now to this peace of mind the possession of wealth greatly contributes; and therefore I say, that, setting one thing against another, of the many advantages which wealth has to give, to a man of sense this is in my opinion the greatest.

Well said, Cephalus, I replied; but as concerning justice, what is it?—to speak the truth and to pay your debts—no more than this? And even to this are there not exceptions? Suppose that a friend when in his right mind has deposited arms with me and he asks for them when he is not in his right mind, ought I to give them back to him? No one would say that I ought or that I should be right in doing so, any more than they would say that I ought always to speak the truth to one who is in his condition.

You are quite right, he replied.

But then, I said, speaking the truth and paying your debts is not a correct definition of justice.

CEPHALUS - SOCRATES – POLEMARCHUS

Quite correct, Socrates, if Simonides is to be believed, said

Polemarchus interposing.

I fear, said Cephalus, that I must go now, for I have to look after the sacrifices, and I hand over the argument to Polemarchus and the company.

Is not Polemarchus your heir? I said.

To be sure, he answered, and went away laughing to the sacrifices.

SOCRATES – POLEMARCHUS

Tell me then, O thou heir of the argument, what did Simonides say, and according to you truly say, about justice?

He said that the repayment of a debt is just, and in saying so he appears to me to be right.

I should be sorry to doubt the word of such a wise and inspired man, but his meaning, though probably clear to you, is the reverse of clear to me. For he certainly does not mean, as we were now saying that I ought to return a return a deposit of arms or of anything else to one who asks for it when he is not in his right senses; and yet a deposit cannot be denied to be a debt.

True.

Then when the person who asks me is not in his right mind I am by no means to make the return?

Certainly not.

When Simonides said that the repayment of a debt was justice, he did not mean to include that case?

Certainly not; for he thinks that a friend ought always to do good to a friend and never evil.

You mean that the return of a deposit of gold which is to the injury of the receiver, if the two parties are friends, is not the repayment of a debt,—that is what you would imagine him to say?

Yes.

And are enemies also to receive what we owe to them?

To be sure, he said, they are to receive what we owe them, and an enemy, as I take it, owes to an enemy that which is due or proper to him—that is to say, evil.

Simonides, then, after the manner of poets, would seem to have spoken darkly of the nature of justice; for he really meant to say that justice is the giving to each man what is proper to him, and this he termed a debt.

That must have been his meaning, he said.

By heaven! I replied; and if we asked him what due or proper thing is given by medicine, and to whom, what answer do you think that he would make to us?

He would surely reply that medicine gives drugs and meat and drink to human bodies.

And what due or proper thing is given by cookery, and to what?

Seasoning to food.

And what is that which justice gives, and to whom?

If, Socrates, we are to be guided at all by the analogy of the preceding instances, then justice is the art which gives good to friends and evil to enemies.

That is his meaning then?

I think so.

And who is best able to do good to his friends and evil to his enemies in time of sickness?

The physician.

Or when they are on a voyage, amid the perils of the sea?

The pilot.

And in what sort of actions or with a view to what result is the just man most able to do harm to his enemy and good to his friends?

In going to war against the one and in making alliances with the other.

But when a man is well, my dear Polemarchus, there is no need of a physician?

No.

And he who is not on a voyage has no need of a pilot?

No.

Then in time of peace justice will be of no use?

I am very far from thinking so.

You think that justice may be of use in peace as well as in war?

Yes.

Like husbandry for the acquisition of corn?

Yes.

Or like shoemaking for the acquisition of shoes,—that is what you mean?

Yes.

And what similar use or power of acquisition has justice in time of peace?

In contracts, Socrates, justice is of use.

And by contracts you mean partnerships?

Exactly.

But is the just man or the skilful player a more useful and better partner at a game of draughts?

The skilful player.

And in the laying of bricks and stones is the just man a more useful or better partner than the builder?

Quite the reverse.

Then in what sort of partnership is the just man a better partner than the harp-player, as in playing the harp the harp-player is certainly a better partner than the just man?

In a money partnership.

Yes, Polemarchus, but surely not in the use of money; for you do not want a just man to be your counsellor the purchase or sale of a horse; a man who is knowing about horses would be better for that, would he not?

Certainly.

And when you want to buy a ship, the shipwright or the pilot would be better?

True.

Then what is that joint use of silver or gold in which the just man is to be preferred?

When you want a deposit to be kept safely.

You mean when money is not wanted, but allowed to lie?

Precisely.

That is to say, justice is useful when money is useless?

That is the inference.

And when you want to keep a pruning-hook safe, then justice is useful to the individual and to the state; but when you want to use it, then the art of the vine-dresser?

Clearly.

And when you want to keep a shield or a lyre, and not to use them, you would say that justice is useful; but when you want to use them, then the art of the soldier or of the musician?

Certainly.

And so of all the other things;—justice is useful when they are useless, and useless when they are useful?

That is the inference.

Then justice is not good for much. But let us consider this further point: Is not he who can best strike a blow in a boxing match or in any kind of fighting best able to ward off a blow?

Certainly.

And he who is most skilful in preventing or escaping from a disease is best able to create one?

True.

And he is the best guard of a camp who is best able to steal a march upon the enemy?

Certainly.

Then he who is a good keeper of anything is also a good thief?

That, I suppose, is to be inferred.

Then if the just man is good at keeping money, he is good at stealing it.

That is implied in the argument.

Then after all the just man has turned out to be a thief. And this is a lesson which I suspect you must have learnt out of Homer; for he, speaking of Autolycus, the maternal grandfather of Odysseus, who is a favourite of his, affirms that

He was excellent above all men in theft and perjury.

And so, you and Homer and Simonides are agreed that justice is an art of theft; to be practised however 'for the good of friends and for the harm of enemies,'—that was what you were saying?

No, certainly not that, though I do not now know what I did say; but I still stand by the latter words.

Well, there is another question: By friends and enemies do we mean those who are so really, or only in seeming?

Surely, he said, a man may be expected to love those whom he thinks good, and to hate those whom he thinks evil.

Yes, but do not persons often err about good and evil: many who are not good seem to be so, and conversely?

That is true.

Then to them the good will be enemies and the evil will be their friends? True.

And in that case they will be right in doing good to the evil and evil to the good?

Clearly.

But the good are just and would not do an injustice?

True.

Then according to your argument it is just to injure those who do no wrong?

Nay, Socrates; the doctrine is immoral.

Then I suppose that we ought to do good to the just and harm to the unjust?

I like that better.

But see the consequence:—Many a man who is ignorant of human nature has friends who are bad friends, and in that case he ought to do harm to them; and he has good enemies whom he ought to benefit; but, if so, we shall be saying the very opposite of that which we affirmed to be the meaning of Simonides.

Very true, he said: and I think that we had better correct an error into which we seem to have fallen in the use of the words 'friend' and 'enemy.'

What was the error, Polemarchus? I asked.

We assumed that he is a friend who seems to be or who is thought good.

And how is the error to be corrected?

We should rather say that he is a friend who is, as well as seems, good; and that he who seems only, and is not good, only seems to be and is not a friend; and of an enemy the same may be said.

You would argue that the good are our friends and the bad our enemies?

Yes.

And instead of saying simply as we did at first, that it is just to do good to our friends and harm to our enemies, we should further say: It is just to do good to our friends when they are good and harm to our enemies when they are evil?

Yes, that appears to me to be the truth.

But ought the just to injure any one at all?

Undoubtedly he ought to injure those who are both wicked and his enemies.

When horses are injured, are they improved or deteriorated?

The latter.

Deteriorated, that is to say, in the good qualities of horses, not of dogs?

Yes, of horses.

And dogs are deteriorated in the good qualities of dogs, and not of horses?

Of course.

And will not men who are injured be deteriorated in that which is the proper virtue of man?

Certainly.

And that human virtue is justice?

To be sure.

Then men who are injured are of necessity made unjust?

That is the result.

But can the musician by his art make men unmusical?

Certainly not.

Or the horseman by his art make them bad horsemen?

Impossible.

And can the just by justice make men unjust, or speaking general can the good by virtue make them bad?

Assuredly not.

Any more than heat can produce cold?

It cannot.

Or drought moisture?

Clearly not.

Nor can the good harm any one?

Impossible.

And the just is the good?

Certainly.

Then to injure a friend or any one else is not the act of a just man, but of the opposite, who is the unjust?

I think that what you say is quite true, Socrates.

Then if a man says that justice consists in the repayment of debts, and that good is the debt which a man owes to his friends, and evil the debt which he owes to his enemies,—to say this is not wise; for it is not true, if, as has been clearly shown, the injuring of another can be in no case just.

I agree with you, said Polemarchus.

Then you and I are prepared to take up arms against any one who attributes such a saying to Simonides or Bias or Pittacus, or any other wise man or seer?

I am quite ready to do battle at your side, he said.

Shall I tell you whose I believe the saying to be?

Whose?

I believe that Periander or Perdiccas or Xerxes or Ismenias the Theban, or some other rich and mighty man, who had a great opinion of his own power, was the first to say that justice is 'doing good to your friends and harm to your enemies.'

Most true, he said.

Yes, I said; but if this definition of justice also breaks down, what other can be offered?

Several times in the course of the discussion Thrasymachus had made an attempt to get the argument into his own hands, and had been put down by the rest of the company, who wanted to hear the end. But when Polemarchus and I had done speaking and there was a pause, he could no longer hold his peace; and, gathering himself up, he came at us like a wild beast, seeking to devour us. We were quite panic-stricken at the sight of him.

The Republic
BOOK I, PART II

Plato

SOCRATES - POLEMARCHUS – THRASYMACHUS

He roared out to the whole company: What folly. Socrates, has taken possession of you all? And why, sillybillies, do you knock under to one another? I say that if you want really to know what justice is, you should not only ask but answer, and you should not seek honour to yourself from the refutation of an opponent, but have your own answer; for there is many a one who can ask and cannot answer. And now I will not have you say that justice is duty or advantage or profit or gain or interest, for this sort of nonsense will not do for me; I must have clearness and accuracy.

I was panic-stricken at his words, and could not look at him without trembling. Indeed I believe that if I had not fixed my eye upon him, I should have been struck dumb: but when I saw his fury rising, I looked at him first, and was therefore able to reply to him.

Thrasymachus, I said, with a quiver, don't be hard upon us. Polemarchus and I may have been guilty of a little mistake in the argument, but I can assure you that the error was not intentional. If we were seeking for a piece of gold, you would not imagine that we were 'knocking under to one another,' and so losing our chance of finding it. And why, when we are seeking for justice, a thing more precious than many pieces of gold, do you say that we are weakly yielding to one another and not doing our utmost to get at the truth? Nay, my good friend, we are most willing and anxious to do so, but the fact is that we cannot. And if so, you people who know all things should pity us and not be angry with us.

Plato, from *The Republic*, trans. Benjamin Jowett, 1888.

How characteristic of Socrates! he replied, with a bitter laugh;—that's your ironical style! Did I not foresee—have I not already told you, that whatever he was asked he would refuse to answer, and try irony or any other shuffle, in order that he might avoid answering?

You are a philosopher, Thrasymachus, I replied, and well know that if you ask a person what numbers make up twelve, taking care to prohibit him whom you ask from answering twice six, or three times four, or six times two, or four times three, 'for this sort of nonsense will not do for me,'—then obviously, that is your way of putting the question, no one can answer you. But suppose that he were to retort, 'Thrasymachus, what do you mean? If one of these numbers which you interdict be the true answer to the question, am I falsely to say some other number which is not the right one?—is that your meaning?'—How would you answer him?

Just as if the two cases were at all alike! he said.

Why should they not be? I replied; and even if they are not, but only appear to be so to the person who is asked, ought he not to say what he thinks, whether you and I forbid him or not?

I presume then that you are going to make one of the interdicted answers?

I dare say that I may, notwithstanding the danger, if upon reflection I approve of any of them.

But what if I give you an answer about justice other and better, he said, than any of these? What do you deserve to have done to you?

Done to me!—as becomes the ignorant, I must learn from the wise—that is what I deserve to have done to me.

What, and no payment! a pleasant notion!

I will pay when I have the money, I replied.

SOCRATES - THRASYMACHUS - GLAUCON

But you have, Socrates, said Glaucon: and you, Thrasymachus, need be under no anxiety about money, for we will all make a contribution for Socrates.

Yes, he replied, and then Socrates will do as he always does—refuse to answer himself, but take and pull to pieces the answer of some one else.

Why, my good friend, I said, how can any one answer who knows, and says that he knows, just nothing; and who, even if he has some faint notions of his own, is told by a man of authority not to utter them? The natural thing is, that the speaker should be some one like yourself who professes to know and can tell what he knows. Will you then kindly answer, for the edification of the company and of myself?

Glaucon and the rest of the company joined in my request and Thrasymachus, as any one might see, was in reality eager to speak; for he thought that he had an excellent answer, and would distinguish himself. But at first he to insist on my answering; at length he consented to begin. Behold, he said, the wisdom of Socrates; he refuses to teach himself, and goes about learning of others, to whom he never even says thank you.

That I learn of others, I replied, is quite true; but that I am ungrateful I wholly deny. Money I have none, and therefore I pay in praise, which is all I have: and how ready I am to praise any one who appears to me to speak well you will very soon find out when you answer; for I expect that you will answer well.

Listen, then, he said; I proclaim that justice is nothing else than the interest of the stronger. And now why do you not me? But of course you won't.

Let me first understand you, I replied. Justice, as you say, is the interest of the stronger. What, Thrasymachus, is the meaning of this? You cannot mean to say that because Polydamas, the pancratiast, is stronger than we are, and finds the eating of beef conducive to his bodily strength, that to eat beef is therefore equally for our good who are weaker than he is, and right and just for us?

That's abominable of you, Socrates; you take the words in the sense which is most damaging to the argument.

Not at all, my good sir, I said; I am trying to understand them; and I wish that you would be a little clearer.

Well, he said, have you never heard that forms of government differ; there are tyrannies, and there are democracies, and there are aristocracies?

Yes, I know.

And the government is the ruling power in each state?

Certainly.

And the different forms of government make laws democratical, aristocratical, tyrannical, with a view to their several interests; and these laws, which are made by them for their own interests, are the justice which they deliver to their subjects, and him who transgresses them they punish as a breaker of the law, and unjust. And that is what I mean when I say that in all states there is the same principle of justice, which is the interest of the government; and as the government must be supposed to have power, the only reasonable conclusion is, that everywhere there is one principle of justice, which is the interest of the stronger.

Now I understand you, I said; and whether you are right or not I will try to discover. But let me remark, that in defining justice you have yourself used the word 'interest' which you forbade me to use. It is true, however, that in your definition the words 'of the stronger' are added.

A small addition, you must allow, he said.

Great or small, never mind about that: we must first enquire whether what you are saying is the truth. Now we are both agreed that justice is interest of some sort, but you go on to say 'of the stronger'; about this addition I am not so sure, and must therefore consider further.

Proceed.

I will; and first tell me, Do you admit that it is just or subjects to obey their rulers?

I do.

But are the rulers of states absolutely infallible, or are they sometimes liable to err?

To be sure, he replied, they are liable to err.

Then in making their laws they may sometimes make them rightly, and sometimes not?

True.

When they make them rightly, they make them agreeably to their interest; when they are mistaken, contrary to their interest; you admit that?

Yes.

And the laws which they make must be obeyed by their subjects,—and that is what you call justice?

Doubtless.

Then justice, according to your argument, is not only obedience to the interest of the stronger but the reverse?

What is that you are saying? he asked.

I am only repeating what you are saying, I believe. But let us consider: Have we not admitted that the rulers may be mistaken about their own interest in what they command, and also that to obey them is justice? Has not that been admitted?

Yes.

Then you must also have acknowledged justice not to be for the interest of the stronger, when the rulers unintentionally command things to be done which are to their own injury. For if, as you say, justice is the obedience which the subject renders to their commands, in that case, O wisest of men, is there any escape from the conclusion that the weaker are commanded to do, not what is for the interest, but what is for the injury of the stronger?

Nothing can be clearer, Socrates, said Polemarchus.

SOCRATES - CLEITOPHON - POLEMARCHUS - THRASYMACHUS

Yes, said Cleitophon, interposing, if you are allowed to be his witness.

But there is no need of any witness, said Polemarchus, for Thrasymachus himself acknowledges that rulers may sometimes command what is not for their own interest, and that for subjects to obey them is justice.

Yes, Polemarchus,—Thrasymachus said that for subjects to do what was commanded by their rulers is just.

Yes, Cleitophon, but he also said that justice is the interest of the stronger, and, while admitting both these propositions, he further acknowledged that the stronger may command the weaker who are his subjects to do what is not for his own interest; whence follows that justice is the injury quite as much as the interest of the stronger.

But, said Cleitophon, he meant by the interest of the stronger what the stronger thought to be his interest,—this was what the weaker had to do; and this was affirmed by him to be justice.

Those were not his words, rejoined Polemarchus.

Never mind, I replied, if he now says that they are, let us accept his statement. Tell me, Thrasymachus, I said, did you mean by justice what the stronger thought to be his interest, whether really so or not?

Certainly not, he said. Do you suppose that I call him who is mistaken the stronger at the time when he is mistaken?

Yes, I said, my impression was that you did so, when you admitted that the ruler was not infallible but might be sometimes mistaken.

You argue like an informer, Socrates. Do you mean, for example, that he who is mistaken about the sick is a physician in that he is mistaken? or that he who errs in arithmetic or grammar is an arithmetician or grammarian at the me when he is making the mistake, in respect of the mistake? True, we say that the physician or arithmetician or grammarian has made a mistake, but this is only a way of speaking; for the fact is that neither the grammarian nor any other person of skill ever makes a mistake in so far as he is what his name implies; they none of them err unless their skill fails them, and then they cease to be skilled artists. No artist or sage or ruler errs at the time when he is what his name implies; though he is commonly said to err, and I adopted the common mode of speaking. But to be perfectly accurate, since you are such a lover of accuracy, we should say that the ruler, in so far as he is the ruler, is unerring, and, being unerring, always commands that which is for his own interest; and the subject is required to execute his commands; and therefore, as I said at first and now repeat, justice is the interest of the stronger.

Indeed, Thrasymachus, and do I really appear to you to argue like an informer?

Certainly, he replied.

And you suppose that I ask these questions with any design of injuring you in the argument?

Nay, he replied, 'suppose' is not the word—I know it; but you will be found out, and by sheer force of argument you will never prevail.

I shall not make the attempt, my dear man; but to avoid any misunderstanding occurring between us in future, let me ask, in what sense do you speak of a ruler or stronger whose interest, as you were saying, he being the superior, it is just that the inferior should execute—is he a ruler in the popular or in the strict sense of the term?

In the strictest of all senses, he said. And now cheat and play the informer if you can; I ask no quarter at your hands. But you never will be able, never.

And do you imagine, I said, that I am such a madman as to try and cheat, Thrasymachus? I might as well shave a lion.

Why, he said, you made the attempt a minute ago, and you failed.

Enough, I said, of these civilities. It will be better that I should ask you a question: Is the physician, taken in that strict sense of which you are speaking, a healer of the sick or a maker of money? And remember that I am now speaking of the true physician.

A healer of the sick, he replied.

And the pilot—that is to say, the true pilot—is he a captain of sailors or a mere sailor?

A captain of sailors.

The circumstance that he sails in the ship is not to be taken into account; neither is he to be called a sailor; the name pilot by which he is distinguished has nothing to do with sailing, but is significant of his skill and of his authority over the sailors.

Very true, he said.

Now, I said, every art has an interest?

Certainly.

For which the art has to consider and provide?

Yes, that is the aim of art.

And the interest of any art is the perfection of it—this and nothing else?

What do you mean?

I mean what I may illustrate negatively by the example of the body. Suppose you were to ask me whether the body is self-sufficing or has wants, I should reply: Certainly the body has wants; for the body may be ill and require to be cured, and has therefore interests to which the art of medicine ministers; and this is the origin and intention of medicine, as you will acknowledge. Am I not right?

Quite right, he replied.

But is the art of medicine or any other art faulty or deficient in any quality in the same way that the eye may be deficient in sight or the ear fail of hearing, and therefore requires another art to provide for the interests of seeing and hearing—has art in itself, I say, any similar liability to fault or defect, and does every art require another supplementary art to provide for its interests, and that another and another without end? Or have the arts to look only after their own interests? Or have they no need either of themselves or of another?—having no faults or defects, they have no need to correct them, either by the exercise of their own art or of any other; they have only to consider the interest of their subject-matter. For every art remains pure and faultless while remaining true—that is to say, while perfect and unimpaired. Take the words in your precise sense, and tell me whether I am not right."

Yes, clearly.

Then medicine does not consider the interest of medicine, but the interest of the body?

True, he said.

Nor does the art of horsemanship consider the interests of the art of horsemanship, but the interests of the horse; neither do any other arts care for themselves, for they have no needs; they care only for that which is the subject of their art?

True, he said.

But surely, Thrasymachus, the arts are the superiors and rulers of their own subjects?

To this he assented with a good deal of reluctance.

Then, I said, no science or art considers or enjoins the interest of the stronger or superior, but only the interest of the subject and weaker?

He made an attempt to contest this proposition also, but finally acquiesced.

Then, I continued, no physician, in so far as he is a physician, considers his own good in what he prescribes, but the good of his patient; for the true physician is also a ruler having the human body as a subject, and is not a mere money-maker; that has been admitted?

Yes.

And the pilot likewise, in the strict sense of the term, is a ruler of sailors and not a mere sailor?

That has been admitted.

And such a pilot and ruler will provide and prescribe for the interest of the sailor who is under him, and not for his own or the ruler's interest?

He gave a reluctant 'Yes.'

Then, I said, Thrasymachus, there is no one in any rule who, in so far as he is a ruler, considers or enjoins what is for his own interest, but always what is for the interest of his subject or suitable to his art; to that he looks, and that alone he considers in everything which he says and does.

When we had got to this point in the argument, and every one saw that the definition of justice had been completely upset, Thrasymachus, instead of replying to me, said: Tell me, Socrates, have you got a nurse?

Why do you ask such a question, I said, when you ought rather to be answering?

Because she leaves you to snivel, and never wipes your nose: she has not even taught you to know the shepherd from the sheep.

What makes you say that? I replied.

Because you fancy that the shepherd or neatherd fattens of tends the sheep or oxen with a view to their own good and not to the good of himself or his master; and you further imagine that the rulers of states, if they are true rulers, never think of their subjects as sheep, and that they are not studying their own advantage day and night. Oh, no; and so entirely astray are you in your ideas about the just and unjust as not even to know that justice and the just are in reality another's good; that is to say, the interest of the ruler and stronger, and the loss of the subject and servant; and injustice the opposite; for the unjust is lord over the truly simple and just: he is the stronger, and his subjects do what is for his interest, and minister to his happiness, which is very far from being their own. Consider further, most foolish Socrates, that the just is always a loser in comparison with the unjust. First of all, in private contracts: wherever the unjust is the partner of the just you will find that, when the partnership is dissolved, the unjust man has always more and the just less. Secondly, in their dealings with the State: when there is an income tax, the just man will pay more and the unjust less on the same amount of income; and when there is anything to be received the one gains nothing and the other much. Observe also what happens when they take an office; there is the just man neglecting his affairs and perhaps suffering other losses, and getting nothing out of the public, because he is just; moreover he is hated by his friends and acquaintance for refusing to serve them in unlawful ways. But all this is reversed in the case of the unjust man. I am speaking, as before, of injustice on a large scale in which the advantage of the unjust is more apparent; and my meaning will be most clearly seen if we turn to that highest form of injustice in which the criminal is the happiest of men, and the sufferers or those who refuse to do injustice are the most miserable—that is to say tyranny, which by fraud and force takes away the property of others, not little by little but wholesale; comprehending in one, things sacred as well as profane, private and public; for which acts of wrong, if he were detected perpetrating any one of them singly, he would be punished and incur great disgrace—they who do such wrong in particular cases are called robbers of temples, and man-stealers and burglars and swindlers and thieves. But when a man besides taking away the money of the citizens has made slaves of them, then, instead of these names of reproach, he is termed happy and blessed, not only by the citizens but by all who hear of his having achieved the consummation of injustice. For mankind censure injustice, fearing that they may be the victims of it and not because they shrink from committing it. And thus, as I have shown, Socrates, injustice, when on a sufficient scale, has more strength and freedom and mastery than justice; and, as I said at first, justice is the interest of the stronger, whereas injustice is a man's own profit and interest.

Thrasymachus, when he had thus spoken, having, like a bathman, deluged our ears with his words, had a mind to go away. But the company would not let him; they insisted that he should remain and defend his position; and I myself added my own humble request that he would not leave us. Thrasymachus, I said to him, excellent man, how suggestive are your remarks! And are you going to run away before you have fairly taught or learned whether they are true or not? Is the attempt to determine the way of man's life so small a matter in your eyes—to determine how life may be passed by each one of us to the greatest advantage?

And do I differ from you, he said, as to the importance of the enquiry?

You appear rather, I replied, to have no care or thought about us, Thrasymachus—whether we live better or worse from not knowing what you say you know, is to you a matter of indifference. Prithee, friend, do not keep your knowledge to yourself; we are a large party; and any benefit which you confer upon us will be amply rewarded. For my own part I openly declare that I am not convinced, and that I do not believe injustice to be more gainful than justice, even if uncontrolled and allowed to have free play. For, granting that there may be an unjust man who is able to commit injustice either by fraud or force, still this does not convince me of the superior advantage of injustice, and there may be others who are in the same predicament with myself. Perhaps we may be wrong; if so, you in your wisdom should convince us that we are mistaken in preferring justice to injustice.

And how am I to convince you, he said, if you are not already convinced by what I have just said; what more can I do for you? Would you have me put the proof bodily into your souls?

Heaven forbid! I said; I would only ask you to be consistent; or, if you change, change openly and let there be no deception. For I must remark, Thrasymachus, if you will recall what was previously said, that although you began by defining the true physician in an exact sense, you did not observe a like exactness when speaking of the shepherd; you thought that the shepherd as a shepherd tends the sheep not with a view to their own good, but like a mere diner or banqueter with a view to the pleasures of the table; or, again, as a trader for sale in the market, and not as a shepherd. Yet surely the art of the shepherd is concerned only with the good of his subjects; he has only to provide the best for them, since the perfection of the art is already ensured whenever all the requirements of it are satisfied. And that was what I was saying just now about the ruler. I conceived that the art of the ruler, considered as ruler, whether in a state or in private life, could only regard the good of his flock or subjects; whereas you seem to think that the rulers in states, that is to say, the true rulers, like being in authority.

Think! Nay, I am sure of it.

Then why in the case of lesser offices do men never take them willingly without payment, unless under the idea that they govern for the advantage not of themselves but of others? Let me ask you a question: Are not the several arts different, by reason of their each having a separate function? And, my dear illustrious friend, do say what you think, that we may make a little progress.

Yes, that is the difference, he replied.

And each art gives us a particular good and not merely a general one—medicine, for example, gives us health; navigation, safety at sea, and so on?

Yes, he said.

And the art of payment has the special function of giving pay: but we do not confuse this with other arts, any more than the art of the pilot is to be confused with the art of medicine, because the health of the pilot may be improved by a sea voyage. You would not be inclined to say, would you, that navigation is the art of medicine, at least if we are to adopt your exact use of language?

Certainly not.

Or because a man is in good health when he receives pay you would not say that the art of payment is medicine?

I should say not.

Nor would you say that medicine is the art of receiving pay because a man takes fees when he is engaged in healing?

Certainly not.

And we have admitted, I said, that the good of each art is specially confined to the art?
Yes.

Then, if there be any good which all artists have in common, that is to be attributed to something of which they all have the common use?

True, he replied.

And when the artist is benefited by receiving pay the advantage is gained by an additional use of the art of pay, which is not the art professed by him?

He gave a reluctant assent to this.

Then the pay is not derived by the several artists from their respective arts. But the truth is, that while the art of medicine gives health, and the art of the builder builds a house, another art attends them which is the art of pay. The various arts may be doing their own business and benefiting that over which they preside, but would the artist receive any benefit from his art unless he were paid as well?

I suppose not.

But does he therefore confer no benefit when he works for nothing?

Certainly, he confers a benefit.

Then now, Thrasymachus, there is no longer any doubt that neither arts nor governments provide for their own interests; but, as we were before saying, they rule and provide for the interests of their subjects who are the weaker and not the stronger—to their good they attend and not to the good of the superior.

And this is the reason, my dear Thrasymachus, why, as I was just now saying, no one is willing to govern; because no one likes to take in hand the reformation of evils which are not his concern without remuneration. For, in the execution of his work, and in giving his orders to another, the true artist does not regard his own interest, but always that of his subjects; and therefore in order that rulers may be willing to rule, they must be paid in one of three modes of payment: money, or honour, or a penalty for refusing.

CHAPTER 3

Aristotle on Friendship

ARISTOTLE (384–322 BCE) was Plato's most gifted student. He was, in many ways, critical of his teacher, but he also retained many of Plato's key assumptions, chief among them, the idea that philosophy is about knowledge.

But where Plato seemed concerned with the knowledge of things beyond what we see around us (justice itself, not merely particular examples of justice), Aristotle was very much concerned with this world, with the things we can see, touch, smell, hear, and taste. Aristotle's approach to philosophy is thus very different than Plato's.

Plato emphasizes the idea that greatest degree to which a thing can *be* is in its universal form: There is justice and then there is *justice*. It's important to see just how different Plato's view of knowledge is from the way we typically understand knowledge and learning: For Plato, the philosopher does not posit a hypothesis and then go out into the world and test it. True knowledge does not need to be tested because it is absolute, not contingent on anything at all.

For Plato, knowledge has to be universal, and if it is to be universal, it cannot assume anything; it cannot be rooted in any particular point of view. This was part of the debate about justice—just simply has to be more than relative to a system installed by a particular ruler.

Aristotle is deeply influenced by the idea that true knowledge must go beyond the senses. He thinks, for instance, that the highest kind of knowledge is completely abstract and practically useless. But, he also thinks, contrary to Plato, that living a good life depends not on turning away from the senses, but rather on taking the small details and intricacies of human social and political life as seriously as possible. To be a good person for Aristotle is not a matter of living up to some abstract idea of justice. On the contrary, being a good person has to do with being a virtuous person, maintaining strong social relationships, and taking seriously the kinds of commitments we have to others. The reading that follows deals with the something Aristotle takes to be central to human life: friendship.

Important Concepts: Friendship; virtue; ergon; doctrine of the mean

ARISTOTLE ON VIRTUE

Friendship is for Aristotle a virtue. What does he mean by this? Today, we typically think of virtue as a moral category—a virtuous person is a good person. Aristotle thinks this way too, but *he understands virtue to refer to what he calls "proper functioning."* The Greek word is ergon.

We still use the word "virtue" in this way when we say that a thing works "by virtue of" some property it has (e.g., the knife cuts well by virtue of its sharpness, balance, and rigidity. Here, virtue refers to a kind of functioning). Aristotle thinks that the virtuous person is the person who functions well, who fulfills his or her *ergon*.

What is a virtue? Aristotle thinks that virtues are dispositions, tendencies to act and feel in certain ways. Coming to the topic at hand, to be a virtuous friend we need to have a disposition to friendly actions and feelings toward our friends. It's not enough to know that we should act in certain ways or reciprocate friendly gestures just because we hope to get something in return. Rather, the virtuous friend genuinely has friendly feelings and chooses actions accordingly.

Aristotle also thinks that making a virtuous choice is about making a choice that accords with a mean. Virtue, here, is a kind of balance between two extremes, both of which would be vices. This is called the *doctrine of the mean*. Consider the following, for instance:

> *Courage* is a virtue; it's the mean between *rashness* and *cowardice*.
> *Friendliness* is a virtue; it's the mean between *obsequiousness* and *quarrelsomeness*.
> *Truthfulness* is the mean between *boastfulness* and *mock modesty*.
> *Pride* is a virtue; it's the mean between *empty vanity* and *excessive humility*.
> Some things (such as spite, envy, theft, etc.) do not admit
> of a mean since they are in themselves bad.[1]

Aristotle points out that all means are relative to individuals. For instance, to be brave in battle amounts to different things for different people. As a philosophy professor, it would be rash for me to charge into battle but cowardly to run and hide. For the trained soldier, on the other hand, it is appropriate to charge into battle; it's courageous. Aristotle writes,

> *Virtue, then, is a state that decides, consisting in a mean, the mean relative to us, which is defined by a reference to reason, that is to say, to the reason by reference to which the prudent person would define it. It's a mean between two vices, one of excess and one of deficiency.*[2]

FRIENDSHIP AS A VIRTUE

Friendship is a virtue, and virtue consists in making decisions based on reason, decisions that aim at finding the right kind of mean between two extremes, where what's right is relative to an individual. So, how can we be a virtuous friend?

One important point is that Aristotle is not talking about friendship as we understand it; he is talking about something that is central to ethics, namely, the cluster of issues that congeal around the various social associations that we form. Hence, because *philia* eclipses our understanding of friendship, it illuminates a much wider moral landscape. *Philia* does not really mean friendship. Some have suggested that love is better translation of *philia*, but Aristotle seems to understand

1 Aristotle dicusses these in *Nicomachean Ethics, Book II, Chapter 7*, starting at 1107a30.
2 Ibid., p. 1107a

something much wider in scope.[3] My mechanic is my friend; all my colleagues are too. So are my wife and child. So is my city counselor. So are my friends, as we typically understand the term today.

But, not just any social relation constitutes friendship. Any old friendly act does not constitute a friendship. The reason is that there is a passive-active distinction in an isolated friendly act, as when, for instance, one helps a person who has dropped his or her belongings on the street. When I help a person collect his or her effects back into his or her handbag, I am committing a friendly act and the other person is receiving the benefits of my action. This is not primarily what we mean by the word friendship, and it is not what Aristotle means either. In the friendly act, there is an active-passive distinction, but between friends there is, or should be, a reciprocity of giving and receiving. When I do something for a friend, my friendly activity is reciprocated by gratitude and the implicit knowledge that my friend would do the same for me. There is a sense in which the friendly acts between friends are already passive, for implicit in them is an expectation of future reciprocity. So, friendship is about reciprocity, and this kind of thing is a basis for all sorts of social, political, and economic relationships.

THREE TYPES OF FRIENDSHIP

Aristotle is master of the philosophical art of making lists, categorizing, distinguishing, and dividing things up. He distinguishes three types of friendship.

1. The first type is *a friendship of expedience*, where the relationship is predicated on some material advantage that is gained.
2. A second type, closely related to the first, is *a friendship for pleasure*, which is similar to an expedient friendship in that the relationship is predicated on the pleasure that each party derives from the other.
3. A third type is the so-called *true friendship*, which is defined by a love for the other person that is based on genuine goodwill toward the other for the other's sake, and not by what the other person can do.

While it is easy to see what Aristotle is getting at in his description of true friends, precisely how a friendship qualifies for this highest, indeed, "complete"[4] friendship is exceedingly unclear.

Of the three types, it is probably only the second (for pleasure) that fits somewhat neatly into our understanding of friendship, but read generously: All three types have something to offer to an understanding of this concept.

Friendships based on expedience are often defined in terms of a simple exchange of goods for services, and are probably the most alien to our common understanding of the word friend.[5] I would not call my mechanic my friend until, perchance, we discover that we have something in common and attempt to develop this mutual interest together, for it is this mutual interest that

---

3   Martha Nussbaum, *The Fragility of Goodness* (Cambridge: Cambridge University Press, 2001), p. 354.
4   *Nicomachean Ethics,* p. 1156b7
5   Ibid., p. 1163b35–1164a1

would allow us to derive pleasure from the relationship. Indeed, Aristotle seems to agree when he says that friends generally enjoy similar things.[6]

It is tempting to think of a friendship of expedience in terms of a relationship in which the two parties use each other for their own purposes, but this is probably not what Aristotle has in mind. It is true that a friendship of expedience is predicated on selfish desire, but this is in the nature of things, such as commercial relationships of exchange. For Aristotle, I am a friend with my mechanic insofar as he keeps my car running and I pay him for his services. There is selfishness on both our parts.

This is very different from the relationship where one friend uses another, since this is often accompanied by a lack of symmetry between friends. I may be a friend with someone strictly because he gets me cheap concert tickets, and he a friend with me because he enjoys my company, but this is not a friendship of expedience, indeed not a friendship at all because there is a lack of symmetry between the respective parties to the friendship. This allows us to eliminate relationships where the people use each other for their own selfish ends from Aristotle's definition of friendship. The way we usually understand relationships based on one party using another can only be friendships in Aristotle's sense, if such using is in the form of exchange of goods or services; that is, without reciprocity there is no friendship.

For Aristotle, *true friends are virtuous*; indeed, without virtue, true friendship is not really possible at all. This requirement that true friendship can only occur between good people, similar in virtue, is a little difficult to swallow. Does Aristotle mean to suggest that only virtuous people can be true friends, that people who are mostly virtuous save for a few moral flaws are incapable of a true friendship? Not only is this insulting to many people who want to consider their friendships genuine, and indeed to consider themselves at least capable of a true friendship, it also seems to elevate true friendship to such heights that it becomes an effectively impossible goal. The reading that follows offers an opportunity for us to explore the importance of all our social relationships.

The Nicomachean Ethics of Aristotle

BOOK VIII

Aristotle

CHAP. I.

Introductory. Reasons for introducing a dissertation on Friendship into this Treatise.

Next would seem properly to follow a dissertation on Friendship: because, in the first place, it is either itself a virtue or connected with virtue; and next it is a thing most necessary for life, since no one would choose to live without friends though he should have all the other good things in the world: and, in fact, men who are rich or possessed of authority and influence are thought

---

6   Ibid., p. 1157b24

Aristotle, from *The Nicomachean Ethics of Aristotle*, trans. Drummond Peercy Chase, pp. 219-229. Oxford University Press, 1865.

to have special need of friends: for where is the use of such prosperity if there be taken away the doing of kindnesses of which friends are the most usual and most commendable objects? Or how can it be kept or preserved without friends? because the greater it is so much the more slippery and hazardous: in poverty moreover and all other adversities men think friends to be their only refuge.

Furthermore, Friendship helps the young to keep from error: the old, in respect of attention and such deficiencies in action as their weakness makes them liable to; and those who are in their prime, in respect of noble deeds; ("They *two* together going;" Homer says, you may remember,) because they are thus more able to devise plans and carry them out.

Again, it seems to be implanted in us by Nature: as, for instance, in the parent towards the offspring and the offspring towards the parent, (not merely in the human species, but likewise in birds and most animals,) and in those of the same tribe towards one another, and specially in men of the same nation; for which reason we commend those men who love their fellows: and one may see in the course of travel how close of kin and how friendly man is to man.

Furthermore, Friendship seems to be the bond of Social Communities, and legislators seem to be more anxious to secure it than Justice even. I mean, Unanimity is somewhat like to Friendship, and this they certainly aim at and specially drive out faction as being inimical.

Again, where people are in Friendship Justice is not required[7]; but, on the other hand, though they are just they need Friendship in addition, and that principle which is most truly just is thought to partake of the nature of Friendship.

Lastly, not only is it a thing necessary but honourable likewise: since we praise those who are fond of friends, and the having numerous friends is thought a matter of credit to a man; some go so far as to hold, that "good man" and "friend" are terms synonymous.

CHAP. II.

A statement of various opinions respecting Friendship.

Yet the disputed points respecting it are not few: some men lay down that it is a kind of resemblance, and that men who are like one another are friends: whence come the common sayings, "Like will to like," "Birds of a feather," and so on. Others, on the contrary, say, that all such come under the maxim, "Two of a trade never agree[8]."

Again, some men push their enquiries on these points higher and reason physically: as Euripides who says,

"The earth by drought consumed doth love the rain,
And the great heaven, overcharged with rain,

---

7 "Owe no man any thing, but to *love* one another: for he that loveth another *hath fulfilled the Law.*" Romans xiii. 8.

8 κεραμεῖς. The Proverb in full is a line from Hesiod, καὶ κεραμεὺς κεραμεῖ κοτέει καὶ τέκτονι τέκτων.

Doth love to fall in showers upon the earth."

Heraclitus, again, maintains, that "contrariety is expedient, and that the best agreement arises from things differing, and that all things come into being in the way of the principle of antagonism."

Empedocles, among others, in direct opposition to these, affirms, that "like aims at like."

These physical questions we will take leave to omit, inasmuch as they are foreign to the present enquiry; and we will examine such as are proper to man and concern moral characters and feelings: as, for instance, "Does Friendship arise among all without distinction, or is it impossible for bad men to be friends'?" and, "Is there but one species of Friendship, or several ?" for they who ground the opinion that there is but one on the fact that Friendship admits of degrees hold that upon insufficient proof; because things which are different in species admit likewise of degrees; (on this point we have spoken before.)

CHAP. III.

Of the object-matter of Friendship.

Our view will soon be cleared on these points when we have ascertained what is properly the object-matter of Friendship: for it is thought that not every thing indiscriminately, but some peculiar matter alone, is the object of this affection; that is to say, what is good, or pleasurable, or useful. Now it would seem that that is useful through which accrues any good or pleasure, and so the objects of Friendship, as absolute Ends, are the good and the pleasurable.

A question here arises; whether it is good absolutely or that which is good to the individuals, for which men feel Friendship, (these two being sometimes distinct:) and similarly in respect of the pleasurable. It seems then that each individual feels it towards that which is good to himself, and that abstractedly it is the real good which is the object of Friendship, and to each individual that which is good to each. It comes then to this; that each individual feels Friendship not for what *is* but for that which *conveys to his mind the impression of being* good to himself. But this will make no real difference, because that which is truly the object of Friendship will also convey this impression to the mind.

There are then three causes from which men feel Friendship: but the term is not applied to the case of fondness for things inanimate because there is no requital of the affection nor desire for the good of those objects: it certainly savours of the ridiculous to say that a man fond of wine wishes well to it: the only sense in which it is true being that he wishes it to be kept safe and sound for his own use and benefit[9]. But to the friend they say one should wish all good for his sake. And when men do thus wish good to another, (he not reciprocating the feeling,) people call them Kindly; because Friendship they describe as being "Kindliness between persons

---

9   In this sense, therefore, is it sung of Mrs. Gilpin, that she
        "two stone bottles found,
        To hold the liquor that she *loved*
        And keep it safe and sound."

who reciprocate it." But must they not add that the feeling must be mutually known? for many men are kindly disposed towards those whom they have never seen but whom they conceive to be amiable or useful: and this notion amounts to the same thing as a real feeling between them.

Well, these are plainly Kindly-disposed towards one another: but how can one call them friends while their mutual feelings are unknown to one another? to complete the idea of Friendship, then, it is requisite that they have kindly feelings towards one another, and wish one another good from one of the aforementioned causes, and that these kindly feelings should be mutually known.

CHAP. IV.

Of the Imperfection of the Friendships based on the motives of Expediency and Pleasure.

As the motives to Friendship differ in kind so do the respective feelings and Friendships. The species then of Friendship are three, in number equal to the objects of it, since in the line of each there may be "mutual affection mutually known."

Now they who have Friendship for one another desire one another's good according to the motive of their Friendship; accordingly they whose motive is utility have no Friendship for one another really, but only in so far as some good arises to them from one another.

And they whose motive is pleasure are in like case: I mean, they have Friendship for men of easy pleasantry, not because they are of a given character but because they are pleasant to themselves. So then they whose motive to Friendship is utility love their friends for what is good to themselves; they whose motive is pleasure do so for what is pleasurable to themselves; that is to say, not in so far as the friend beloved *is* but in so far as he is useful or pleasurable. These Friendships then are a matter of result: since the object is not beloved in that he is the man he is but in that he furnishes advantage or pleasure as the case may be.

Such Friendships are of course very liable to dissolution if the parties do not continue alike: I mean, that the others cease to have any Friendship for them when they are no longer pleasurable or useful. Now it is the nature of utility not to be permanent but constantly varying: so, of course, when the motive which made them friends is vanished, the Friendship likewise dissolves; since it existed only relatively to those circumstances.

Friendship of this kind is thought to exist principally among the old; (because men at that time of life pursue not what is pleasurable but what is profitable;) and in such, of men in their prime and of the young, as are given to the pursuit of profit. They that are such have no intimate intercourse with one another; for sometimes they are not even pleasurable to one another: nor, in fact, do they desire such intercourse unless their friends are profitable to them, because they are pleasurable only in so far as they have hopes of advantage. With these Friendships is commonly ranked that of hospitality.

But the Friendship of the young is thought to be based on the motive of pleasure: because they live at the beck and call of passion and generally pursue what is pleasurable to themselves and the object of the present moment: and as their age changes so likewise do their pleasures.

This is the reason why they form and dissolve Friendships rapidly: since the Friendship changes with the pleasurable object and such pleasure changes quickly.

The young are also much given up to Love; this passion being, in great measure, a matter of impulse and based on pleasure: for which cause they conceive Friendships and quickly drop them, changing often in the same day: but these wish for society and intimate intercourse with their friends, since they thus attain the object of their Friendship.

CHAP. V.

On the perfections of the Friendship based on virtue, and the imperfections of the other two kinds.

That then is perfect Friendship which subsists between those who are good and whose similarity consists in their goodness: for these men wish one another's good in similar ways; in so far as they are good, (and good they are in themselves); and those are specially friends who wish good to their friends for their sakes, because they feel thus towards them on their own account and not as a mere matter of result; so the Friendship between these men continues to subsist so long as they are good; and goodness, we know, has in it a principle of permanence.

Moreover, each party is good abstractedly and also relatively to his friend, for all good men are not only abstractedly good but also useful to one another. Such friends are also mutually pleasurable because all good men are so abstractedly, and also relatively to one another inasmuch as to each individual those actions are pleasurable which correspond to his nature, and all such as are like them. Now when men are good these will be always the same, or at least similar.

Friendship then under these circumstances is permanent, as we should reasonably expect, since it combines in itself all the requisite qualifications of friends. I mean, that Friendship of whatever kind is based upon good or pleasure, (either abstractedly or relatively to the person entertaining the sentiment of Friendship,) and results from a similarity of some sort; and to this kind belong all the aforementioned requisites in the parties themselves, because in this the parties are similar, and so on[10]: moreover, in it there is the abstractedly good and the abstractedly pleasant, and as these are specially the object-matter of Friendship so the feeling and the state of Friendship is found most intense and most excellent in men thus qualified.

Rare it is probable Friendships of this kind will be, because men of this kind are rare. Besides, all requisite qualifications being presupposed, there is farther required time and intimacy: for, as the proverb says, men cannot know one another "till they have eaten the requisite quantity of salt together;" nor can they in fact admit one another to intimacy, much less be friends, till each

---

10   Cardwell's reading, *ταύτη γὰρ ὅμοιοι, καὶ τὰ λοιπά*, is here adopted, as yielding a better sense than Bekker's.

has appeared to the other and been proved to be a fit object of Friendship. They who speedily commence an interchange of friendly actions may be said to wish to be friends, but they are not so unless they are also proper objects of Friendship and mutually known to be such: that is to say, a desire for Friendship may arise quickly but not Friendship itself.

Well, this Friendship is perfect both in respect of the time and in all other points; and exactly the same and similar results accrue to each party from the other; which ought to be the case between friends.

The friendship based upon the pleasurable is, so to say, a copy of this, since the good are sources of pleasure to one another: and that based on utility likewise, the good being also useful to one another. Between men thus connected Friendships are most permanent when the same result accrues to both from one another, pleasure, for instance; and not merely so but from the same source, as in the case of two men of easy pleasantry; and not as it is in that of a lover and the object of his affection, these not deriving their pleasure from the same causes, but the former from seeing the latter and the latter from receiving the attentions of the former: and when the bloom of youth fades the Friendship sometimes ceases also, because then the lover derives no pleasure from seeing and the object of his affection ceases to receive the attentions which were paid before: in many cases, however, people so connected continue friends, if being of similar tempers they have come from custom to like one another's disposition.

Where people do not interchange pleasure but profit in matters of Love, the Friendship is both less intense in degree and also less permanent: in fact, they who are friends because of advantage commonly part when the advantage ceases; for, in reality, they never were friends of one another but of the advantage.

So then it appears that from motives of pleasure or profit bad men may be friends to one another, or good men to bad men, or men of neutral character to one of any character whatever: but disinterestedly, for the sake of one another, plainly the good alone can be friends; because bad men have no pleasure even in themselves unless in so far as some advantage arises.

And further, the Friendship of the good is alone superior to calumny; it not being easy for men to believe a third person respecting one whom they have long tried and proved: there is between good men mutual confidence, and the feeling that one's friend would never have done one wrong, and all other such things as are expected in Friendship really worthy the name; but in the other kinds there is nothing to prevent all such suspicions.

I call them Friendships, because since men commonly give the name of friends to those who are connected from motives of profit, (which is justified by political language, for alliances between states are thought to be contracted with a view to advantage,) and to those who are attached to one another by the motive of pleasure, (as children are,) we may perhaps also be allowed to call such persons friends, and say there are several species of Friendship; primarily and specially that of the good, in that they are good, and the rest only in the way of resemblance: I mean, people connected otherwise are friends in that way in which there arises to them somewhat good and some mutual resemblance, (because, we must remember, the pleasurable is good to those who are fond of it.)

These secondary Friendships, however, do not combine very well; that is to say, the same persons do not become friends by reason of advantage and by reason of the pleasurable, for these matters of result are not often combined. And Friendship having been divided into these kinds, bad men will be friends by reason of pleasure or profit, this being their point of resemblance; while the good are friends for one another's sake, that is, in so far as they are good.

These last may be termed abstractedly and simply friends, the former as a matter of result and termed friends from their resemblance to these last.

CHAP. VI.

On the method of sustaining Friendship.

Further; just as in respect of the different virtues some men are termed good in respect of a certain inward state, others in respect of acts of working, so is it in respect of Friendship: I mean, they who live together take pleasure in, and impart good to, one another: but they who are asleep or are locally separated do not perform acts, but only are in such a state as to act in a friendly way if they acted at all: distance has in itself no direct effect upon Friendship, but only prevents the acting it out: yet, if the absence be protracted, it is thought to cause a forgetfulness even of the Friendship: and hence it has been said, "many and many a Friendship doth want of intercourse destroy."

Accordingly, neither the old nor the morose appear to be calculated for Friendship, because the pleasurableness in them is small, and no one can spend his days in company with that which is positively painful or even not pleasurable; since to avoid the painful and aim at the pleasurable is one of the most obvious tendencies of human nature. They who get on with one another very fairly, but are not in habits of intimacy, are rather like people having kindly feelings towards one another than friends; nothing being so characteristic of friends as the living with one another, because the necessitous desire assistance, and the happy companionship, they being the last persons in the world for solitary existence: but people cannot spend their time together unless they are mutually pleasurable and take pleasure in the same objects, a quality which is thought to appertain to the Friendship of companionship.

CHAPTER 4

Cultivation and Artifice

A Debate between Mengzi and Xunzi on Human Nature and Goodness[1]

U P UNTIL NOW, we have been focusing on the Western philosophical tradition, and this text will, in general, focus on philosophy as it is practiced in the West. It is an unfortunate contingency of the history of philosophy that professional academic philosophy does not pay much attention to philosophical traditions from other parts of the world. This is highly unfortunate since there are rich histories of philosophy that originate in places such as China, Africa, India, and in the indigenous traditions here in North America and around the world. In this chapter, we will explore a classic debate between two Chinese philosophers about human nature and the role of moral cultivation.

Important Concepts: Cultivation; four beginnings; ritual; distinction

Both Mengzi and Xunzi lived during the second half of the Zhou dynasty (1040–221 BCE), during the Warring States period (403–221 BCE) in classical Chinese history. Dating either of these figures exactly is a difficult task, but we know that Mengzi was a very early follower of Confucius and that Xunzi lived a little later, distinguishing himself by providing a novel and compelling version of Confucianism that differed in important respects from the interpretation offered by Mengzi. If you have heard of any Chinese philosopher at all, you have probably heard of Confucius, or Kongzi. *One of the things that distinguishes the Confucian tradition from other classical Chinese traditions (Taoism, for instance) is its emphasis on ritual practice and moral cultivation as central to the proper development of the human being.* In a famous passage, Kongzi summarizes his idea of the path of moral development:

> The Master said, "At fifteen I set my mind upon learning; at thirty I took
> my place in society; at forty I became free of doubts; at fifty I understood

---

1   Thanks to Brian Bruya, whose comments on this section helped me to avoid several infelicities of terminology and interpretation.

Heaven's Mandate; at sixty my ear was attuned; and at seventy I could follow my heart's desire without overstepping the bounds of propriety."[2]

One thing to note is that this is an awfully long path—it's not until seventy that one's desires can be properly in line with the demands of morality. This takes effort, resolve, and a long life of practice. Within the Confucian tradition, there is considerable debate about just what the role of this practice of moral cultivation actually is. Mengzi argues that cultivation develops something inherently good in human nature. Cultivation hones and develops a human being's inner goodness to reveal the virtuous truth of the human heart. Xunzi, on the other hand, argues that human nature inherently tends toward bad action and that the good we find in people and in the arrangement of human life is due strictly to deliberate effort to steer ourselves away from the tendency toward bad actions.

MENGZI, VIRTUE, AND THE CULTIVATION OF GOODNESS

Mengzi thinks that we have inherently good natures. This is best illustrated in the reading that follows, where Mengzi cites the example of seeing a child about to fall into a well. Anyone would immediately react with "alarm and distress," which indicates that we have a natural tendency to goodness, to want to help those in need and to feeling compassion toward others. But, this idea that we have a natural tendency toward goodness does not mean that we are *born good*; rather, it means that we are *born with a natural capacity for goodness*. This distinction is important. Being born *with a natural capacity for* goodness means that our goodness requires moral cultivation; it's not something that we have by nature. One must be careful not to interpret Mengzi as saying that we must somehow force ourselves to be good. We must find a balance; that is, proper cultivation consists in allowing our good nature to develop naturally. Put another way, we must get out of the way of goodness by creating conditions amenable to its development.

As an illustration of this idea, Mengzi cites a humorous anecdote.

> Do not be like the man from Song. Among the people of the state of Song, there was one who, concerned lest his grain not grow, pulled on it. Wearily, he returned home, and said to his family, 'Today I am worn out. I helped the grain to grow.' His son rushed out and looked at it. The grain was withered.[3]

The point here is to illustrate how much harm can be done by trying too hard to help nature do what it naturally does. Pulling on a young seedling to help it grow is surely ridiculous; no less ridiculous, Mengzi wants to suggest, is trying to forces ourselves to be good when goodness is in

---

2   Kongzi, "The Analects 2.4," in *Readings in Classical Chinese Philosophy*, second edition, eds. Philip J. Ivanoe and Bryan W. Van Norden (Indianapolis: Hackett, 2001), 5.
3   Mengzi, "The Mengzi 2A2," in *Readings in Classical Chinese Philosophy*, 127.

our nature. But Mengzi continues in his anecdote; simply leaving the grain alone to grow is not the answer either: "Those who abandon it [the grain], thinking it will not help, are those who do not weed the grain."[4] Simply leaving the grain alone is to step away from the opportunity to create conditions amenable to the grain's growth. Just like the cultivation of grain, the cultivation of our natural goodness requires a delicate balance of not interfering with natural development and creating the conditions required for growth.

In the following selection, Mengzi makes an argument for the four beginnings (*si duan*). Each "beginning" can be identified both by an indwelling virtue and its corresponding feeling. The virtue of benevolence corresponds to the feeling of compassion; the virtue of righteousness to disdain; the virtue of propriety to deference; the virtue of wisdom to approval and disapproval.

—

Chapter 6

Mencius

1. Mencius said, 'All men have a mind which cannot bear to see the sufferings of others.

2. 'The ancient kings had this commiserating mind, and they, as a matter of course, had likewise a commiserating government. When with a commiserating mind was practised a commiserating government, to rule the kingdom was as easy a matter as to make anything go round in the palm.

3. 'When I say that all men have a mind which cannot bear to see the sufferings of others, my meaning may be illustrated thus:—even now-a-days, if men suddenly see a child about to fall into a well, they will without exception experience a feeling of alarm and distress. They will feel so, not as a ground on which they may gain the favour of the child's parents, nor as a ground on which they may seek the praise of their neighbours and friends, nor from a dislike to the reputation of having been unmoved by such a thing.

4. 'From this case we may perceive that the feeling of commiseration is essential to man, that the feeling of shame and dislike is essential to man, that the feeling of modesty and complaisance is essential to man, and that the feeling of approving and disapproving is essential to man.

5. 'The feeling of commiseration is the principle of benevolence. The feeling of shame and dislike is the principle of righteousness. The feeling of modesty and complaisance is the principle of propriety. The feeling of approving and disapproving is the principle of knowledge.

6. 'Men have these four principles just as they have their four limbs. When men, having these four principles, yet say of themselves that they cannot develop them, they play the thief with themselves, and he who says of his prince that he cannot develop them plays the thief with his prince.

---

4   Ibid.

Mencius (Mengzi), Selections from "The Mencius," *Chinese Classics*, vol. 2, trans. James Legge, pp. 22-23. Oxford University Press, 1895.

7. 'Since all men have these four principles in themselves, let them know to give them all their development and completion, and the issue will be like that of fire which has begun to burn, or that of a spring which has begun to find vent. Let them have their complete development, and they will suffice to love and protect all within the four seas. Let them be denied that development, and they will not suffice for a man to serve his parents with.'

Chapters 21 and 22

Mencius

Chapter 21

1. The philosopher Kâo said, 'Man's nature is like the ch'î-willow, and righteousness is like a cup or a bowl. The fashioning benevolence and righteousness out of man's nature is like the making cups and bowls from the ch'î-willow.'

2. Mencius replied, 'Can you, leaving untouched the nature of the willow, make with it cups and bowls? You must do violence and injury to the willow, before you can make cups and bowls with it. If you must do violence and injury to the willow in order to make cups and bowls with it, on your principles you must in the same way do violence and injury to humanity in order to fashion from it benevolence and righteousness! Your words, alas! would certainly lead all men on to reckon benevolence and righteousness to be calamities.'

1. The philosopher Kâo said, 'Man's nature is like water whirling round in a corner. Open a passage for it to the east, and it will flow to the east; open a passage for it to the west, and it will flow to the west. Man's nature is indifferent to good and evil, just as the water is indifferent to the east and west.'

2. Mencius replied, 'Water indeed will flow indifferently to the east or west, but will it flow indifferently up or down? The tendency of man's nature to good is like the tendency of water to flow downwards. There are none but have this tendency to good, just as all water flows downwards.

3. 'Now by striking water and causing it to leap up, you may make it go over your forehead, and, by damming and leading it you may force it up a hill;—but are such movements according to the nature of water? It is the force applied which causes them. When men are made to do what is not good, their nature is dealt with in this way.'

1. The philosopher Kâo said, 'Life is what we call nature!'

2. Mencius asked him, 'Do you say that by nature you mean life, just as you say that white is white?' 'Yes, I do,' was the reply. Mencius added, 'Is the whiteness of a white feather like that of white snow, and the whiteness of white snow like that of white jade?' Kâo again said 'Yes.'

3. 'Very well,' pursued Mencius. 'Is the nature of a dog like the nature of an ox, and the nature of an ox like the nature of a man?'

Mencius (Mengzi), Selections from "The Mencius," *Chinese Classics*, vol. 2, trans. James Legge, pp. 72-79. Oxford University Press, 1895.

1. The philosopher Kâo said, 'To enjoy food and delight in colours is nature. Benevolence is internal and not external; righteousness is external and not internal.'

2. Mencius asked him, 'What is the ground of your saying that benevolence is internal and righteousness external?' He replied, 'There is a man older than I, and I give honour to his age. It is not that there is first in me a principle of such reverence to age. It is just as when there is a white man, and I consider him white; according as he is so externally to me. On this account, I pronounce of righteousness that it is external.'

3. Mencius said, 'There is no difference between our pronouncing a white horse to be white and our pronouncing a white man to be white. But is there no difference between the regard with which we acknowledge the age of an old horse and that with which we acknowledge the age of an old man? And what is it which is called righteousness?—the fact of a man's being old? or the fact of our giving honour to his age?'

4. Kâo said, 'There is my younger brother;—I love him. But the younger brother of a man of Ch'in I do not love: that is, the feeling is determined by myself, and therefore I say that benevolence is internal. On the other hand, I give honour to an old man of Ch'û, and I also give honour to an old man of my own people: that is, the feeling is determined by the age, and therefore I say that righteousness is external.'

5. Mencius answered him, 'Our enjoyment of meat roasted by a man of Ch'in does not differ from our enjoyment of meat roasted by ourselves. Thus, what you insist on takes place also in the case of such things, and will you say likewise that our enjoyment of a roast is external?'

1. The disciple Mang Chî asked Kung-tû, saying, 'On what ground is it said that righteousness is internal?'

2. Kung-tû replied, 'We therein act out our feeling of respect, and therefore it is said to be internal.'

3. The other objected, 'Suppose the case of a villager older than your elder brother by one year, to which of them would you show the greater respect?' 'To my brother,' was the reply. 'But for which of them would you first pour out wine at a feast?' 'For the villager.' Mang Chî argued, 'Now your feeling of reverence rests on the one, and now the honour due to age is rendered to the other;—this is certainly determined by what is without, and does not proceed from within.'

4. Kung-tû was unable to reply, and told the conversation to Mencius. Mencius said, 'You should ask him, "Which do you respect most,—your uncle, or your younger brother?" He will answer, "My uncle." Ask him again, "If your younger brother be personating a dead ancestor, to which do you show the greater respect,—to him or to your uncle?" He will say, "To my younger brother." You can go on, "But where is the respect due, as you said, to your uncle?" He will reply to this, "I show the respect to my younger brother, because of the position which he occupies," and you can likewise say, "So my respect to the villager is because of the position which he occupies. Ordinarily, my respect is rendered to my elder brother; for a brief season, on occasion, it is rendered to the villager."'

5. Mang Chî heard this and observed, 'When respect is due to my uncle, I respect him, and when respect is due to my younger brother, I respect him;—the thing is certainly determined by

what is without, and does not proceed from within.' Kung-tû replied, 'In winter we drink things hot, in summer we drink things cold; and so, on your principle, eating and drinking also depend on what is external!'

1. The disciple Kung-tû said, 'The philosopher Kâo says, "Man's nature is neither good nor bad."

2. 'Some say, "Man's nature may be made to practise good, and it may be made to practise evil, and accordingly, under Wan and Wû, the people loved what was good, while under Yû and Lî, they loved what was cruel."

3. 'Some say, "The nature of some is good, and the nature of others is bad. Hence it was that under such a sovereign as Yâo there yet appeared Hsiang; that with such a father as Kû-sâu there yet appeared Shun; and that with Châu for their sovereign, and the son of their elder brother besides, there were found Ch'î, the viscount of Wei, and the prince Pî-Kan.

4. 'And now you say, "The nature is good." Then are all those wrong?'

5. Mencius said, 'From the feelings proper to it, it is constituted for the practice of what is good. This is what I mean in saying that the nature is good.

6. 'If men do what is not good, the blame cannot be imputed to their natural powers.

7. 'The feeling of commiseration belongs to all men; so does that of shame and dislike; and that of reverence and respect; and that of approving and disapproving. The feeling of commiseration implies the principle of benevolence; that of shame and dislike, the principle of righteousness; that of reverence and respect, the principle of propriety; and that of approving and disapproving, the principle of knowledge. Benevolence, righteousness, propriety, and knowledge are not infused into us from without. We are certainly furnished with them. And a different view is simply owing to want of reflection. Hence it is said, "Seek and you will find them. Neglect and you will lose them." Men differ from one another in regard to them;—some as much again as others, some five times as much, and some to an incalculable amount:—it is because they cannot carry out fully their natural powers.

8. 'It is said in the Book of Poetry,

"Heaven in producing mankind,
Gave them their various faculties and relations with their specific laws.
These are the invariable rules of nature for all to hold,
And all love this admirable virtue."

Confucius said, "The maker of this ode knew indeed the principle of our nature!" We may thus see that every faculty and relation must have its law, and since there are invariable rules for all to hold, they consequently love this admirable virtue.'

1. Mencius said, 'In good years the children of the people are most of them good, while in bad years the most of them abandon themselves to evil. It is not owing to any difference of their natural powers conferred by Heaven that they are thus different. The abandonment is owing to the circumstances through which they allow their minds to be ensnared and drowned in evil.

2. 'There now is barley.—Let it be sown and covered up; the ground being the same, and the time of sowing likewise the same, it grows rapidly up, and, when the full time is come, it is all found to be ripe. Although there may be inequalities of produce, that is owing to the difference of the soil, as rich or poor, to the unequal nourishment afforded by the rains and dews, and to the different ways in which man has performed his business in reference to it.

3. 'Thus all things which are the same in kind are like to one another;—why should we doubt in regard to man, as if he were a solitary exception to this? The sage and we are the same in kind.

4. 'In accordance with this the scholar Lung said, "If a man make hempen sandals without knowing the size of people's feet, yet I know that he will not make them like baskets." Sandals are all like one another, because all men's feet are like one another.

5. 'So with the mouth and flavours;—all mouths have the same relishes. Yî-yâ only apprehended before me what my mouth relishes. Suppose that his mouth in its relish for flavours differed from that of other men, as is the case with dogs or horses which are not the same in kind with us, why should all men be found following Yî-yâ in their relishes? In the matter of tastes all the people model themselves after Yî-yâ; that is, the mouths of all men are like one another.

6. 'And so also it is with the ear. In the matter of sounds, the whole people model themselves after the music-master K'wang; that is, the ears of all men are like one another.

7. 'And so also it is with the eye. In the case of Tsze-tû, there is no man but would recognise that he was beautiful. Any one who would not recognise the beauty of Tsze-tû must have no eyes.

8. 'Therefore I say,—Men's mouths agree in having the same relishes; their ears agree in enjoying the same sounds; their eyes agree in recognising the same beauty:—shall their minds alone be without that which the similarly approve? What is it then of which they similarly approve? It is, I say, the principles of our nature, and the determinations of righteousness. The sages only apprehended before me that of which my mind approves along with other men. Therefore the principles of our nature and the determinations of righteousness are agreeable to my mind, just as the flesh of grass and grain-fed animals is agreeable to my mouth.'

1. Mencius said, 'The trees of the Niû mountain were once beautiful. Being situated, however, in the borders of a large State, they were hewn down with axes and bills;—and could they retain their beauty? Still through the activity of the vegetative life day and night, and the nourishing influence of the rain and dew, they were not without buds and sprouts springing forth, but then came the cattle and goats and browsed upon them. To these things is owing the bare and stripped appearance of the mountain, and when people now see it, they think it was never finely wooded. But is this the nature of the mountain?

2. 'And so also of what properly belongs to man;—shall it be said that the mind of any man was without benevolence and righteousness? The way in which a man loses his proper goodness of mind is like the way in which the trees are denuded by axes and bills. Hewn down day after day, can it—the mind—retain its beauty? But there is a development of its life day and night, and in the calm air of the morning, just between night and day, the mind feels in a degree those desires and aversions which are proper to humanity, but the feeling is not strong, and it

is fettered and destroyed by what takes place during the day. This fettering taking place again and again, the restorative influence of the night is not sufficient to preserve the proper goodness of the mind; and when this proves insufficient for that purpose, the nature becomes not much different from that of the irrational animals, and when people now see it, they think that it never had those powers which I assert. But does this condition represent the feelings proper to humanity?

3. 'Therefore, if it receive its proper nourishment, there is nothing which will not grow. If it lose its proper nourishment, there is nothing which will not decay away.

4. 'Confucius said, "Hold it fast, and it remains with you. Let it go, and you lose it. Its outgoing and incoming cannot be defined as to time or place." It is the mind of which this is said!'

Chapter 22

1. Mencius said, 'It is not to be wondered at that the king is not wise!

2. 'Suppose the case of the most easily growing thing in the world;—if you let it have one day's genial heat, and then expose it for ten days to cold, it will not be able to grow. It is but seldom that I have an audience of the king, and when I retire, there come all those who act upon him like the cold. Though I succeed in bringing out some buds of goodness, of what avail is it?

3. 'Now chess-playing is but a small art, but without his whole mind being given, and his will bent, to it, a man cannot succeed at it. Chess Ch'iû is the best chess-player in all the kingdom. Suppose that he is teaching two men to play.—The one gives to the subject his whole mind and bends to it all his will, doing nothing but listening to Chess Ch'iû. The other, although he seems to be listening to him, has his whole mind running on a swan which he thinks is approaching, and wishes to bend his bow, adjust the string to the arrow, and shoot it. Although he is learning along with the other, he does not come up to him. Why?—because his intelligence is not equal? Not so.'

1. Mencius said, 'I like fish, and I also like bear's paws. If I cannot have the two together, I will let the fish go, and take the bear's paws. So, I like life, and I also like righteousness. If I cannot keep the two together, I will let life go, and choose righteousness.

2. 'I like life indeed, but there is that which I like more than life, and therefore, I will not seek to possess it by any improper ways. I dislike death indeed, but there is that which I dislike more than death, and therefore there are occasions when I will not avoid danger.

3. 'If among the things which man likes there were nothing which he liked more than life, why should he not use every means by which he could preserve it? If among the things which man dislikes there were nothing which he disliked more than death, why should he not do everything by which he could avoid danger?

4. 'There are cases when men by a certain course might preserve life, and they do not employ it; when by certain things they might avoid danger, and they will not do them.

5. 'Therefore, men have that which they like more than life, and that which they dislike more than death. They are not men of distinguished talents and virtue only who have this mental nature. All men have it; what belongs to such men is simply that they do not lose it.

6.   'Here are a small basket of rice and a platter of soup, and the case is one in which the getting them will preserve life, and the want of them will be death;—if they are offered with an insulting voice, even a tramper will not receive them, or if you first tread upon them, even a beggar will not stoop to take them.

7.   'And yet a man will accept of ten thousand chung, without any consideration of propriety or righteousness. What can the ten thousand chung add to him? When he takes them, is it not that he may obtain beautiful mansions, that he may secure the services of wives and concubines, or that the poor and needy of his acquaintance may be helped by him?

8.   'In the former case the offered bounty was not received, though it would have saved from death, and now the emolument is taken for the sake of beautiful mansions. The bounty that would have preserved from death was not received, and the emolument is taken to get the service of wives and concubines. The bounty that would have saved from death was not received, and the emolument is taken that one's poor and needy acquaintance may be helped by him. Was it then not possible likewise to decline this? This is a case of what is called—"Losing the proper nature of one's mind."'

1.   Mencius said, 'Benevolence is man's mind, and righteousness is man's path.

2.   'How lamentable is it to neglect the path and not pursue it, to lose this mind and not know to seek it again!

3.   'When men's fowls and dogs are lost, they know to seek for them again, but they lose their mind, and do not know to seek for it.

4.   'The great end of learning is nothing else but to seek for the lost mind.'

1.   Mencius said, 'Here is a man whose fourth finger is bent and cannot be stretched out straight. It is not painful, nor does it incommode his business, and yet if there be any one who can make it straight, he will not think the way from Ch'in to Ch'û far to go to him; because his finger is not like the finger of other people.

2.   'When a man's finger is not like those of other people, he knows to feel dissatisfied, but if his mind be not like that of other people, he does not know to feel dissatisfaction. This is called—"Ignorance of the relative importance of things."'

Mencius said, 'Anybody who wishes to cultivate the t'ung or the tsze, which may be grasped with both hands, perhaps with one, knows by what means to nourish them. In the case of their own persons, men do not know by what means to nourish them. Is it to be supposed that their regard of their own persons is inferior to their regard for a t'ung or tsze? Their want of reflection is extreme.'

1.   Mencius said, 'There is no part of himself which a man does not love, and as he loves all, so he must nourish all. There is not an inch of skin which he does not love, and so there is not an inch of skin which he will not nourish. For examining whether his way of nourishing be good or not, what other rule is there but this, that he determine by reflecting on himself where it should be applied?

2. 'Some parts of the body are noble, and some ignoble; some great, and some small. The great must not be injured for the small, nor the noble for the ignoble. He who nourishes the little belonging to him is a little man, and he who nourishes the great is a great man.

3. 'Here is a plantation-keeper, who neglects his wû and chiâ, and cultivates his sour jujube-trees;—he is a poor plantation-keeper.

4. 'He who nourishes one of his fingers, neglecting his shoulders or his back, without knowing that he is doing so, is a man who resembles a hurried wolf.

5. 'A man who only eats and drinks is counted mean by others;—because he nourishes what is little to the neglect of what is great.

6. 'If a man, fond of his eating and drinking, were not to neglect what is of more importance, how should his mouth and belly be considered as no more than an inch of skin?'

1. The disciple Kung-tû said, 'All are equally men, but some are great men, and some are little men;—how is this?' Mencius replied, 'Those who follow that part of themselves which is great are great men; those who follow that part which is little are little men.'

2. Kung-tû pursued, 'All are equally men, but some follow that part of themselves which is great, and some follow that part which is little;—how is this?' Mencius answered, 'The senses of hearing and seeing do not think, and are obscured by external things. When one thing comes into contact with another, as a matter of course it leads it away. To the mind belongs the office of thinking. By thinking, it gets the right view of things; by neglecting to think, it fails to do this. These—the senses and the mind—are what Heaven has given to us. Let a man first stand fast in the supremacy of the nobler part of his constitution, and the inferior part will not be able to take it from him. It is simply this which makes the great man.'

1. Mencius said, 'There is a nobility of Heaven, and there is a nobility of man. Benevolence, righteousness, self-consecration, and fidelity, with unwearied joy in these virtues;—these constitute the nobility of Heaven. To be a kung, a ch'ing, or a tâ-fû;—this constitutes the nobility of man.

2. 'The men of antiquity cultivated their nobility of Heaven, and the nobility of man came to them in its train.

3. 'The men of the present day cultivate their nobility of Heaven in order to seek for the nobility of man, and when they have obtained that, they throw away the other:—their delusion is extreme. The issue is simply this, that they must lose that nobility of man as well.'

2. 'The honour which men confer is not good honour. Those whom Châo the Great ennobles he can make mean again.

3. 'It is said in the Book of Poetry,
"He has filled us with his wine,
He has satiated us with his goodness."
"Satiated us with his goodness," that is, satiated us with benevolence and righteousness, and he who is so satiated, consequently, does not wish for the fat meat and fine millet of men. A

good reputation and far-reaching praise fall to him, and he does not desire the elegant embroidered garments of men.'

1. Mencius said, 'Benevolence subdues its opposite just as water subdues fire. Those, however, who now-a-days practise benevolence do it as if with one cup of water they could save a whole waggon-load of fuel which was on fire, and when the flames were not extinguished, were to say that water cannot subdue fire. This conduct, moreover, greatly encourages those who are not benevolent.

2. 'The final issue will simply be this—the loss of that small amount of benevolence.'

2. 'A master-workman, in teaching others, uses the compass and square, and his pupils do the same.'

XUNZI, ARTIFICE, AND THE CULTIVATION OF GOODNESS

As was noted previously, Xunzi is in direct disagreement with Mengzi about the human nature. While it might be difficult to see how Mengzi (human nature is good) and Xunzi (human nature is bad) could be any further apart in their basic orientation, they agree that human goodness requires cultivation. But, where Mengzi thinks that the aim of cultivation is to reveal a naturally good human nature, Xunzi thinks that cultivation is necessary to steer human beings in the right direction, away from the tendency to engage in bad actions. It is not that Xunzi thinks that people are naturally bad, and it is certainly not that he thinks people are inherently evil. It's that he thinks that we lack any inborn tendency to goodness. In fact, Xunzi seems to think that without cultivation, humans are no better than animals. Comparing his thinking directly to Mengzi, Xunzi writes,

> Mengzi says: People's nature is good. I say: This is not so. In every case, both in ancient times and in the present, what everyone under Heaven calls good is being correct, ordered, peaceful, and controlled. What they call bad is being deviant, dangerous, unruly, and chaotic. This is the distinction between good and bad. Now does he really think that people's nature is originally correct, ordered, peaceful, and controlled? Then what use would there be for sage-kings? What use for ritual and the standards of righteousness?[5]

Xunzi clearly thinks, then, that human nature is such that it is originally and by nature in a state of unruly chaos, pulled in different directions and with a tendency to do bad things. Anyone who has ever been a teenager can empathize with the sentiment of Xunzi's argument, here. Xunzi's insight in the context of the tradition of Confucian thought is that if we follow these tendencies, we shall end up miserable, struggling against ourselves and others for desires that only lead to discord. It is because of this that humans desire to become good. Humans are unique in that they have the creative and intellectual power to see past these natural tendencies and work

---

5   Xunzi, "Human Nature is Bad," in *Readings in Classical Chinese Philosophy*, 301.

Excerpts from: Xunzi, "The Xunzi," *Readings in Classical Chinese Philosophy*, ed. Philip J. Ivanoe and Bryan W. Van Norden, trans. Eric L. Hutton, pp. 257, 266, 274, 276, 301. Copyright © 2001 by Hackett Publishing Company, Inc.

to better themselves through deliberate effort, and the way that we better ourselves, for Xunzi, is through careful, rigorous, mindful, and faithful practice of ritual.

So, *what is ritual?* This is an important concept in Confucian thought, but it is a concept that does not have any clear cognate in Western thinking. Xunzi explains that the ancient sage-kings established ritual to satisfy people's desire to sufficiently quell their desires and thus avoid the struggle and conflict that arises when many people seek the same objects of desire. "Thus," Xunzi writes,

> [R]itual is a means of nurture. Meats and grains, the five flavors and various spices and means to nurture the mouth. Fragrances and perfumes are means to nurture the nose. Carving and inlay, insignias and patterns are means to nurture the eyes. Bells and drums, pipes and chimes, lutes and zithers are means to nurture the ears. Homes and palaces, cushions and beds, tables and mats are means to nurture the body. Thus, ritual is a means of nurture.[6]

Ritual thus helps us to become human, to bring order out of chaos and provide the kind of nurturing that humans need to flourish and develop as human beings. So important is ritual to Xunzi's thought that it plays a role not only in human relations, but is also a name for the natural order of the world. Xunzi writes,

> By ritual, Heaven and earth harmoniously combine;
> By ritual, the sun and the moon radiantly shine;
> By ritual, the four seasons in progression arise;
> By ritual, the stars move orderly across the skies;
> By ritual, the great rivers through their courses flow;
> By ritual, the ten thousand things all thrive and grow;
> By ritual, for love and hate proper measure is made;
> By ritual, on joy and anger fit limits are laid.
> By ritual, compliant subordinates are created,
> By ritual, enlightened leaders are generated;
> With ritual, all things can change yet not bring chaos,
> But deviate from ritual and you face only loss.[7]

Ritual is thus viewed as necessary for a properly ordered life in the universe. Everything we can possibly achieve is due to an effort to live within the confines of ritual. Indeed, all human achievement is for Xunzi a kind of artifice (something made by humankind) that results from an effort to make human life better, to harmonize our relationships with ourselves, others, and the world

---

6   Xunzi, "Discourse on Ritual," in *Readings in Classical Chinese Philosophy*, 274.

7   Xunzi, "Discourse on Ritual," 276.

around us. The key to this power, this ability to get past our natural inclinations, is the human capacity for making subtle distinctions.

> What is that by which humans are human? I say: It is because they have distinctions. Desiring food when hungry, desiring warmth when cold, desiring rest when tired, liking the beneficial and hating the harmful—these are the things people have from birth [...] However, that by which human are human is not that they are special in having two legs and no feathers, but that they have distinctions [...] The birds and the beasts have fathers and sons but not the intimate relation of father and son. They have the male sex and the female sex but no differentiation between male and female. And so among human ways, none is without distinctions. Of distinctions, none are greater than social divisions, and of social divisions, none are greater than rituals, and of rituals none are greater than those of the sage-kings.[8]

Exactly what Xunzi means by "distinctions" is not perfectly clear, but he seems to be thinking primarily about the practices and divisions that make up the landscape of human social, moral, and political lives. What makes us human is the way in which we deliberately organize our lives to help us be more than what we were simply born with. In other places, Xunzi also explains this in terms of technical accomplishment:

> One who makes use of a chariot and horses has not thereby improved his feet, but he can now go a thousand li. One who makes use of a boat and oars has not thereby become able to swim, but he can now cross rivers and streams. The gentleman is not different from others by birth. Rather, he is good at making use of things.[9]

The difference between Mengzi and Xunzi is very clear. To be able to accomplish great things, it is not enough to develop what we already have. Both in our social lives and in how we achieve technical mastery, we realize what it means to be human through ingenuity, creativity, and deliberate effort.

---

8   Xunzi, "Against Physiognomy," in *Readings in Classical Chinese Philosophy*, 266.
9   Xunzi, "An Exhortation to Learning," in *Readings in Classical Chinese Philosophy*, 257.

CHAPTER 5

Epictetus and Stoicism

I N THE SEVEN hundred years or so after Plato and Aristotle, there emerged a proliferation of schools of philosophy. This time is generally broken up into two main periods: Hellenistic philosophy (300 BCE–100 CE), including epicureanism and early stoicism, and the imperial schools (100–400 CE), including skepticism and later stoicism (of which Epictetus is a part).

In general, all the schools of classical antiquity agreed that philosophy ought to be practically oriented—it ought to make our lives better. Without that, what's the point of doing philosophy at all? In the ancient world, philosophy was practice; it was life. One would see one's philosophy teachers around town; one would see how they live, how they behave. Perhaps one would even mimic them. This idea of philosophy being a kind of way of life, providing practical guidance for living, is unfortunately something that can today be quite foreign from formal academic philosophy. Open any professional academic journal in philosophy or attend any professional conference and you will be met with highly technical debates, many of which have quite a tenuous link with anything that is of any concern to anyone who is not a professional philosopher.

You have probably heard the term "stoic" before. It has connotations of being detached, letting the world go by, and not letting it affect you negatively. This is a pretty good summary of stoic philosophy. The stoics are so called because they met in the stoa, the portico, the arched entrance ways to the city. Epictetus is perhaps one of the most well-known of the large and famous lines of stoic philosophers. Marcus Aurelius (the Roman emperor) was also a stoic. The contrast between Epictetus and Aurelius gives you a sense about just how widely appealing and influential stoicism was, and still is. Epictetus began life as a slave, studied philosophy on his own, and apparently became rippled at some point in his life. Marcus Aurelius, on the other hand, was a Roman Emperor.

Important Concepts: Nature; virtue; lazy argument; wisdom

Epictetus (55–135 CE) is famous for his widely read *Echeiridion* (literally, "handbook"), probably written for his many students as a general guide to help them through the stoic teachings. The *Encheiridion* was meant to be read and re-read, something I still enjoy doing. The text is a remarkably calming one to read, and almost anyone who reads it finds something in it to connect with. Its core message, captured right in the opening lines, "Some things are up to us and some are not up to us," is deceptively simple. The complexity of the claim begins to appear as soon as we begin to think seriously about just what is up to us and what is not.

How do we know what is up to us? Epictetus held that our desires, judgments, expectations, actions, etc. are up to us, while things such as our reputations, political situations, natural events, etc. are not up to us. The stoics thought that by just figuring out this distinction and acting accordingly, we could not fail to be happy. This is of course no easy task. Our actions are intimately linked to the world and to how our lives turn out, but there is also a way in which we are subject to a world we have no control over. Consider, for instance, whether we experience anxiety because of the pressures placed on us by other people and the external world (things we cannot control) or because of our own judgments about and reactions to events in our lives (things that are up to us). In most cases, anxiety is probably the result of a bit of both. The stoic insight here is that since we have no power over the former, we're much better off focusing on the latter. Trying to effect changes in the external world or in other people is a frustrating task at best, but making changes in ourselves is something that is much more reasonably within our reach.

But, the stoic insight goes much deeper than this merely normative prescription to focus our efforts on changing ourselves rather than changing the world. It is simply a fact for the stoics that certain things are out of our control. *The natural world is a world of absolute necessity over which we have no influence whatsoever, and this natural necessity is precisely the way it should be; the nature cannot and should not be any different. Nature is perfectly rational since only what is necessary happens in nature and whatever happens in nature is always right.* This means that proper reasoning tracks nature; our logic, if it is correct, is the logic of nature. Nature is *never* mistaken; *we* are mistaken! We all have our preferences, but things can prove that these preferences are mistaken. *To be virtuous is to live according to nature, and living according to nature is to live according to reason.* Virtue is completely rational. The goal, then, is harmonize your preferences with what happens by nature. *True wisdom is the alignment of one's desires with the rational order of the universe.*

One of the persistent problems with this view concerns the deceptively simple opening lines of the text, "Some things are up to us and some are not up to us." If the goal is to align one's desires with the rational order of the universe and this order is one of those things that is not up to us, then how do we know where to draw the line? Consider paragraph IV of the *Enchiridion*. There, Epictetus is speaking of going to a public bath and advising us to adjust our expectations to what typically happens at baths: "[S]ome persons pouring out, others pushing in, others scolding, others pilfering." The question we much ask ourselves is the extent to which such things are things that we should elect to live with. It is certainly good advice to not get bothered by the actions of others, but surely there are things that we should be bothered by, that should get us "out of humor at things that happen." Epictetus's own example of stealing is a good example. Should I not be bothered by someone stealing my wallet at a public pool? How far should we take this? What if someone violently assaults me? Is this just what people do at the bath? What is the rational order of nature? And what, exactly, is up to us? It seems that there are a certain set of cases where it would be reasonable for us to try to change things, where there is an issue of social justice.

We can see this issue another way, too. Before the development of pharmaceutical antibiotics, a bacterial infection could easily lead to something as serious as the loss of a limb, organ failure, or even death. Does this mean that salmonella or tuberculosis are part of the order of nature that is not up to us? Should we not even bother going to a doctor, then? *This is a version of what has been called the "lazy argument"; it's the argument that since things are fated for us, there is no point going to a doctor—we're going to get better or not, the doctor cannot affect your situation one way or the other. If we're going to get sick and even die, this is just our fate, something we have no control over.*

If you think there is something wrong with this reasoning, then you have begun to sense the complexity of stoic philosophy. What can we control? When would we be better off not acting at all? Why should I consult a physician if it's my fate to get sick? Fate, after all, is totally rational; it's the rational order of the universe. So, the deep question, again, is where the line between what is not up to us and what is up to us is drawn. How are we supposed to know when we have the freedom to act and make a difference? How do we know that our action is not in vain?

Epictetus does offer some resources to help us think through this problem. Consider section XXXII, where he suggests that we should always share in danger when it is the right thing to do. Apollo, as the story goes, threw a person out of the temple for not coming to the aid of his friend. No fortune teller can tell us what is right—we always have to decide this for ourselves, using reason. For while we may not have any power over what events come to pass, knowledge of the causes of things allows us to use reason to decide on the right course of action. Coming back to the lazy argument, this means that the sick person should consult a physician because the sick person is ignorant of causes. There might well be a cure in the rational order and the doctor is the one qualified to find it. Whether there is a cure depends on my finding it! Again, recall section XXXII: Whether my friend dies depends on whether or not I will intervene to save him.

The Enchiridion

Epictetus

I

There are things which are within our power, and there are things which are beyond our power. Within our power are opinion, aim, desire, aversion, and, in one word, whatever affairs are our own. Beyond our power are body, property, reputation, office, and, in one word, whatever are not properly our own affairs.

Now the things within our power are by nature free, unrestricted, unhindered; but those beyond our power are weak, dependent, restricted, alien. Remember, then, that if you attribute freedom to things by nature dependent and take what belongs to others for your own, you will

Epictetus, *The Enchiridion*, ed. Arrian, trans. Thomas Wentwork Higginson. Little, Brown and Company, 1865.

be hindered, you will lament, you will be disturbed, you will find fault both with gods and men. But if you take for your own only that which is your own and view what belongs to others just as it really is, then no one will ever compel you, no one will restrict you; you will find fault with no one, you will accuse no one, you will do nothing against your will; no one will hurt you, you will not have an enemy, nor will you suffer any harm.

Aiming, therefore, at such great things, remember that you must not allow yourself any inclination, however slight, toward the attainment of the others; but that you must entirely quit some of them, and for the present postpone the rest. But if you would have these, and possess power and wealth likewise, you may miss the latter in seeking the former; and you will certainly fail of that by which alone happiness and freedom are procured.

Seek at once, therefore, to be able to say to every unpleasing semblance, "You are but a semblance and by no means the real thing." And then examine it by those rules which you have; and first and chiefly by this: whether it concerns the things which are within our own power or those which are not; and if it concerns anything beyond our power, be prepared to say that it is nothing to you.

II

Remember that desire demands the attainment of that of which you are desirous; and aversion demands the avoidance of that to which you are averse; that he who fails of the object of his desires is disappointed; and he who incurs the object of his aversion is wretched. If, then, you shun only those undesirable things which you can control, you will never incur anything which you shun; but if you shun sickness, or death, or poverty, you will run the risk of wretchedness. Remove [the habit of] aversion, then, from all things that are not within our power, and apply it to things undesirable which are within our power. But for the present, altogether restrain desire; for if you desire any of the things not within our own power, you must necessarily be disappointed; and you are not yet secure of those which are within our power, and so are legitimate objects of desire. Where it is practically necessary for you to pursue or avoid anything, do even this with discretion and gentleness and moderation.

III

With regard to whatever objects either delight the mind or contribute to use or are tenderly beloved, remind yourself of what nature they are, beginning with the merest trifles: if you have a favorite cup, that it is but a cup of which you are fond of—for thus, if it is broken, you can bear it; if you embrace your child or your wife, that you embrace a mortal—and thus, if either of them dies, you can bear it.

IV

When you set about any action, remind yourself of what nature the action is. If you are going to bathe, represent to yourself the incidents usual in the bath—some persons pouring out, others pushing in, others scolding, others pilfering. And thus you will more safely go about this action if you say to yourself, "I will now go to bathe and keep my own will in harmony with nature." And so with regard to every other action. For thus, if any impediment arises in bathing, you will be able to say, "It was not only to bathe that I desired, but to keep my will in harmony with nature; and I shall not keep it thus if I am out of humor at things that happen."

V

Men are disturbed not by things, but by the views which they take of things. Thus death is nothing terrible, else it would have appeared so to Socrates. But the terror consists in our notion of death, that it is terrible. When, therefore, we are hindered or disturbed, or grieved, let us never impute it to others, but to ourselves—that is, to our own views. It is the action of an uninstructed person to reproach others for his own misfortunes; of one entering upon instruction, to reproach himself; and one perfectly instructed, to reproach neither others nor himself.

VI

Be not elated at any excellence not your own. If a horse should be elated, and say, "I am handsome," it might be endurable. But when you are elated and say, "I have a handsome horse," know that you are elated only on the merit of the horse. What then is your own? The use of the phenomena of existence. So that when you are in harmony with nature in this respect, you will be elated with some reason; for you will be elated at some good of your own.

VII

As in a voyage, when the ship is at anchor, if you go on shore to get water, you may amuse yourself with picking up a shellfish or a truffle in your way, but your thoughts ought to be bent toward the ship, and perpetually attentive, lest the captain should call, and then you must leave all these things, that you may not have to be carried on board the vessel, bound like a sheep; thus likewise in life, if, instead of a truffle or shellfish, such a thing as a wife or a child be granted you, there is no objection; but if the captain calls, run to the ship, leave all these things, and never look behind. But if you are old, never go far from the ship, lest you should be missing when called for.

VIII

Demand not that events should happen as you wish; but wish them to happen as they do happen, and you will go on well.

IX

Sickness is an impediment to the body, but not to the will unless itself pleases. Lameness is an impediment to the leg, but not to the will; and say this to yourself with regard to everything that happens. For you will find it to be an impediment to something else, but not truly to yourself.

X

Upon every accident, remember to turn toward yourself and inquire what faculty you have for its use. If you encounter a handsome person, you will find continence the faculty needed; if pain, then fortitude; if reviling, then patience. And when thus habituated, the phenomena of existence will not overwhelm you.

XI

Never say of anything, "I have lost it," but, "I have restored it." Has your child died? It is restored. Has your wife died? She is restored. Has your estate been taken away? That likewise is restored. "But it was a bad man who took it." What is it to you by whose hands he who gave it has demanded it again? While he permits you to possess it, hold it as something not your own, as do travelers at an inn.

XII

If you would improve, lay aside such reasonings as these: "If I neglect my affairs, I shall not have a maintenance; if I do not punish my servant, he will be good for nothing." For it were better to die of hunger, exempt from grief and fear, than to live in affluence with perturbation; and it is better that your servant should be bad than you unhappy.

Begin therefore with little things. Is a little oil spilled or a little wine stolen? Say to yourself, "This is the price paid for peace and tranquillity; and nothing is to be had for nothing." And when you call your servant, consider that it is possible he may not come at your call; or, if he does, that he may not do what you wish. But it is not at all desirable for him, and very undesirable for you, that it should be in his power to cause you any disturbance.

XIII

If you would improve, be content to be thought foolish and dull with regard to externals. Do not desire to be thought to know anything; and though you should appear to others to be somebody, distrust yourself. For be assured, it is not easy at once to keep your will in harmony with nature and to secure externals; but while you are absorbed in the one, you must of necessity neglect the other.

XIV

If you wish your children and your wife and your friends to live forever, you are foolish, for you wish things to be in your power which are not so, and what belongs to others to be your own. So likewise, if you wish your servant to be without fault, you are foolish, for you wish vice not to be vice but something else. But if you wish not to be disappointed in your desires, that is in your own power. Exercise, therefore, what is in your power. A man's master is he who is able to confer or remove whatever that man seeks or shuns. Whoever then would be free, let him wish nothing, let him decline nothing, which depends on others; else he must necessarily be a slave.

XV

Remember that you must behave as at a banquet. Is anything brought round to you? Put out your hand and take a moderate share. Does it pass by you? Do not stop it. Is it not yet come? Do not yearn in desire toward it, but wait till it reaches you. So with regard to children, wife, office, riches; and you will some time or other be worthy to feast with the gods. And if you do not so much as take the things which are set before you, but are able even to forego them, then you will not only be worthy to feast with the gods, but to rule with them also. For, by thus doing, Diogenes and Heraclitus, and others like them, deservedly became divine, and were so recognized.

XVI

When you see anyone weeping for grief, either that his son has gone abroad or that he has suffered in his affairs, take care not to be overcome by the apparent evil, but discriminate and be ready to say, "What hurts this man is not this occurrence itself—for another man might not be hurt by it—but the view he chooses to take of it." As far as conversation goes, however, do not disdain to accommodate yourself to him and, if need be, to groan with him. Take heed, however, not to groan inwardly, too.

XVII

Remember that you are an actor in a drama of such sort as the Author chooses—if short, then in a short one; if long, then in a long one. If it be his pleasure that you should enact a poor man, or a cripple, or a ruler, or a private citizen, see that you act it well. For this is your business—to act well the given part, but to choose it belongs to another.

XVIII

When a raven happens to croak unluckily, be not overcome by appearances, but discriminate and say, "Nothing is portended to me, either to my paltry body, or property, or reputation, or children, or wife. But to me all portents are lucky if I will. For whatsoever happens, it belongs to me to derive advantage therefrom."

XIX

You can be unconquerable if you enter into no combat in which it is not in your own power to conquer. When, therefore, you see anyone eminent in honors or power, or in high esteem on any other account, take heed not to be bewildered by appearances and to pronounce him happy; for if the essence of good consists in things within our own power, there will be no room for envy or emulation. But, for your part, do not desire to be a general, or a senator, or a consul, but to be free; and the only way to this is a disregard of things which lie not within our own power.

XX

Remember that it is not he who gives abuse or blows, who affronts, but the view we take of these things as insulting. When, therefore, anyone provokes you, be assured that it is your own opinion which provokes you. Try, therefore, in the first place, not to be bewildered by appearances. For if you once gain time and respite, you will more easily command yourself.

XXI

Let death and exile, and all other things which appear terrible, be daily before your eyes, but death chiefly; and you will never entertain an abject thought, nor too eagerly covet anything.

XXII

If you have an earnest desire toward philosophy, prepare yourself from the very first to have the multitude laugh and sneer, and say, "He is returned to us a philosopher all at once"; and, "Whence this supercilious look?" Now, for your part, do not have a supercilious look indeed, but keep steadily to those things which appear best to you, as one appointed by God to this particular station. For remember that, if you are persistent, those very persons who at first ridiculed will afterwards admire you. But if you are conquered by them, you will incur a double ridicule.

XXIII

If you ever happen to turn your attention to externals, for the pleasure of anyone, be assured that you have ruined your scheme of life. Be content, then, in everything, with being a philosopher; and if you wish to seem so likewise to anyone, appear so to yourself, and it will suffice you.

XXIV

Let not such considerations as these distress you: "I shall live in discredit and be nobody anywhere." For if discredit be an evil, you can no more be involved in evil through another than in baseness. Is it any business of yours, then, to get power or to be admitted to an entertainment? By no means. How then, after all, is this discredit? And how it is true that you will be nobody anywhere when you ought to be somebody in those things only which are within your own power, in which you may be of the greatest consequence? "But my friends will be unassisted." What do you mean by "unassisted"? They will not have money from you, nor will you make them Roman citizens. Who told you, then, that these are among the things within our own power, and not rather the affairs of others? And who can give to another the things which he himself has not? "Well, but get them, then, that we too may have a share." If I can get them with the preservation of my own honor and fidelity and self-respect, show me the way and I will get them; but if you require me to lose my own proper good, that you may gain what is no good, consider how unreasonable and foolish you are. Besides, which would you rather have, a sum of money or a faithful and honorable friend? Rather assist me, then, to gain this character than require me to do those things by which I may lose it. Well, but my country, say you, as far as depends upon me, will be unassisted. Here, again, what assistance is this you mean? It will not have porticos nor baths of your providing? And what signifies that? Why, neither does a smith provide it with shoes, nor a shoemaker with arms. It is enough if everyone fully performs his own proper business. And were you to supply it with another faithful and honorable citizen, would not he be of use to it? Yes. Therefore neither are you yourself useless to it. "What place, then," say you, "shall I hold in the state?" Whatever you can hold with the preservation of your fidelity and honor. But if, by desiring to be useful to that, you lose these, how can you serve your country when you have become faithless and shameless?

XXV

Is anyone preferred before you at an entertainment, or in courtesies, or in confidential intercourse? If these things are good, you ought to rejoice that he has them; and if they are evil, do not be grieved that you have them not. And remember that you cannot be permitted to rival others in externals without using the same means to obtain them. For how can he who will not haunt the door of any man, will not attend him, will not praise him, have an equal share with him who does these things? You are unjust, then, and unreasonable if you are unwilling to pay the price for which these things are sold, and would have them for nothing. For how much are lettuces sold? An obulus, for instance. If another, then, paying an obulus, takes the lettuces, and you, not paying it, go without them, do not imagine that he has gained any advantage over you. For as he has the lettuces, so you have the obulus which you did not give. So, in the present case, you have not been invited to such a person's entertainment because you have not paid him the price for which a supper is sold. It is sold for praise; it is sold for attendance. Give him, then, the value if it be for your advantage. But if you would at the same time not pay the one, and yet receive the other, you are unreasonable and foolish. Have you nothing, then, in place of the supper? Yes, indeed, you have—not to praise him whom you do not like to praise; not to bear the insolence of his lackeys.

XXVI

The will of nature may be learned from things upon which we are all agreed. As when our neighbor's boy has broken a cup, or the like, we are ready at once to say, "These are casualties that will happen"; be assured, then, that when your own cup is likewise broken, you ought to be affected just as when another's cup was broken. Now apply this to greater things. Is the child or wife of another dead? There is no one who would not say, "This is an accident of mortality." But if anyone's own child happens to die, it is immediately, "Alas! how wretched am I!" It should be always remembered how we are affected on hearing the same thing concerning others.

XXVII

As a mark[1] is not set up for the sake of missing the aim, so neither does the nature of evil exist in the world.

---

1   Happiness, the effect of virtue, is the mark which God has set up for us to aim at. Our missing it is no work of His; nor so properly anything real, as a mere negative and failure of our own.

XXVIII

If a person had delivered up your body to some passer-by, you would certainly be angry. And do you feel no shame in delivering up your own mind to any reviler, to be disconcerted and confounded?

XXIX[2]

In every affair consider what precedes and what follows, and then undertake it. Otherwise you will begin with spirit, indeed, careless of the consequences, and when these are developed, you will shamefully desist. "I would conquer at the Olympic Games." But consider what precedes and what follows, and then, if it be for your advantage, engage in the affair. You must conform to rules, submit to a diet, refrain from dainties; exercise your body, whether you choose it or not, at a stated hour, in heat and cold; you must drink no cold water, and sometimes no wine—in a word, you must give yourself up to your trainer as to a physician. Then, in the combat, you may be thrown into a ditch, dislocate your arm, turn your ankle, swallow an abundance of dust, receive stripes [for negligence], and, after all, lose the victory. When you have reckoned up all this, if your inclination still holds, set about the combat. Otherwise, take notice, you will behave like children who sometimes play wrestlers, sometimes gladiators, sometimes blow a trumpet, and sometimes act a tragedy, when they happen to have seen and admired these shows. Thus you too will be at one time a wrestler, and another a gladiator; now a philosopher, now an orator; but nothing in earnest. Like an ape you mimic all you see, and one thing after another is sure to please you, but is out of favor as soon as it becomes familiar. For you have never entered upon anything considerately; nor after having surveyed and tested the whole matter, but carelessly, and with a halfway zeal. Thus some, when they have seen a philosopher and heard a man speaking like Euphrates[3]—though, indeed, who can speak like him?—have a mind to be philosophers, too. Consider first, man, what the matter is, and what your own nature is able to bear. If you would be a wrestler, consider your shoulders, your back, your thighs; for different persons are made for different things. Do you think that you can act as you do and be a philosopher, that you can eat, drink, be angry, be discontented, as you are now? You must watch, you must labor, you must get the better of certain appetites, must quit your acquaintances, be despised by your servant, be laughed at by those you meet; come off worse than others in everything—in offices, in honors, before tribunals. When you have fully considered all these things, approach, if you please—that is, if, by parting with them, you have a mind to purchase serenity, freedom, and tranquillity. If not, do not come hither; do not, like children, be now a philosopher, then a publican, then an orator, and then one of Caesar's officers. These things are not consistent.

---

2   Chapter XV of the third book of the Discourses, which, with the exception of some very trifling differences, is the same as chapter XXIX of the Enchiridion.—Ed.

3   Euphrates was a philosopher of Syria, whose character is described, with the highest encomiums, by Pliny the Younger, Letters I. 10.

You must be one man, either good or bad. You must cultivate either your own reason or else externals; apply yourself either to things within or without you—that is, be either a philosopher or one of the mob.

XXX

Duties are universally measured by relations. Is a certain man your father? In this are implied taking care of him, submitting to him in all things, patiently receiving his reproaches, his correction. But he is a bad father. Is your natural tie, then, to a good father? No, but to a father. Is a brother unjust? Well, preserve your own just relation toward him. Consider not what he does, but what you are to do to keep your own will in a state conformable to nature, for another cannot hurt you unless you please. You will then be hurt when you consent to be hurt. In this manner, therefore, if you accustom yourself to contemplate the relations of neighbor, citizen, commander, you can deduce from each the corresponding duties.

XXXI

Be assured that the essence of piety toward the gods lies in this—to form right opinions concerning them, as existing and as governing the universe justly and well. And fix yourself in this resolution, to obey them, and yield to them, and willingly follow them amidst all events, as being ruled by the most perfect wisdom. For thus you will never find fault with the gods, nor accuse them of neglecting you. And it is not possible for this to be affected in any other way than by withdrawing yourself from things which are not within our own power, and by making good or evil to consist only in those which are. For if you suppose any other things to be either good or evil, it is inevitable that, when you are disappointed of what you wish or incur what you would avoid, you should reproach and blame their authors. For every creature is naturally formed to flee and abhor things that appear hurtful and that which causes them; and to pursue and admire those which appear beneficial and that which causes them. It is impracticable, then, that one who supposes himself to be hurt should rejoice in the person who, as he thinks, hurts him, just as it is impossible to rejoice in the hurt itself. Hence, also, a father is reviled by his son when he does not impart the things which seem to be good; and this made Polynices and Eteocles[4] mutually enemies—that empire seemed good to both. On this account the husbandman reviles the gods; [and so do] the sailor, the merchant, or those who have lost wife or child. For where our interest is, there, too, is piety directed. So that whoever is careful to regulate his desires and aversions as he ought is thus made careful of piety likewise. But it also becomes incumbent on everyone to offer libations and sacrifices and first fruits, according to the customs of his country, purely, and not heedlessly nor negligently; not avariciously, nor yet extravagantly.

---

4   The two inimical sons of Oedipus, who killed each other in battle.—Ed.

XXXII

When you have recourse to divination, remember that you know not what the event will be, and you come to learn it of the diviner; but of what nature it is you knew before coming; at least, if you are of philosophic mind. For if it is among the things not within our own power, it can by no means be either good or evil. Do not, therefore, bring with you to the diviner either desire or aversion—else you will approach him trembling—but first clearly understand that every event is indifferent and nothing to you, of whatever sort it may be; for it will be in your power to make a right use of it, and this no one can hinder. Then come with confidence to the gods as your counselors; and afterwards, when any counsel is given you, remember what counselors you have assumed, and whose advice you will neglect if you disobey. Come to divination as Socrates prescribed, in cases of which the whole consideration relates to the event, and in which no opportunities are afforded by reason or any other art to discover the matter in view. When, therefore, it is our duty to share the danger of a friend or of our country, we ought not to consult the oracle as to whether we shall share it with them or not. For though the diviner should forewarn you that the auspices are unfavorable, this means no more than that either death or mutilation or exile is portended. But we have reason within us; and it directs us, even with these hazards, to stand by our friend and our country. Attend, therefore, to the greater diviner, the Pythian God, who once cast out of the temple him who neglected to save his friend.[5]

XXXIII

Begin by prescribing to yourself some character and demeanor, such as you may preserve both alone and in company.

Be mostly silent, or speak merely what is needful, and in few words. We may, however, enter sparingly into discourse sometimes, when occasion calls for it; but let it not run on any of the common subjects, as gladiators, or horse races, or athletic champions, or food, or drink—the vulgar topics of conversation—and especially not on men, so as either to blame, or praise, or make comparisons. If you are able, then, by your own conversation, bring over that of your company to proper subjects; but if you happen to find yourself among strangers, be silent.

Let not your laughter be loud, frequent, or abundant.

Avoid taking oaths, if possible, altogether; at any rate, so far as you are able.

Avoid public and vulgar entertainments; but if ever an occasion calls you to them, keep your attention upon the stretch, that you may not imperceptibly slide into vulgarity. For be assured that if a person be ever so pure himself, yet, if his companion be corrupted, he who converses with him will be corrupted likewise.

---

5   This refers to an anecdote given in full by Simplicius, in his commentary on this passage, of a man assaulted and killed on his way to consult the oracle, while his companion, deserting him, took refuge in the temple till cast out by the Deity.—Tr.

Provide things relating to the body no further than absolute need requires, as meat, drink, clothing, house, retinue. But cut off everything that looks toward show and luxury.

Before marriage guard yourself with all your ability from unlawful intercourse with women; yet be not uncharitable or severe to those who are led into this, nor boast frequently that you yourself do otherwise.

If anyone tells you that a certain person speaks ill of you, do not make excuses about what is said of you, but answer: "He was ignorant of my other faults, else he would not have mentioned these alone."

It is not necessary for you to appear often at public spectacles; but if ever there is a proper occasion for you to be there, do not appear more solicitous for any other than for yourself—that is, wish things to be only just as they are, and only the best man to win; for thus nothing will go against you. But abstain entirely from acclamations and derision and violent emotions. And when you come away, do not discourse a great deal on what has passed and what contributes nothing to your own amendment. For it would appear by such discourse that you were dazzled by the show.

Be not prompt or ready to attend private recitations; but if you do attend, preserve your gravity and dignity, and yet avoid making yourself disagreeable.

When you are going to confer with anyone, and especially with one who seems your superior, represent to yourself how Socrates or Zeno[6] would behave in such a case, and you will not be at a loss to meet properly whatever may occur.

When you are going before anyone in power, fancy to yourself that you may not find him at home, that you may be shut out, that the doors may not be opened to you, that he may not notice you. If, with all this, it be your duty to go, bear what happens and never say to yourself, "It was not worth so much"; for this is vulgar, and like a man bewildered by externals.

In company, avoid a frequent and excessive mention of your own actions and dangers. For however agreeable it may be to yourself to allude to the risks you have run, it is not equally agreeable to others to hear your adventures. Avoid likewise an endeavor to excite laughter, for this may readily slide you into vulgarity, and, besides, may be apt to lower you in the esteem of your acquaintance. Approaches to indecent discourse are likewise dangerous. Therefore, when anything of this sort happens, use the first fit opportunity to rebuke him who makes advances that way, or, at least, by silence and blushing and a serious look show yourself to be displeased by such talk.

XXXIV

If you are dazzled by the semblance of any promised pleasure, guard yourself against being bewildered by it; but let the affair wait your leisure, and procure yourself some delay. Then bring to your mind both points of time—that in which you shall enjoy the pleasure, and that in which you will repent and reproach yourself, after you have enjoyed it—and set before you, in opposition to these, how you will rejoice and applaud yourself if you abstain. And even though it

---

6   Reference is to Zeno of Cyprus (335–263 b.c.), the founder of the Stoic school.—Ed.

should appear to you a seasonable gratification, take heed that its enticements and allurements and seductions may not subdue you, but set in opposition to this how much better it is to be conscious of having gained so great a victory.

XXXV

When you do anything from a clear judgment that it ought to be done, never shrink from being seen to do it, even though the world should misunderstand it; for if you are not acting rightly, shun the action itself; if you are, why fear those who wrongly censure you?

XXXVI

As the proposition, "either it is day or it is night," has much force in a disjunctive argument, but none at all in a conjunctive one, so, at a feast, to choose the largest share is very suitable to the bodily appetite, but utterly inconsistent with the social spirit of the entertainment. Remember, then, when you eat with another, not only the value to the body of those things which are set before you, but also the value of proper courtesy toward your host.

XXXVII

If you have assumed any character beyond your strength, you have both demeaned yourself ill in that and quitted one which you might have supported.

XXXVIII

As in walking you take care not to tread upon a nail, or turn your foot, so likewise take care not to hurt the ruling faculty of your mind. And if we were to guard against this in every action, we should enter upon action more safely.

XXXIX

The body is to everyone the proper measure of its possessions, as the foot is of the shoe. If, therefore, you stop at this, you will keep the measure; but if you move beyond it, you must necessarily be carried forward, as down a precipice; as in the case of a shoe, if you go beyond its fitness to the foot, it comes first to be gilded, then purple, and then studded with jewels. For to that which once exceeds the fit measure there is no bound.

XL

Women from fourteen years old are flattered by men with the title of mistresses. Therefore, perceiving that they are regarded only as qualified to give men pleasure, they begin to adorn themselves, and in that to place all their hopes. It is worthwhile, therefore, to try that they may perceive themselves honored only so far as they appear beautiful in their demeanor and modestly virtuous.

XLI

It is a mark of want of intellect to spend much time in things relating to the body, as to be immoderate in exercises, in eating and drinking, and in the discharge of other animal functions. These things should be done incidentally and our main strength be applied to our reason.

XLII

When any person does ill by you, or speaks ill of you, remember that he acts or speaks from an impression that it is right for him to do so. Now it is not possible that he should follow what appears right to you, but only what appears so to himself. Therefore, if he judges from false appearances, he is the person hurt, since he, too, is the person deceived. For if anyone takes a true proposition to be false, the proposition is not hurt, but only the man is deceived. Setting out, then, from these principles, you will meekly bear with a person who reviles you, for you will say upon every occasion, "It seemed so to him."

XLIII

Everything has two handles: one by which it may be borne, another by which it cannot. If your brother acts unjustly, do not lay hold on the affair by the handle of his injustice, for by that it cannot be borne, but rather by the opposite—that he is your brother, that he was brought up with you; and thus you will lay hold on it as it is to be borne.

XLIV

These reasonings have no logical connection: "I am richer than you, therefore I am your superior." "I am more eloquent than you, therefore I am your superior." The true logical connection is rather this: "I am richer than you, therefore my possessions must exceed yours." "I am more eloquent than you, therefore my style must surpass yours." But you, after all, consist neither in property nor in style.

XLV

Does anyone bathe hastily? Do not say that he does it ill, but hastily. Does anyone drink much wine? Do not say that he does ill, but that he drinks a great deal. For unless you perfectly understand his motives, how should you know if he acts ill? Thus you will not risk yielding to any appearances but such as you fully comprehend.

XLVI

Never proclaim yourself a philosopher, nor make much talk among the ignorant about your principles, but show them by actions. Thus, at an entertainment, do not discourse how people ought to eat, but eat as you ought. For remember that thus Socrates also universally avoided all ostentation. And when persons came to him and desired to be introduced by him to philosophers, he took them and introduced them; so well did he bear being overlooked. So if ever there should be among the ignorant any discussion of principles, be for the most part silent. For there is great danger in hastily throwing out what is undigested. And if anyone tells you that you know nothing, and you are not nettled at it, then you may be sure that you have really entered on your work. For sheep do not hastily throw up the grass to show the shepherds how much they have eaten, but, inwardly digesting their food, they produce it outwardly in wool and milk. Thus, therefore, do you not make an exhibition before the ignorant of your principles, but of the actions to which their digestion gives rise.

XLVII

When you have learned to nourish your body frugally, do not pique yourself upon it; nor, if you drink water, be saying upon every occasion, "I drink water." But first consider how much more frugal are the poor than we, and how much more patient of hardship. If at any time you would inure yourself by exercise to labor and privation, for your own sake and not for the public, do not attempt great feats; but when you are violently thirsty, just rinse your mouth with water, and tell nobody.

XLVIII

The condition and characteristic of a vulgar person is that he never looks for either help or harm from himself, but only from externals. The condition and characteristic of a philosopher is that he looks to himself for all help or harm. The marks of a proficient are that he censures no one, praises no one, blames no one, accuses no one; says nothing concerning himself as being anybody or knowing anything. When he is in any instance hindered or restrained, he accuses himself; and if he is praised, he smiles to himself at the person who praises him; and if he is censured, he makes no defense. But he goes about with the caution of a convalescent, careful of interference with anything that is doing well but not yet quite secure. He restrains desire; he transfers his aversion to those things only which thwart the proper use of our own will; he employs his energies moderately in all directions; if he appears stupid or ignorant, he does not care; and, in a word, he keeps watch over himself as over an enemy and one in ambush.

XLIX

When anyone shows himself vain on being able to understand and interpret the works of Chrysippus,[7] say to yourself: "Unless Chrysippus had written obscurely, this person would have had nothing to be vain of. But what do I desire? To understand nature, and follow her. I ask, then, who interprets her; and hearing that Chrysippus does, I have recourse to him. I do not understand his writings. I seek, therefore, one to interpret them." So far there is nothing to value myself upon. And when I find an interpreter, what remains is to make use of his instructions. This alone is the valuable thing. But if I admire merely the interpretation, what do I become more than a grammarian, instead of a philosopher, except, indeed, that instead of Homer I interpret Chrysippus? When anyone, therefore, desires me to read Chrysippus to him, I rather blush when I cannot exhibit actions that are harmonious and consonant with his discourse.

L

Whatever rules you have adopted, abide by them as laws, and as if you would be impious to transgress them; and do not regard what anyone says of you, for this, after all, is no concern of yours. How long, then, will you delay to demand of yourself the noblest improvements, and in no instance to transgress the judgments of reason? You have received the philosophic principles with which you ought to be conversant; and you have been conversant with them. For what other master, then, do you wait as an excuse for this delay in self-reformation? You are no longer a boy but a grown man. If, therefore, you will be negligent and slothful, and always add procrastination to procrastination, purpose to purpose, and fix day after day in which you will attend to yourself, you will insensibly continue to accomplish nothing and, living and dying, remain of vulgar mind. This instant, then, think yourself worthy of living as a man grown up and a proficient. Let whatever appears to be the best be to you an inviolable law. And if any instance of pain or pleasure, glory or disgrace, be set before you, remember that now is the combat, now the Olympiad comes on, nor can it be put off; and that by one failure and defeat honor may be lost or—won. Thus Socrates became perfect, improving himself by everything, following reason alone. And though you are not yet a Socrates, you ought, however, to live as one seeking to be a Socrates.

---

7   Chrysippus (c. 280–207 B.C.) was a Stoic philosopher who became head of the Stoa after Cleanthes. His works, which are lost, were most influential and were generally accepted as the authoritative interpretation of orthodox Stoic philosophy.—Ed.

LI

The first and most necessary topic in philosophy is the practical application of principles, as, We ought not to lie; the second is that of demonstrations as, Why it is that we ought not to lie; the third, that which gives strength and logical connection to the other two, as, Why this is a demonstration. For what is demonstration? What is a consequence? What a contradiction? What truth? What falsehood? The third point is then necessary on account of the second; and the second on account of the first. But the most necessary, and that whereon we ought to rest, is the first. But we do just the contrary. For we spend all our time on the third point and employ all our diligence about that, and entirely neglect the first. Therefore, at the same time that we lie, we are very ready to show how it is demonstrated that lying is wrong.

Upon all occasions we ought to have these maxims ready at hand:
Conduct me, Zeus, and thou, O Destiny,
Wherever your decrees have fixed my lot.
I follow cheerfully; and, did I not,
Wicked and wretched, I must follow still.[8]
Who'er yields properly to Fate is deemed
Wise among men, and knows the laws of Heaven.[9]
And this third:
"O Crito, if it thus pleases the gods, thus let it be."[10]
"Anytus and Melitus may kill me indeed; but hurt me they cannot."[11]

---

8   Cleanthes, in Diogenes Laertius, quoted also by Seneca, Epistle 107.
9   Euripides, Fragments.
10   Plato, Crito, Chap. XVII.
11   Plato, Apology, Chap. XVIII.

CHAPTER 6

Reasoning about God

Augustine, Anselm, and Aquinas

W ITH THE MIDDLE Ages (475–1492) the history of philosophy in the West makes a decisive move to unite the intellectual values of argument, rigor, and philosophical inquiry with a Christian belief system. Augustine lived from 354–430. By this time, Europe had undergone a major shift to Christianity as the dominant belief system. It was in 306 that the famous emperor Constantine the Great succeeded in capturing the throne of Rome, and he remained there until 337. In 313, Constantine and his colleague Licinius passed the Edict of Milan, sometimes called the Law of Religious Toleration, which declared Christianity to be a legitimate religion and made it so that Christians could practice without fear of persecution. Christianity had been around since about 200 BCE, or so. At first, it was practiced as a small cult religion, but it grew and Constantine himself converted to Christianity in 312. Before Constantine took power, Christians had to practice in secret and were subjected to terrible persecution, as were practitioners of other religious cults.

Of course, this political change and the shift to Christianity as a religion officially endorsed by the state did not mean that the whole of ancient thinking and philosophy had been left behind. The idea of an immortal soul and the idea of some form of absolute being that is not subject to time and natural law are both quite at home in ancient thought and are important parts of Christianity, and indeed the Abrahamic tradition in general. *Another important idea that carries over well from ancient Greek thought is the idea that the universe has a rational order.* Recall that the stoics put a great faith in the rationality of nature. For them, nature is never mistaken, no matter how senseless it may seem from our human point of view. What changes for Christian philosophers is that this natural rational order is divinized; that is, God is becomes the source of reason and of the rational order of the universe.

We can see this most clearly in the thinking of people like Augustine, Anselm, and Aquinas, all of which we will explore in what follows.

Important Concepts: Credo *ut intelligam*; the problem of evil; ontological argument, cosmological argument; deductive versus inductive.

Philosophy in the Christian world becomes a tool for understanding God: The better the knowledge of nature, the better the knowledge of God's message. But there is no such thing as a Christian philosophy; there is Christianity and there is philosophy. Philosophy is a tool for Christianity, nothing more. Faith is first! We use our faith to guide our understanding. Philosophy is a tool in this task of understanding. We see the force of this faith-first methodological injunction nowhere more clearly than in the thinking of St. Augustine and St. Anselm. Both thinkers employ the basic method of *Credo ut intelligam*, a Latin phrase meaning "I believe in order that I may understand," used explicitly by St. Anselm but adapted from a formula original to St. Augustine. The idea is that faith comes first and that faith is necessary to order to be able to understand anything at all about God's creation.

This approach leads to some famous difficulties. The problem of evil, for instance, is one that has received considerable attention all the way from the ancient world to today; while it is a problem that seems impossible to deny the real existence of evil in the world, the traditional concept of the Christian God does not seem compatible with evil. Traditionally, God is conceived as all powerful (omnipotent), all knowing (omniscient), and all good (omnibenevolent). But, if God is all these things, why would God make a world that contains evil in it? God is omnibenevolent, so it can't be because God thinks evil is a good thing. God is omnipotent, so it's not that God could not make a world that does not contain evil. And God is omniscient, so it's not that God missed something or made some mistake. If faith comes first, then it is difficult to see how we can square the belief in God with our experience of a world that undoubtedly contains evil. Just the conviction that human beings have free will seems to imply that evil is at least possible, since if evil was not possible for us, we would not be free to choose whichever course of action we want. The selection from Augustine represents an effort to attempt to think through part of this problem.

AUGUSTINE (354–430)

St. Augustine was an extremely prolific writer who left us with some of the most philosophically rich and beautiful texts in the Christian philosophical tradition. In a famous text, *On the Free Choice of Will*, Augustine tackles some of the great puzzles surrounding human freedom in its compatibility with the existence of the traditional God that is familiar to the Abrahamic traditions. Like many early Christian philosophers, Augustine was trying to provide rational arguments to both support faith and to defend faith against its detractors.

One central question, still interesting and relevant today, is whether God can be thought to have given humans free will. The problem is that free will can be used to sin, so if God gave us the power to sin, it seems that God is (at least indirectly) responsible for evil in the world. But, this is unthinkable because, as we have seen, God, by definition, is wholly good. Augustine solves this problem in a preliminary way by pointing out that without free will, we would be able to do neither good nor evil since when one cannot choose how to act, one cannot be responsible for that action, and so cannot be said to be doing good or evil at all. Free will is, in this way, a prerequisite for good. In this way, Augustine shows that God simply had to make human beings free since it's the only way to ensure that we make genuinely good choices. The upshot here is that we can of course still err, but it also places evil into the realm of human responsibility. God may well have granted us the power to choose evil, but we still have to choose it. This can be seen as a kind of solution to the problem of evil, but it's worth considering whether it makes sense to think the problem can be solved so easily, simply by making humans responsible. Could an omnibenevolent God really create a world in which some of the things humans do to one another are even possible?

ANSELM (1033–1109)

Like Augustine, Anselm wants to try to understand God and how belief in God can be justified in the face of the world. As previously explained, they both follow the faith-first methodological injunction to believe in God in order to understand the world, God's creation. St. Anselm's *Proslogion*, from which we have a selection, is a series of puzzles about God that seem to resist understanding. How can God be both just and merciful when justice often seems to require stern punishment? How can God be omnipotent if God cannot do everything? God cannot make what is true into something false. How can God be thought to exist? The *Proslogion* deals with such questions by praying to God, not for guidance, but for understanding. Anselm wants to understand his faith, and he writes to help others understand theirs.

One important thing to keep in mind when reading Anselm is that he was writing for Monks, or at least other believers. For someone like Anselm, not believing in God would be almost unthinkable, something only a fool would entertain. What makes Anselm (and Augustine) a philosopher is that he is trying to use the philosophical tools of reason and rational argument to provide the faithful with the tools necessary for understanding their own faith.

The selection that follows is from the section of the *Proslogion* where Anselm is trying to understand how belief in God can be rationally justified. Anselm's solution is the original formulation of the rightly famous ontological argument, an argument not necessarily for God's existence, but rather for why belief in God is rationally justifiable. There's a subtle difference, here. We'll see in the next section that St. Aquinas's approach to this topic amounts to an actual argument for God's existence, a reason why even the nonbeliever ought to believe. Anselm, remember, is a monk writing for monks, a believer writing for believers—he is not trying to convince the nonbeliever. God's existence is assumed as a premise in an argument that proves God's existence as real. Some people have pointed out that this commits the fallacy of arguing in a circle (look this up), but I will let you decide whether you think this is a problem.

The ontological argument is so called because it turns on the nature of God's existence. "Ontological" means having to do with existence, and "ontology" is the study of being and existence.

God's real existence, so the argument goes, logically follows from the nature of God's existence, from the kind of thing that God is. At its most basic, the argument is as follows:

1. God is something than which nothing greater can be thought.
2. It is greater to exist in reality than in the understanding alone.
3. Therefore, God exists in reality.

If you think there is something fishy going on here, you're not alone. Philosophers have been discussing this argument for over a thousand years. Try to use this summary to guide you through the reading. Try to figure out how Anselm is coming to his conclusion.

———

Proslogion

Anselm

CHAPTER I

Exhortation of the mind to the contemplation of God. —It casts aside cares, and excludes all thoughts save that of God, that it may seek Him. Man was created to see God. Man by sin lost the blessedness for which he was made, and found the misery for which he was not made. He did not keep this good when he could keep it easily. Without God it is ill with us. Our labors and attempts are in vain without God. Man cannot seek God, unless God himself teaches him; nor find him, unless he reveals himself. God created man in his image, that he might be mindful of him, think of him, and love him. The believer does not seek to understand, that he may believe, but he believes that he may understand: for unless he believed he would not understand [...]

CHAPTER II

Truly there is a God, although the fool hath said in his heart, There is no God.

AND so, Lord, do thou, who dost give understanding to faith, give me, so far as thou knowest it to be profitable, to understand that thou art as we believe; and that thou art that which we believe. And indeed, we believe that thou art a being than which nothing greater can be conceived. Or is there no such nature, since the fool hath said in his heart, there is no God? (Psalms 14:1). But, at any rate, this very fool, when he hears of this being of which I speak—a being than which nothing greater can be conceived—understands what he hears, and what he understands is in his understanding; although he does not understand it to exist.

For, it is one thing for an object to be in the understanding, and another to understand that the object exists. When a painter first conceives of what he will afterwards perform, he has it in his understanding, but he does not yet understand it to be, because he has not yet performed

Anselm, *Selections from Works of St. Anselm*, trans. Sidney Norton Deane, 1903.

it. But after he has made the painting, he both has it in his understanding, and he understands that it exists, because he has made it.

Hence, even the fool is convinced that something exists in the understanding, at least, than which nothing greater can be conceived. For, when he hears of this, he understands it. And whatever is understood, exists in the understanding. And assuredly that, than which nothing greater can be conceived, cannot exist in the understanding alone. For, suppose it exists in the understanding alone: then it can be conceived to exist in reality; which is greater.

Therefore, if that, than which nothing greater can be conceived, exists in the understanding alone, the very being, than which nothing greater can be conceived, is one, than which a greater can be conceived. But obviously this is impossible. Hence, there is no doubt that there exists a being, than which nothing greater can be conceived, and it exists both in the understanding and in reality.

CHAPTER III

God cannot be conceived not to exist. —God is that, than which nothing greater can be conceived. —That which can be conceived not to exist is not God.

AND it assuredly exists so truly, that it cannot be conceived not to exist. For, it is possible to conceive of a being which cannot be conceived not to exist; and this is greater than one which can be conceived not to exist. Hence, if that, than which nothing greater can be conceived, can be conceived not to exist, it is not that, than which nothing greater can be conceived. But this is an irreconcilable contradiction. There is, then, so truly a being than which nothing greater can be conceived to exist, that it cannot even be conceived not to exist; and this being thou art, O Lord, our God.

So truly, therefore, dost thou exist, O Lord, my God, that thou canst not be conceived not to exist; and rightly. For, if a mind could conceive of a being better than thee, the creature would rise above the Creator; and this is most absurd. And, indeed, whatever else there is, except thee alone, can be conceived not to exist. To thee alone, therefore, it belongs to exist more truly than all other beings, and hence in a higher degree than all others. For, whatever else exists does not exist so truly, and hence in a less degree it belongs to it to exist. Why, then, has the fool said in his heart, there is no God (Psalms 14:1), since it is so evident, to a rational mind, that thou dost exist in the highest degree of all? Why, except that he is dull and a fool?

CHAPTER IV

How the fool has said in his heart what cannot be conceived. —A thing may be conceived in two ways: (1) when the word signifying it is conceived; (2) when the thing itself is understood As far as the word goes, God can be conceived not to exist; in reality he cannot.

BUT how has the fool said in his heart what he could not conceive; or how is it that he could not conceive what he said in his heart? since it is the same to say in the heart, and to conceive.

But, if really, nay, since really, he both conceived, because he said in his heart; and did not say in his heart, because he could not conceive; there is more than one way in which a thing is said in the heart or conceived. For, in one sense, an object is conceived, when the word signifying it is conceived; and in another, when the very entity, which the object is, is understood.

In the former sense, then, God can be conceived not to exist; but in the latter, not at all. For no one who understands what fire and water are can conceive fire to be water, in accordance with the nature of the facts themselves, although this is possible according to the words. So, then, no one who understands what God is can conceive that God does not exist; although he says these words in his heart, either without any or with some foreign, signification. For, God is that than which a greater cannot be conceived. And he who thoroughly understands this, assuredly understands that this being so truly exists, that not even in concept can it be nonexistent. Therefore, he who understands that God so exists, cannot conceive that he does not exist.

I thank thee, gracious Lord, I thank thee; because what I formerly believed by thy bounty, I now so understand by thine illumination, that if I were unwilling to believe that thou dost exist, I should not be able not to understand this to be true.

CHAPTER V

God is whatever it is better to be than not to be; and he, as the only self-existent being, creates all things from nothing.

WHAT art thou, then, Lord God, than whom nothing greater can be conceived? But what art thou, except that which, as the highest of all beings, alone exists through itself, and creates all other things from nothing? For, whatever is not this is less than a thing which can be conceived of. But this cannot be conceived of thee. What good, therefore, does the supreme Good lack, through which every good is? Therefore, thou art just, truthful, blessed, and whatever it is better to be than not to be. For it is better to be just than not just; better to be blessed than not blessed.

AQUINAS (1215–1274)

One of the important things to know about Aquinas, and one of the things that makes his philosophy—his Christian philosophy—unique is that for him theology and philosophy are separate sciences: Theology moves from God to things; philosophy moves from things to God. And there is no conflict between faith and rationality because truth is always consistent with truth. If we derive things from God and infer God from things, then the answers we get on both paths will be consistent because they both reveal the same truth. Aquinas, just like Augustine and Anselm, would have found it preposterous to not believe in God, but philosophy, for Aquinas, does not begin with belief; that is, faith does not come first for the philosopher. This is an important distinction between the Augustine/Anselm approach and Aquinas's approach. Aquinas thinks he can provide good reasons to believe in God that even the nonbeliever can accept.

This difference in approach explains that different types of argument we see in Anselm and Aquinas. Anselm uses *deduction* to prove God's existence, which means that he derives the conclusion that God exists from the definition of God itself. The way the argument is set up, if one accepts the truth of the premises, the conclusion follows by necessity. Aquinas, on the other hand, uses *induction* to prove God's existence since he begins with evidence and concludes from this evidence that God exists.

The difference between these approaches motivates a debate between Anselm and Aquinas about whether God's existence is self-evident. What does "self-evident" mean? Self-evident propositions are ones that contain the predicate in the subject. Self-evident propositions would be things such as, "If A is shorter than B, then B is taller than A." The idea here is that once you understand the proposition, you don't need anything else to assent to it as true—understanding it is enough. This is precisely the characteristic that Anselm thinks the proposition "God exists" has. Consider that for Anselm the ontological argument is an attempt to fully articulate the logic behind the claim that God exists. For him, God's existence is self-evident since, as Anselm shows, to understand what God is commits one to accepting God's existence.

Aquinas does not agree. Aquinas points out that self-evident propositions simply cannot be denied, but all sorts of people deny that God exists—this alone is evidence that God exists is not self-evident. Aquinas addresses this issue by pointing out that something can be self-evident in two ways: (a) in itself, not to us; and (b) in itself, also to us. God exists is self-evident only to God because no other being has the capacity to know the essence of God. Aquinas's critique of Anselm, then, is that the concept of God does not imply the existence of God, at least not to us. Notice how this fleshes out the difference between Anselm's *deductive* and Aquinas's *inductive* argument. Anselm thinks that God's real existence simply follows from the definition of God, but Aquinas does not think that a philosopher should accept God's existence before finding evidence for God in the world. God's existence can thus not be *derived*, but it can be logically inferred through an *inductive* argument. Aquinas is a member of the school of natural theology, a school of theology that thinks that God's existence can be proven by appeal to the natural world, to the works of God. As philosophers, however, we always have to point to finite things to demonstrate an infinite God. It is only in theology that we can begin with faith and move from God to things. Perhaps you can see how philosophy and theology can complement one another.

The selection that follows is from Aquinas's massive *Summa Theologica*, from the section where Aquinas "proves" God's existence. The proofs are a little easier to follow than Anselm's argument, if only because they are clearly divided into five different proofs, the argument from motion, the argument from efficient causes, the argument from possibility and necessity, the argument from the gradation of being, and the argument from design. The first three arguments share a very similar structure. See if you can discern this structure.

Summa Theologica

St. Thomas Aquinas

FIRST ARTICLE [I, Q. 2, Art. 1]

Whether the Existence of God Is Self-Evident?

Objection 1: It seems that the existence of God is self-evident. Now those things are said to be self-evident to us the knowledge of which is naturally implanted in us, as we can see in regard to first principles. But as Damascene says (De Fide Orth. i, 1,3), "the knowledge of God is naturally implanted in all." Therefore the existence of God is self-evident.

Obj. 2: Further, those things are said to be self-evident which are known as soon as the terms are known, which the Philosopher (1 Poster. iii) says is true of the first principles of demonstration. Thus, when the nature of a whole and of a part is known, it is at once recognized that every whole is greater than its part. But as soon as the signification of the word "God" is understood, it is at once seen that God exists. For by this word is signified that thing than which nothing greater can be conceived. But that which exists actually and mentally is greater than that which exists only mentally. Therefore, since as soon as the word "God" is understood it exists mentally, it also follows that it exists actually. Therefore the proposition "God exists" is self-evident.

Obj. 3: Further, the existence of truth is self-evident. For whoever denies the existence of truth grants that truth does not exist: and, if truth does not exist, then the proposition "Truth does not exist" is true: and if there is anything true, there must be truth. But God is truth itself: "I am the way, the truth, and the life" (John 14:6) Therefore "God exists" is self-evident.

On the contrary, No one can mentally admit the opposite of what is self-evident; as the Philosopher (Metaph. iv, lect. vi) states concerning the first principles of demonstration. But the opposite of the proposition "God is" can be mentally admitted: "The fool said in his heart, There is no God" (Ps. 52:1). Therefore, that God exists is not self-evident.

I answer that, A thing can be self-evident in either of two ways: on the one hand, self-evident in itself, though not to us; on the other, self-evident in itself, and to us. A proposition is self-evident because the predicate is included in the essence of the subject, as "Man is an animal," for animal is contained in the essence of man. If, therefore the essence of the predicate and subject be known to all, the proposition will be self-evident to all; as is clear with regard to the first principles of demonstration, the terms of which are common things that no one is ignorant of, such as being and non-being, whole and part, and such like. If, however, there

St. Thomas Aquinas, *Selections from Summa Theologica*, trans. Fathers of the English Dominican Province.

are some to whom the essence of the predicate and subject is unknown, the proposition will be self-evident in itself, but not to those who do not know the meaning of the predicate and subject of the proposition. Therefore, it happens, as Boethius says (Hebdom., the title of which is: "Whether all that is, is good"), "that there are some mental concepts self-evident only to the learned, as that incorporeal substances are not in space." Therefore I say that this proposition, "God exists," of itself is self-evident, for the predicate is the same as the subject, because God is His own existence as will be hereafter shown (Q. 3, Art. 4). Now because we do not know the essence of God, the proposition is not self-evident to us; but needs to be demonstrated by things that are more known to us, though less known in their nature—namely, by effects.

Reply Obj. 1: To know that God exists in a general and confused way is implanted in us by nature, inasmuch as God is man's beatitude. For man naturally desires happiness, and what is naturally desired by man must be naturally known to him. This, however, is not to know absolutely that God exists; just as to know that someone is approaching is not the same as to know that Peter is approaching, even though it is Peter who is approaching; for many there are who imagine that man's perfect good which is happiness, consists in riches, and others in pleasures, and others in something else.

Reply Obj. 2: Perhaps not everyone who hears this word "God" understands it to signify something than which nothing greater can be thought, seeing that some have believed God to be a body. Yet, granted that everyone understands that by this word "God" is signified something than which nothing greater can be thought, nevertheless, it does not therefore follow that he understands that what the word signifies exists actually, but only that it exists mentally. Nor can it be argued that it actually exists, unless it be admitted that there actually exists something than which nothing greater can be thought; and this precisely is not admitted by those who hold that God does not exist.

Reply Obj. 3: The existence of truth in general is self-evident but the existence of a Primal Truth is not self-evident to us.

SECOND ARTICLE [I, Q. 2, Art. 2]

Whether It Can Be Demonstrated That God Exists?

Objection 1: It seems that the existence of God cannot be demonstrated. For it is an article of faith that God exists. But what is of faith cannot be demonstrated, because a demonstration produces scientific knowledge; whereas faith is of the unseen (Heb. 11:1). Therefore it cannot be demonstrated that God exists.

Obj. 2: Further, the essence is the middle term of demonstration. But we cannot know in what God's essence consists, but solely in what it does not consist; as Damascene says (De Fide Orth. i, 4). Therefore we cannot demonstrate that God exists.

Obj. 3: Further, if the existence of God were demonstrated, this could only be from His effects. But His effects are not proportionate to Him, since He is infinite and His effects are finite; and between the finite and infinite there is no proportion. Therefore, since a cause cannot be demonstrated by an effect not proportionate to it, it seems that the existence of God cannot be demonstrated.

On the contrary, The Apostle says: "The invisible things of Him are clearly seen, being understood by the things that are made" (Rom. 1:20). But this would not be unless the existence of God could be demonstrated through the things that are made; for the first thing we must know of anything is whether it exists.

I answer that, Demonstration can be made in two ways: One is through the cause, and is called a priori, and this is to argue from what is prior absolutely. The other is through the effect, and is called a demonstration a posteriori; this is to argue from what is prior relatively only to us. When an effect is better known to us than its cause, from the effect we proceed to the knowledge of the cause. And from every effect the existence of its proper cause can be demonstrated, so long as its effects are better known to us; because since every effect depends upon its cause, if the effect exists, the cause must pre-exist. Hence the existence of God, in so far as it is not self-evident to us, can be demonstrated from those of His effects which are known to us.

Reply Obj. 1: The existence of God and other like truths about God, which can be known by natural reason, are not articles of faith, but are preambles to the articles; for faith presupposes natural knowledge, even as grace presupposes nature, and perfection supposes something that can be perfected. Nevertheless, there is nothing to prevent a man, who cannot grasp a proof, accepting, as a matter of faith, something which in itself is capable of being scientifically known and demonstrated.

Reply Obj. 2: When the existence of a cause is demonstrated from an effect, this effect takes the place of the definition of the cause in proof of the cause's existence. This is especially the case in regard to God, because, in order to prove the existence of anything, it is necessary to accept as a middle term the meaning of the word, and not its essence, for the question of its essence follows on the question of its existence. Now the names given to God are derived from His effects; consequently, in demonstrating the existence of God from His effects, we may take for the middle term the meaning of the word "God".

Reply Obj. 3: From effects not proportionate to the cause no perfect knowledge of that cause can be obtained. Yet from every effect the existence of the cause can be clearly demonstrated, and so we can demonstrate the existence of God from His effects; though from them we cannot perfectly know God as He is in His essence.

THIRD ARTICLE [I, Q. 2, Art. 3]

Whether God Exists?

Objection 1: It seems that God does not exist; because if one of two contraries be infinite, the other would be altogether destroyed. But the word "God" means that He is infinite goodness. If, therefore, God existed, there would be no evil discoverable; but there is evil in the world. Therefore God does not exist.

Obj. 2: Further, it is superfluous to suppose that what can be accounted for by a few principles has been produced by many. But it seems that everything we see in the world can be accounted for by other principles, supposing God did not exist. For all natural things can be reduced to one principle which is nature; and all voluntary things can be reduced to one principle which is human reason, or will. Therefore there is no need to suppose God's existence.

On the contrary, It is said in the person of God: "I am Who am." (Ex. 3:14)

I answer that, The existence of God can be proved in five ways.

The first and more manifest way is the argument from motion. It is certain, and evident to our senses, that in the world some things are in motion. Now whatever is in motion is put in motion by another, for nothing can be in motion except it is in potentiality to that towards which it is in motion; whereas a thing moves inasmuch as it is in act. For motion is nothing else than the reduction of something from potentiality to actuality. But nothing can be reduced from potentiality to actuality, except by something in a state of actuality. Thus that which is actually hot, as fire, makes wood, which is potentially hot, to be actually hot, and thereby moves and changes it. Now it is not possible that the same thing should be at once in actuality and potentiality in the same respect, but only in different respects. For what is actually hot cannot simultaneously be potentially hot; but it is simultaneously potentially cold. It is therefore impossible that in the same respect and in the same way a thing should be both mover and moved, i.e. that it should move itself. Therefore, whatever is in motion must be put in motion by another. If that by which it is put in motion be itself put in motion, then this also must needs be put in motion by another, and that by another again. But this cannot go on to infinity, because then there would be no first mover, and, consequently, no other mover; seeing that subsequent movers move only inasmuch as they are put in motion by the first mover; as the staff moves only because it is put in motion by the hand. Therefore it is necessary to arrive at a first mover, put in motion by no other; and this everyone understands to be God.

The second way is from the nature of the efficient cause. In the world of sense we find there is an order of efficient causes. There is no case known (neither is it, indeed, possible) in which a thing is found to be the efficient cause of itself; for so it would be prior to itself, which is impossible. Now in efficient causes it is not possible to go on to infinity, because in all efficient causes following in order, the first is the cause of the intermediate cause, and the intermediate is the cause of the ultimate cause, whether the intermediate cause be several, or only one. Now to take away the cause is to take away the effect. Therefore, if there be no first cause among efficient causes, there will be no ultimate, nor any intermediate cause. But if in efficient causes it is possible to go on to infinity, there will be no first efficient cause, neither will there be an ultimate effect, nor any intermediate efficient causes; all of which is plainly false. Therefore it is necessary to admit a first efficient cause, to which everyone gives the name of God.

The third way is taken from possibility and necessity, and runs thus. We find in nature things that are possible to be and not to be, since they are found to be generated, and to corrupt, and consequently, they are possible to be and not to be. But it is impossible for these always to exist, for that which is possible not to be at some time is not. Therefore, if everything is possible not to be, then at one time there could have been nothing in existence. Now if this were true, even now there would be nothing in existence, because that which does not exist only begins to exist by something already existing. Therefore, if at one time nothing was in existence, it would have been impossible for anything to have begun to exist; and thus even now nothing would be in existence—which is absurd. Therefore, not all beings are merely possible, but there must exist something the existence of which is necessary. But every necessary thing either has its necessity caused by another, or not. Now it is impossible to go on to infinity in necessary things which have their necessity caused by another, as has been already proved in regard to efficient causes. Therefore we cannot but postulate the existence of some being having of itself its own necessity, and not receiving it from another, but rather causing in others their necessity. This all men speak of as God.

The fourth way is taken from the gradation to be found in things. Among beings there are some more and some less good, true, noble and the like. But more and less are predicated of different things, according as they resemble in their different ways something which is the maximum, as a thing is said to be hotter according as it more nearly resembles that which is hottest; so that there is something which is truest, something best, something noblest and, consequently, something which is uttermost being; for those things that are greatest in truth are greatest in being, as it is written in Metaph. ii. Now the maximum in any genus is the cause of all in that genus; as fire, which is the maximum heat, is the cause of all hot things. Therefore there must also be something which is to all beings the cause of their being, goodness, and every other perfection; and this we call God.

The fifth way is taken from the governance of the world. We see that things which lack intelligence, such as natural bodies, act for an end, and this is evident from their acting always, or nearly always, in the same way, so as to obtain the best result. Hence it is plain that not fortuitously, but designedly, do they achieve their end. Now whatever lacks intelligence cannot move towards an end, unless it be directed by some being endowed with knowledge and intelligence; as the arrow is shot to its mark by the archer. Therefore some intelligent being exists by whom all natural things are directed to their end; and this being we call God.

Reply Obj. 1: As Augustine says (Enchiridion xi): "Since God is the highest good, He would not allow any evil to exist in His works, unless His omnipotence and goodness were such as to bring good even out of evil." This is part of the infinite goodness of God, that He should allow evil to exist, and out of it produce good.

Reply Obj. 2: Since nature works for a determinate end under the direction of a higher agent, whatever is done by nature must needs be traced back to God, as to its first cause. So also whatever is done voluntarily must also be traced back to some higher cause other than human reason or will, since these can change or fail; for all things that are changeable and capable of defect must be traced back to an immovable and self-necessary first principle, as was shown in the body of the Article.

PART TWO

The Modern World

THE DEVELOPMENT OF philosophy in the early modern world can be characterized by a change in the understanding of the very project of philosophy, especially natural philosophy, or natural science. In the ancient world and all the way through the middle ages, the mainstream understanding of the universe was heavily influenced by ancient texts, especially from Aristotle, which worked their way into the Christian conception of the world. As we saw in Part I, Aristotle's work was taken up by Christian philosophers, such as Aquinas, and was developed into a system of natural theology that understood the world as God's creation. This influence of Aristotelian philosophy and science on church doctrine is staggering. Aquinas's philosophy was the basis of the official doctrine of the Catholic Church until the 1950s, and Aquinas based much of his thinking on arguments he found in Aristotle. Aristotle documented and categorized everything so completely that it was difficult to imagine that there was anything he had not considered and formulated an answer to.

THE CHALLENGE OF THE RENAISSANCE

But already during the Renaissance (c. fourteenth to seventeenth centuries), the dominance of the Christian worldview begins to sow the seeds of its own eventually waning influence. The Renaissance is generally understood as the intellectual and cultural transition between the middle ages and the modern world, and many Renaissance thinkers develop new and creative ways to at square the Christian philosophies of the middle ages with newly emerging ideas of humanity as free from any form of divine decree. One of the most famous Renaissance thinkers, Pico della Mirandola (1463–1494) argues, for instance, that humankind is a unique creation of God, unique precisely because humankind has no determinate place in nature, no particular role to play, no destiny that is already set out in the mind of the creator. Humankind is a child of God, yes, but humankind, unlike all other creatures in creation, is free! Pico writes,

> The nature of all other creatures is defined and restricted within laws which We have laid down; you, by contrast, impeded by no such restrictions, may, by your own free will, to whose custody We have assigned you, trace for yourself the lineaments of your own nature. I have placed you at the very center of the world, so that from that vantage point you may with greater ease glance round about you on all that the world contains. We have made you a creature neither of heaven nor of earth, neither mortal nor immortal, in order that you may, as the free and proud shaper of your own being, fashion yourself in the form you may prefer. It will be in your power to descend to the lower, brutish forms of life; you will be able, through your own decision, to rise again to the superior orders whose life is divine.[1]

At the time, Pico's work was regarded as heresy. Since while Pico's religiosity was deeply embedded in the middle ages, his celebration of human freedom to find its own place in the world is a direct threat to the authority of the church. After all, if humankind really is the "proud shaper of its own being," able to "fashion itself in the form it prefers," the church has very little sovereignty over how humans make their decisions about what they are to become. This sentiment of individual freedom become definitive of the Enlightenment around three hundred years later, and Pico's thinking was deeply influential for modern thinkers who wanted to challenge religious authority. Today, Pico's work can be read as a transitional text between the religiosity of the middle ages and the incipient secularism of the modern world.

THE MECHANICAL UNIVERSE

By the sixteenth century, the dominance of Aristotelian science began to wane as the new experimental sciences were developed by people such as Francis Bacon (1561–1626) Galileo (1564–1642), and Newton (1642–1727). With these thinkers, the understanding of the universe as fundamentally the work of a creator, God, is exchanged for the idea of the universe as fundamentally mathematical; that is, to understand the universe is, for someone like Galileo, to have penetrated to its mathematical foundation. Recall that for Aquinas, philosophy and theology

---

1   Giovanni Pico della Mirandola, *Oration on the Dignity of Man*, trans. A. Robert Caponigri (Chicago: Henry Regnery Company, 1956), 7–8.

are like two sides of the same coin: In philosophy we start from the world and explain God; in theology, we start from God and explain the world. There is no room here for thinking that the universe is anything but God's creation. But, when Galileo looked up at the stars, he did not see the heavens; he did not see a world apart from our own, governed by its own celestial laws. No, Galileo saw the whole universe as one, governed by the same mechanical laws, mathematical at its core.

Developing Nicolai Copernicus's (1473–1543) work that showed that the sun and not the earth is the center of our solar system, Galileo showed beyond any reasonable doubt that the earth orbits the sun and that planetary motion is explicable using the same physics and mathematics that hold here on Earth. Galileo is, in this way, right at the beginning of an important shift in thinking about the nature of the universe. Instead of a creation conceived in the divine mind, the universe comes to be understood as an indifferent mechanism, of which the earth is just a part. This new mechanical conception of nature had the result, starting with Galileo, of disenchanting nature. For Galileo, nature has no values; it's indifferent, a mere machine. This was a radical view at the time. There is no heaven; we live in a big, meaningless universe.

This was obviously not a view that the Church could accept, and so Galileo was locked away and labelled a heretic. Still, he refused to retract his claims; he refused to apologize for his heresy. A heretic is not a person who makes a mistake and then corrects him- or herself. A heretic is a person who steadfastly refuses to toe the line. Galileo was a heretic because he refused to accept the authority of the Church over the authority of his own reason, his own senses. Under the threat of torture, however, he took it all back and admitted the error of his reason in the face of religious doctrine. He remained under house arrest until his death. Still, the damage had been done. Galileo may have crumbled under the brutal authority, but his work never disappeared.

One of the most consequential results of Galileo's thinking is that the human mind comes to be understood as the sole source of meaningfulness in an indifferent universe. The universe on its own, after all, is an indifferent mechanism. It does not take long for philosophers to take this idea very seriously and draw a strong distinction between the mind and the world. The philosopher Susan Bordo (1947–) has characterized this era as one of deep "epistemological insecurity."[2] People like Galileo had shown that we are not the center of the universe. But even more importantly (and destabilizing), this showed just how very wrong we can be about some basic assumptions. Imagine finding out that our place in the universe is completely different than how we imagine it today. This kind of realization naturally puts into question the reliability of our senses. Our ability to understand the world is thrown into doubt and we begin to question the reliability of our knowledge of the external world. We are thus left with the problem of how we can know that our minds adequately represent the external world.

---

2   Susan Bordo, *The Flight to Objectivity: Essays on Cartesianism and Culture.* (Albany: SUNY Press, 1987), 33–44.

RENÉ DESCARTES, SKEPTICISM, AND SUBSTANCE DUALISM

One famous philosopher, René Descartes (1596–1650) goes so far as to argue that there are two kinds of substances in the world: There is mental substance (thinking things) and material substance (extended things). Descartes is what we in philosophy call a "dualist," since he thinks that there are two basic kinds of things in the world.

Descartes starts by pointing out that when we're dreaming, we can't distinguish between reality and the dream—the dream is a convincing copy of reality. Given this, what's to stop us from concluding that we are dreaming now, or that memories we've had are actually memories of dreams? Take a second to think about this. Have you ever been unsure about whether a memory you're having is of a dream or reality? I have. Have you ever woken up still under the assumption that what you dreamt really happened? That's happened to me, too. Have you ever wanted to return to a dream? I sure have. I had a great one last night! If you answer yes to any of these questions, perhaps you can see Descartes's point about the difficulty in distinguishing dreams from reality.

Descartes then deepens his skepticism about our ability to distinguish reality by employing a famous thought experiment. Imagine that there is an evil demon who is deceiving us at every turn, giving us false impressions of reality, tricking us into believing falsities about our bodies and about other people, implanting into us false memories, and constantly tricking us into thinking that our logical and mathematical deductions are true when they're not. It's important to see that Descartes is not speculating that there is an evil demon like this in the world, nor that we are subject to that kind of deception, by any means. Descartes's point is just that if this kind of thing is even remotely possible, if it is even thinkable, then we must be on guard against it. The only way to place knowledge on a firm foundation is to doubt everything that can possibly be doubted, and the evil demon thought experiment is a good way to imagine all the things that are susceptible to doubt.

From all this, Descartes concludes that the one thing we simply cannot doubt is that we are thinking, since in order to doubt that we are thinking, we must be thinking. Thus, "I think, therefore I am." This simply cannot be false. Whatever else we doubt, we simply cannot doubt that the very thing that is doing all this doubting does in fact exist. Thus, the one thing Descartes can be sure of is his own existence as a thinking thing, as thinking things, mental substance. Thus, Descartes shows us that there must be two kinds of things, material and mental.

The twentieth-century philosopher Richard Rorty (1931–2007) has characterized this shift we see in Galileo and (especially) Descartes as the invention of the mind, the philosophical conception of an inner arena of ideas. Rorty's central book *Philosophy and the Mirror of Nature* argues that Western philosophy has always assumed that there is a strong distinction between the way the world appears to us and the way the world "really is." In the modern world, however, we end up with a dichotomy between extended, material substance and thinking, mental substance. In other words, we get a strong distinction between mind and world. From this distinction, we get the pervasive idea that knowledge is just an accurate representation of reality, what in philosophy we call the "representational theory of knowledge." With this is born the modern discipline of *epistemology*, or the study of the nature, sources, and limits of knowledge; the study of what we can know and how we can claim to know it.

Descartes's argument has been extremely influential—so much so that many find the argument intuitively compelling still today. But Descartes's dualism is not without its problems, and it was certainly not without its detractors. The philosopher Margaret Cavendish, for instance, developed powerful responses to Descartes's dualism by questioning how any interaction between mind and matter could then be possible.[3] The first selection in this next part of the text is from Thomas Hobbes, who shared Cavendish's suspicions about dualism and who developed a thoroughgoing materialism that saw the world, and everything in it, all the way down to human emotion, as parts of a vastly complicated mechanism—no mental substance, no dualism, just matter, all of it connected through a vastly complicated web of causal relations. Let us turn to Hobbes.

---

3   Margaret Cavendish, "Section 1, Letter XXXV," *Philosophical Letters*. Retrieved from http://www.gutenberg.org/files/53679/53679-h/53679-h.htm.

CHAPTER 7

Thomas Hobbes

Human Nature and Politics

H OBBES (1588–1679) WAS a gifted student and attended Oxford at the age of eighteen. When he graduated, he worked as a tutor for a wealthy family and had the opportunity to travel, spending considerable time in continental Europe and having the good fortune of meeting several of the period's greatest thinkers, people such as Descartes, Galileo, and Margaret Cavendish; he even worked for Francis Bacon, the father of experimental science.

Important Concepts: Materialism; Leviathan; sovereign; natural versus artificial; natural law; state of nature

Hobbes, like many of the great minds of his time, was swept up by the ongoing revolution in science and philosophy. *Hobbes is a materialist* and he works with what is called a *corpuscular* theory of the material universe. This means that he thinks the universe is governed by the interaction of individual parts. We saw in the introduction to this section that Descartes divided everything into two kinds of substances, mind and matter. Because of this, Descartes was called a dualist. The way in which Descartes arrives at this conclusion is famously expressed in his *cogito ergo sum* argument—noticing that he could be deceived by everything except that he was a thinking thing (for he had to be something to be deceived), Descartes concluded that mind (thinking substance) and body (material substance) were distinct things.

Hobbes throws this out entirely. *Everything is matter*. The only distinction is between natural bodies and artificial bodies. This is significant as much for Hobbes's political philosophy as much as it is for his thinking as a whole. Absolutely *everything* is treated as moving parts that interact and finally explain the movement of the whole. Hobbes then extends the corpuscular picture of the universe: mind and action, morality and politics.

Leviathan, from which our selections are drawn, is one of the great works of Western philosophy. Hobbes is a wonderful writer. His style is difficult to read and sometimes I think his sentence structure is modeled on the chaotic state of nature he describes in the second selection, excerpted later. Is this what sentences look like before we submit ourselves to the rule of a comprehensible system of punctuation? But, struggling though his difficult style pays dividends since the text is one of the most elegant extensions of materialistic philosophy to the problem of socio-political organization. Nobody interested in philosophy in the modern world can afford to neglect Hobbes.

One of the most expressive passages in the *Leviathan* is its introduction. It is, to my mind, one of the greatest introductions ever written to any philosophical work. In it, Hobbes articulates his view of humankind and the world as modeled on a machine, with intricate moving parts, all governed by laws of motion and interaction.

———

Leviathan

Thomas Hobbes

Nature (the Art whereby God hath made and governes the World) is by the *Art* of man, as in many other things, so in this also imitated, that it can make an Artificial Animal. For seeing life is but a motion of Limbs, the beginning whereof is in some principall part within; why may we not say, that all *Automata* (Engines that move themselves by springs and wheeles as doth a watch) have an artificiall life? For what is the *Heart*, but a *Spring*; and the *Nerves*, but so many *Strings*; and the *Joynts*, but so many *Wheeles*, giving motion to the whole Body, such as was intended by the Artificer? *Art* goes yet further, imitating that Rationall and most excellent worke of Nature, *Man*. For by Art is created that great LEVIATHAN called a COMMON-WEALTH, or STATE, (in latine CIVITAS) which is but an Artificiall Man; though of greater stature and strength than the Naturall, for whose protection and defence it was intended; and in which, the *Soveraignty* is an Artificiall *Soul*, as giving life and motion to the whole body; The *Magistrates*, and other *Officers* of Judicature and Execution, artificiall *Joynts; Reward* and *Punishment* (by which fastned to the seate of the Soveraignty, every joynt and member is moved to perform his duty) are the *Nerves*, that do the same in the Body Naturall; The *Wealth* and *Riches* of all the particular members, are the *Strength; Salus Populi* (the *peoples safety*) its *Businesse; Counsellors*, by whom all things needfull for it to know, are suggested unto it, are the *Memory; Equity* and *Lawes*, an artificiall *Reason* and *Will; Concord, Health; Sedition, Sicknesse* and *Civill war, Death*. Lastly, the *Pacts* and *Covenants*, by which the parts of this Body Politique were at first made, set together, and united, resemble that *Fiat*, or the *Let us make man*, pronounced by God in the Creation. [2]

To describe the Nature of this Artificiall man, I will consider

> First, the *Matter* thereof, and the *Artificer*; both which is *Man*.
> Secondly, *How*, and by what *Covenants* it is made; what are the *Rights* and just *Power* or *Authority* of a *Soveraigne*; and what it is that *preserveth* and *dissolveth* it.
> Thirdly, what is a *Christian Common-wealth*.
> Lastly, what is the *Kingdome of Darkness*.

Concerning the first, there is a saying much usurped of late, That *Wisedome* is acquired, not by reading of *Books*, but of *Men*. Consequently whereunto, those persons, that for the

Thomas Hobbes, *Selection from Leviathan*, pp. xviii-xx, 1651.

most part can give no other proof of being wise, take great delight to shew what they think they have read in men, by uncharitable censures of one another behind their backs. But there is another saying not of late understood, by which they might learn truly to read one another, if they would take the pains; and that is, *Nosce teipsum, Read thy self*: which was not meant, as it is now used, to countenance, either the barbarous state of men in power, towards their inferiors; or to encourage men of low degree, to a sawcie behaviour towards their betters; But to teach us, that for the similitude of the thoughts, and Passions of one man, to the thoughts, and Passions of another, whosoever looketh into himself, and considereth what he doth, when he does *think, opine, reason, hope, feare,* &c, and upon what grounds; he shall thereby read and know, what are the thoughts, and Passions of all other men, upon the like occasions. I say the similitude of *Passions*, which are the same in all men, *desire, feare, hope,* &c; not the similitude of the *objects* of the Passions, which are the things *desired, feared, hoped,* &c: for these the constitution individuall, and particular education do so vary, and they are so easie to be kept from our knowledge, that the characters of mans heart, blotted and confounded as they are, with dissembling, lying, counterfeiting, and erroneous doctrines, are legible onely to him that searcheth hearts. And though by mens actions wee do discover their designe sometimes; yet to do it without comparing them with our own, and distinguishing all circumstances, by which the case may come to be altered, is to decypher without a key, and be for the most part deceived, by too much trust, or by too much diffidence; as he that reads, is himself a good or evil man.

But let one man read another by his actions never so perfectly, it serves him onely with his acquaintance, which are but few. He that is to govern a whole Nation, must read in himself, not this, or that particular man; but Man-kind: which though it be hard to do, harder than to learn any Language, or Science; yet, when I shall have set down my own reading orderly, and perspic-uously, the pains left another, will be onely to consider, if he also find not the same in himself. For this kind of Doctrine, admitteth no other Demonstration. [3]

"For what is the *Heart,* but a *Spring*; and the *Nerves,* but so many *Strings.*" I just love that image. You don't have to agree with Hobbes that humankind is best understood as a kind of automaton to find the image he paints in the introduction a beautiful and compelling one, but Hobbes's genius is really to be found in his next move, where he distinguishes the work of God (nature) and the work of humankind (art) to argue that the proper activity of humankind is the creation of an "artificial man" in the form of a political organization, the state. Humankind, for Hobbes, is not a naturally political animal. Politics is an *art*; it's *artificial*. Naturally, we are brutes, driven by selfish desires that inevitably throw us into a state of discord with ourselves and others. But, the artifice of politics allows us to be more than what we are simply by our natures. It's worth considering here just how similar Hobbes is to Xunzi, who, as we recall from that chapter, thinks that social organization is the primary form of distinction, something that elevates humankind above natural inclination.

Hobbes is famous for his idea of "the state of nature," something that emerges as a kind of thought experiment in which Hobbes attempts to imagine what people would be like simply by nature, without the artifice of the state. As we shall see in the selection, the state of nature is a state of brutal and ruthless competition. In a constant state of enmity and war, it makes for a life that is "nasty, brutish, and short."

But, the thought experiment itself is not the interesting part. Hobbes uses the thought experiment to describe the process through which the political organization of the state could be rationally and legitimately set up, giving a sovereign ultimate authority in matters of dispute between people. Hobbes reasons in the following way:

We are all more or less equal in our ability to achieve our ends. Some of us are strong, some cunning, some charming. This means that whenever two people happen to desire the same thing, they become enemies locked in a battle for the object of desire. So, in seeking one's own end (one's own conservation through the steady increase in power), one ends up seeking only to destroy. This state of constant war is the state of nature, and in this state of nature there is no place for law, no place for right, no place for justice. But there is a saving grace. Men desire peace; they fear death; they want nothing more than to live comfortably, but they also desire to defend themselves against those who would get in the way of this peace. These last two are, respectively, the first, most fundamental laws of nature. Notice the use of this term "nature." *It's a law of nature*, not a civil law, not a rule of conduct—this is what people do *by nature*. We desire peace, but our desire to protect ourselves leads to war. The second law of nature gives a rationally justified version of the golden rule. We surrender some freedom; we take only that amount of freedom that we would grant to others. Out of this surrendering of rights and freedoms grows a *contract*, and out of this contract emerges a *pact*, or *covenant*, an agreement to deliver on the terms of the contract at a later date. *Justice* consists in the honoring of covenants.

I noted that Hobbes's use of the term "nature" to describe the laws that govern our social agreements. As he states in the introduction, the state is *another nature*; it's no mere imitation. The state is a natural configuration chosen by rational people for the sake of protection and flourishing. It is derived from human nature itself, and because of this it is natural.

———

Leviathan

CHAPTERS 13 AND 14

Thomas Hobbes

CHAP. XIII.

Of the NATURALL CONDITION *of Mankind, as concerning their Felicity, and Misery.*
 Nature hath made men so equall, in the faculties of body, and mind; as that though there bee found one man sometimes manifestly stronger in body, or of quicker mind then another; yet when all is reckoned together, the difference between man, and man, is not so considerable, as that one man can thereupon claim to himselfe any benefit, to which another may not pretend,

Thomas Hobbes, *Selection from Leviathan*, pp. 81-90, 1651.

as well as he. For as to the strength of body, the weakest has strength enough to kill the strongest, either by secret machination, or by confederacy with others, that are in the same danger with himselfe.

Men by nature Equall.

And as to the faculties of the mind, (setting aside the arts grounded upon words, and especially that skill of proceeding upon generall, and infallible rules, called Science; which very few have, and but in few things; as being not a native faculty, born with us; nor attained, (as Prudence,) while we look after somewhat els,) I find yet a greater equality amongst men, than that of strength. For Prudence, is but Experience; which equall time, equally bestowes on all men, in [61] those things they equally apply themselves unto. That which may perhaps make such equality incredible, is but a vain conceipt of ones owne wisdome, which almost all men think they have in a greater degree, than the Vulgar; that is, than all men but themselves, and a few others, whom by Fame, or for concurring with themselves, they approve. For such is the nature of men, that howsoever they may acknowledge many others to be more witty, or more eloquent, or more learned; Yet they will hardly believe there be many so wise as themselves: For they see their own wit at hand, and other mens at a distance. But this proveth rather that men are in that point equall, than unequall. For there is not ordinarily a greater signe of the equall distribution of any thing, than that every man is contented with his share.

From this equality of ability, ariseth equality of hope in the attaining of our Ends. And therefore if any two men desire the same thing, which neverthe-lesse they cannot both enjoy, they become enemies; and in the way to their End, (which is principally their owne conservation, and sometimes their delectation only,) endeavour to destroy, or subdue one an other. And from hence it comes to passe, that where an Invader hath no more to feare, than an other

From Equality proceeds Diffidence.

mans single power; if one plant, sow, build, or possesse a convenient Seat, others may probably be expected to come prepared with forces united, to dispossesse, and deprive him, not only of the fruit of his labour, but also of his life, or liberty. And the Invader again is in the like danger of another.

And from this diffidence of one another, there is no way for any man to secure himselfe, so reasonable, as Anticipation; that is, by force, or wiles, to master the persons of all men he can, so long, till he see no other power great enough to endanger him: And this is no more than his own conservation requireth, and is generally allowed. Also because there be some, that taking pleasure in contemplating their own power in the acts of conquest, which they pursue farther than their security requires; if others, that otherwise would be glad to be at ease within modest bounds, should not by invasion increase their power, they would not be able, long time, by standing only on their defence, to subsist. And by consequence, such augmentation of dominion over men, being necessary to a mans conservation, it ought to be allowed him.

Againe, men have no pleasure, (but on the contrary a great deale of griefe) in keeping company, where there is no power able to over-awe them all. For every man looketh that his companion should value

From Diffidence Warre.

him, at the same rate he sets upon himselfe: And upon all signes of contempt, or undervaluing, naturally endeavours, as far as he dares (which amongst them that have no common power to keep them in quiet, is far enough to make them destroy each other,) to extort a greater value from his contemners, by dommage; and from others, by the example.

So that in the nature of man, we find three principall causes of quarrell. First, Competition; Secondly, Diffidence; Thirdly, Glory. [62]

The first, maketh men invade for Gain; the second, for Safety; and the third, for Reputation. The first use Violence, to make themselves Masters of other mens persons, wives, children, and cattell; the second, to defend them; the third, for trifles, as a word, a smile, a different opinion, and any other signe of undervalue, either direct in their Persons, or by reflexion in their Kindred, their Friends, their Nation, their Profession, or their Name.

Hereby it is manifest, that during the time men live without a common Power to keep them all in awe, they are in that condition which is called Warre; and such a warre, as is of every man, against every man. For WARRE, consisteth not in Battell onely, or the act of fighting; but in a tract of *time*, wherein the Will to contend by Battell is sufficiently known: and therefore the notion of Time, is to be considered in the nature of Warre; as it is in the nature of Weather. For as the nature of Foule weather, lyeth not in a showre or two of rain; but in an inclination thereto of many dayes together: So the nature of War, consisteth not in actual fighting; but in the known disposition thereto, during all the time there is no assurance to the contrary. All other time is PEACE.

Out of Civil States, there is alwayes Warre *of every one against every one.*

Whatsoever therefore is consequent to a time of Warre, where every man is Enemy to every man; the same is consequent to the time, wherein men live without other security, than what their own strength, and their own invention shall furnish them withall. In such condition, there is no place for Industry; because the fruit thereof is uncertain: and consequently no Culture of the Earth; no Navigation, nor use of the commodities that may be imported by Sea; no commodious Building; no Instruments of moving, and removing such things as require much force; no Knowledge of the face of the Earth; no account of Time; no Arts; no Letters; no Society; and which is worst of all, continuall feare, and danger of violent death; And the life of man, solitary, poore, nasty, brutish, and short.

The Incommodities of such a War.

It may seem strange to some man, that has not well weighed these things; that Nature should thus dissociate, and render men apt to invade, and destroy one another: and he may therefore, not trusting to this Inference, made from the Passions, desire perhaps to have the same confirmed by Experience. Let him therefore consider with himselfe, when taking a journey, he armes himselfe, and seeks to go well accompanied; when going to sleep, he locks his dores; when even in his house he locks his chests; and this when he knowes there bee Lawes, and publike Officers, armed, to revenge all injuries shall bee done him; what opinion he has of his fellow subjects, when he rides armed; of his fellow Citizens, when he locks his dores; and of his children, and servants, when he locks his chests. Does he not there as much accuse mankind by his actions, as I do by my words ? But neither of us accuse mans nature in it. The Desires, and other Passions of man, are in themselves no Sin. No more are the Actions, that proceed from those Passions, till they know a Law that forbids them: which till Lawes be made they cannot know: nor can any Law be made, till they have agreed upon the Person that shall make it. [63]

It may peradventure be thought, there was never such a time, nor condition of warre as this; and I believe it was never generally so, over all the world: but there are many places, where they live so now. For the savage people in many places of *America*, except the government of small Families, the concord whereof dependeth on naturall lust, have no government at all; and live at this day in that brutish manner, as I said before. Howsoever, it may be perceived what manner of life there would be, where there were no common Power to feare; by the manner of life, which men that have formerly lived under a peacefull government, use to degenerate into, in a civill Warre.

But though there had never been any time, wherein particular men were in a condition of warre one against another; yet in all times, Kings, and Persons of Soveraigne authority, because of their Independency, are in continuall jealousies, and in the state and posture of Gladiators; having their weapons pointing, and their eyes fixed on one another; that is, their Forts, Garrisons, and Guns upon the Frontiers of their Kingdomes; and continuall Spyes upon their neighbours; which is a posture of War. But because they uphold thereby, the Industry of their Subjects; there does not follow from it, that misery, which accompanies the Liberty of particular men.

To this warre of every man against every man, this also is consequent; that nothing can be Unjust. The notions of Right and Wrong, Justice and Injustice have there no place. Where there is no common Power, there is no Law: where no Law, no Injustice. Force, and Fraud, are in warre, the two Cardinall vertues. Justice, and Injustice are none of the Faculties neither of the Body, nor Mind. If they were, they might be in a man that were alone in the world, as well as his Senses, and Passions. They are Qualities, that relate to men in Society, not in Solitude. It is consequent also to the same condition, that there be no Propriety, no Dominion, no *Mine* and *Thine* distinct; but onely that to be every mans, that he can get; and for so long, as he can keep it. And thus much for the ill condition, which man by meer Nature is actually placed in; though with a possibility to come out of it, consisting partly in the Passions, partly in his Reason.

In such a Warre, nothings is Unjust.

The Passions that encline men to Peace, are Feare of Death; Desire of such things as are necessary to commodious living; and a Hope by their Industry to obtain them. And Reason suggesteth convenient Articles of Peace, upon which men may to agreement. These Articles, are they, which otherwise are called the Lawes of Nature: whereof I shall speak more particularly, in the two following Chapters. [64]

The Passions that incline men to Peace.

CHAP. XIV.

Of the first and second Naturall Lawes, *and of* Contracts.

The Right Of Nature, which Writers commonly call *Jus Naturale,* is the Liberty each man hath, to use his own power, as he will himselfe, for the preservation of his own Nature; that is to say, of his own Life; and consequently, of doing any thing, which in *Right of Nature what.* his own Judgement, and Reason, hee shall conceive to be the aptest means thereunto.

By Liberty, is understood, according to the proper signification of the word, the absence of externall Impediments: which Impediments, may oft take away part of a mans power to do what *Liberty what.* hee would; but cannot hinder him from using the power left him, according as his judgement, and reason shall dictate to him.

A Law of Nature, *(Lex Naturalis,)* is a Precept, or generall Rule, found out by Reason, by which a man is forbidden to do, that, which is destructive of his life, or taketh away the means *A Law of Nature* of preserving the same; and to omit, that, by which he thinketh it may *what.* be best preserved. For though they that speak of this subject, use to confound *Jus,* and *Lex, Right* and *Law;* yet they ought to be distinguished; because Right, consisteth in liberty to do, or to forbeare; Whereas Law, determineth, and bindeth to one of them: so that Law, and Right, differ *Difference of* as much, as Obligation, and Liberty; which in one and the same matter *Right and Law* are inconsistent.

And because the condition of Man, (as hath been declared in the precedent Chapter) is a condition of Warre of every one against every one; in which case every one is governed by his *Naturally every* own Reason; and there is nothing he can make use of, that may not be a *man has Right* help unto him, in preserving his life against his enemyes; It followeth, that *to every thing.* in such a condition, every man has a Right to every thing; even to one anothers body. And therefore, as long as this naturall Right of every man to every thing endureth, there can be no security to any man, (how strong or wise soever he be,) of living out the time, which Nature ordinarily alloweth men to live. And consequently it is a precept, or generall rule of Reason, *That every man, ought to endeavour* *The Fundamentall* *Peace, as farre as he has hope of obtaining it; and when he cannot obtain* *Law of Nature.* *it, that be may seek, and use, all helps, and advantages of Warre.* The first branch of which Rule, containeth the first, and Fundamentall Law of Nature; which is, *to seek Peace, and follow it.* The Second, the summe of the Right of Nature; which is, *By all means we can, to defend our selves.*

From this Fundamentall Law of Nature, by which men are commanded to endeavour Peace, is derived this second Law; *That a man be willing when others are so too, as farre-forth, as* *for Peace, and* [65] *defence of himselfe be shall think it necessary, to* *The se[c]ond* *lay down this right to all things; and be contented with so much liberty* *Law of Nature.* *against other men, as he would allow other men against himselfe.* For as long as every man holdeth this Right, of doing any thing he liketh; so long are all men in the condition of Warre. But if other men will not lay down their Right, as well as he; then there is no Reason for any one, to devest himselfe of his: For that were to expose himselfe to Prey, (which no man is bound to) rather than to dispose himselfe to Peace. This is that Law of the Gospell; *Whatsoever you require that others should do to you, that do ye to them.* And that Law of all men, *Quod tibi fieri non vis, alteri ne feceris.*

To *lay downe* a mans *Right* to any thing, is to *devest* himselfe of the *Liberty,* of hindring another of the benefit of his own Right to the same. For he that renounceth, or passeth away his Right, giveth not to any other man a Right which he had not before; because there is nothing to which every man had not Right by Nature: but onely standeth out of his way, that he may enjoy his own origi- nall Right, without hindrance from him; not without hindrance from another. So that the effect which redoundeth to one man, by another mans defect of Right, is but so much diminution of impediments to the use of his own Right originall.

What it is to lay down a Right.

Right is layd aside, either by simply Renouncing it; or by Transferring it to another. By *Simply* Renouncing; when he cares not to whom the benefit thereof redoundeth. By Transferring; when he intendeth the benefit thereof to some certain person, or persons. And when a man hath in either manner abandoned, or granted away his Right; then is he said to be Obliged, or Bound, not to hinder those, to whom such Right is granted, or abandoned, from the benefit of it: and that he *Ought,* and it is his Duty, not to make voyd that voluntary act of his own: and that such hindrance is Injustice, and Injury, as being *Sine Jure;* the Right being before renounced, or transferred. So that *Injury,* or *Injustice,* in the controversies of the world, is somewhat like to that, which in the disputations of Scholers is called *Absurdity.* For as it is there called an Absurdity, to contradict what one maintained in the Beginning: so in the world, it is called Injustice, and Injury, voluntarily to undo that, which from the beginning he had voluntarily done. The way by which a man either simply Renounceth, or Transferreth his Right, is a Declara- tion, or Signification, by some voluntary and sufficient signe, or signes, that he doth so Renounce, or Transferre; or hath so Renounced, or Transferred the same, to him that accepteth it. And these Signes are either Words onely, or Actions onely; or (as it hap- peneth most often) both Words, and Actions. And the same are the Bonds, by which men are bound, and obliged: Bonds, that have their strength, not from their own Nature, (for nothing is more easily broken then a mans word,) but from Feare of some evill consequence upon the rupture.

Renouncing a Right what it is.

Transferring Right what.

Obligation.

Duty.

Injustice.

Whensoever a man Transferreth his Right, or Renounceth it; it is either in consideration of some Right reciprocally transferred to [66] himselfe; or *for* some other good he hopeth for thereby. For it is a vol- untary act; and of the voluntary acts of every man, the object is some

Not all Rights are alienable.

Good to himselfe. And therefore there be some Rights, which no man can be understood by any words, or other signes, to have abandoned, or transferred. As first a man cannot lay down the right of resisting them, that assault him by force, to take away his life; because he cannot be understood to ayme thereby, at any Good to himselfe. The same may be sayd of Wounds, and Chayns, and Imprisonment; both because there is no benefit consequent to such patience; as there is to the patience of suffering another to be wounded, or imprisoned: as also because a man cannot tell, when he seeth men proceed against him by violence, whether they intend his death or not. And lastly the motive, and end for which this renouncing, and transferring of Right is introduced, is nothing else but the security of a mans person, in his life, and in the means of so preserving life, as not to be weary of it. And therefore if a man by words, or other signes, seem to despoyle himselfe of the End, for which those signes were intended; he is not to be understood as if he meant it, or that it was his will; but that he was ignorant of how such words and actions were to be interpreted.

Contract what. The mutuall transferring of Right, is that which men call CONTRACT.

There is difference, between transferring of Right to the Thing; and transferring, or tradition, that is, delivery of the Thing it selfe. For the Thing may be delivered together with the Translation of the Right; as in buying and selling with ready mony; or exchange of goods, or lands: and it may be delivered some time after.

Again, one of the Contractors, may deliver the Thing contracted for on his part, and leave the other to perform his part at some determinate time after, and in the mean time be trusted; and

Covenant what. then the Contract on his part, is called PACT, or COVENANT: Or both parts may contract now, to performe hereafter: in which cases, he that is to performe in time to come, being trusted, his performance is called *Keeping of Promise,* or Faith; and the fayling of performance (if it be voluntary) *Violation of Faith.*

CHAPTER 8

John Locke

Freedom, Property, and the Limits of Political Power

RECALL THAT FOR Hobbes, people are fundamentally selfish, seeking only their own peace. It is only in the context of this fundamentally selfish drive that the human agreement to sacrifice some of our natural freedom makes any sense. Things are quite different with John Locke (1632–1704), for whom people are fundamentally free and equal, with a fundamental right to property. It's not really that Hobbes and Locke disagree. Rather, it's a matter of emphasis. Hobbes seems to think that freedom is a political problem to be solved by people working together, while Locke seems to think that freedom is something we all already have, so the problem is to remove as many limitations as possible. Locke's thinking has been extremely influential in the subsequent development of Western political thought. Indeed, so thoroughly imbedded in American culture is the idea that all people are fundamentally free and equal with a basic right to accumulate property that many Americans find it hard to see that this idea is not without its problematic presuppositions. Indeed, just the idea that freedom is something we already have by nature is not at all clear. I mean, what good is freedom if a person has no access to essential resources such as nutritious food, medical care, and economic security? One thing we can take from Hobbes is that freedom does not mean much in the abstract, and it is especially worthless if we are living in a state in which we are only free to fight with one another.

Important Concepts: Freedom; political power; public good; property.

One way to understand Locke's emphasis on the primacy of equality, individual liberty, and the basic freedom from external rule is to see that his *Two Treatises on Government*, from which our selection is drawn, is written in the context of the exclusion crisis. This was a plot led by the Earl of Shaftesbury to exclude the brother of King Charles II, James, from assuming the crown. It was revealed that James was a Catholic, and Catholic rule in France had been tyrannical. Wanting to avoid that, several protestant leaders sought to exclude James from the natural succession of kings. Locke was extremely critical of the divine right of kings. Indeed, the "First Treatise" in the *Two Treatises on Government* is dedicated to a systematic critique of this idea in the work of the political theorist Robert Filmer (c. 1588–1653). Locke hated everything about authoritarian rule, and his "Second Treatise," the part of the *Two Treatises* we are reading, represents his effort to articulate the limits of legitimate political rule.

In this way, perhaps the best way to begin the reading is by focusing on *the definition of political power that is* offered at the end of chapter 1. It's a power to make and *enforce* laws, dole out *punishment* (capital and otherwise) for the sake of *regulating* and *preserving* property. So, there are powers of enforcement and these extend all the way to the punishment of death, but only in the interest of regulating and preserving property. It's also a power that is meant to *employ the force of the community* in the execution of law and the protection of the commonwealth. *But, all this only for the PUBLIC GOOD.*

It's also illuminating to notice how different Locke's state of nature is from Hobbes's. For Locke, the state of nature is a state of perfect freedom, while for Hobbes there is no freedom in the state of nature. And notice how much closer Locke is to the American tendency to regard freedom as the most basic and fundamental right. But, freedom for Hobbes is a moral and political problem; it's a problem of how to remove hindrances from human activity and to create a state in which freedom is possible. This is the case for Locke, too, in a sense. But Locke's problem is to build a community around an *assumption* of perfect equality between people, and on the *assumption* that we are, by nature, free. Hobbes never makes any such assumption. Instead, Hobbes observes that without the artifice of the state, humans will rarely, if ever, have a chance to be free. In this way, it is significant that Locke distinguishes the state of nature from the state of war. The state of nature is one of peace and perfect equality, where no one person has natural authority over anyone else. War is a human act; it's something we have to do, that we have to engage in, and the person who wages such war is fully responsible for its consequences.

Another important feature of the selection is Locke's understanding of the natural right we all have to accumulate property. In the state of nature, for Locke, we are indeed equal, but, as Locke argues, God never intended this absolute equality to last. The industrious and the rational gradually come to enjoy superiority because they gradually mix their labor with nature to acquire property, and this property is perishable, so money is required so that people may be motivated to amass wealth without fear of loss.

This defense of the right to accumulate property does not come without a serious qualification regarding moral responsibility. Locke thinks the property owner has a responsibility to treat the property with respect, not to waste it so that others may benefit from it. It's worth asking whether Locke's thinking would support a law enforcing the redistribution of resources to those prepared to treat it more responsibly. And what would Locke say about environmentally devastating use of property, things such as oil extraction, destruction of environmentally sensitive areas for commercial development, etc? Such things are arguable waste resources so that future generations cannot benefit from them. We have no natural right to any property other than ourselves. Any property acquired through labor could have been acquired by anyone else, and so we are all accountable to others in the proper use of that property. Nothing gives anyone the right to abuse and waste what we all share.

Second Treatise of Government

John Locke

CHAPTER 1: AN ESSAY CONCERNING THE TRUE ORIGINAL, EXTENT AND END OF CIVIL GOVERNMENT

Sect. 1. It having been shewn in the foregoing discourse,

(1). That Adam had not, either by natural right of fatherhood, or by positive donation from God, any such authority over his children, or dominion over the world, as is pretended:

(2). That if he had, his heirs, yet, had no right to it:

(3). That if his heirs had, there being no law of nature nor positive law of God that determines which is the right heir in all cases that may arise, the right of succession, and consequently of bearing rule, could not have been certainly determined:

(4). That if even that had been determined, yet the knowledge of which is the eldest line of Adam's posterity, being so long since utterly lost, that in the races of mankind and families of the world, there remains not to one above another, the least pretence to be the eldest house, and to have the right of inheritance:

All these premises having, as I think, been clearly made out, it is impossible that the rulers now on earth should make any benefit, or derive any the least shadow of authority from that, which is held to be the fountain of all power, Adam's private dominion and paternal jurisdiction; so that he that will not give just occasion to think that all government in the world is the product only of force and violence, and that men live together by no other rules but that of beasts, where the strongest carries it, and so lay a foundation for perpetual disorder and mischief, tumult, sedition and rebellion, (things that the followers of that hypothesis so loudly cry out against) must of necessity find out another rise of government, another original of political power, and another way of designing and knowing the persons that have it, than what Sir Robert Filmer hath taught us.

Sect. 2. To this purpose, I think it may not be amiss, to set down what I take to be political power; that the power of a MAGISTRATE over a subject may be distinguished from that of a FATHER over his children, a MASTER over his servant, a HUSBAND over his wife, and a LORD over his slave. All which distinct powers happening sometimes together in the same man, if he be considered under these different relations, it may help us to distinguish these powers one from wealth, a father of a family, and a captain of a galley.

Sect. 3. POLITICAL POWER, then, I take to be a RIGHT of making laws with penalties of death, and consequently all less penalties, for the regulating and preserving of property, and of employing the force of the community, in the execution of such laws, and

John Locke, *Selection from Second Treatise of Government*, 1690.

in the defence of the commonwealth from foreign injury; and all this only for the public good.

CHAPTER. II: OF THE STATE OF NATURE

Sect. 4. TO understand political power right, and derive it from its original, we must consider, what state all men are naturally in, and that is, a state of perfect freedom to order their actions, and dispose of their possessions and persons, as they think fit, within the bounds of the law of nature, without asking leave, or depending upon the will of any other man.

A state also of equality, wherein all the power and jurisdiction is reciprocal, no one having more than another; there being nothing more evident, than that creatures of the same species and rank, promiscuously born to all the same advantages of nature, and the use of the same faculties, should also be equal one amongst another without subordination or subjection, unless the lord and master of them all should, by any manifest declaration of his will, set one above another, and confer on him, by an evident and clear appointment, an undoubted right to dominion and sovereignty.

Sect. 5. This equality of men by nature, the judicious Hooker looks upon as so evident in itself, and beyond all question, that he makes it the foundation of that obligation to mutual love amongst men, on which he builds the duties they owe one another, and from whence he derives the great maxims of justice and charity. His words are,

The like natural inducement hath brought men to know that it is no less their duty, to love others than themselves; for seeing those things which are equal, must needs all have one measure; if I cannot but wish to receive good, even as much at every man's hands, as any man can wish unto his own soul, how should I look to have any part of my desire herein satisfied, unless myself be careful to satisfy the like desire, which is undoubtedly in other men, being of one and the same nature? To have any thing offered them repugnant to this desire, must needs in all respects grieve them as much as me; so that if I do harm, I must look to suffer, there being no reason that others should shew greater measure of love to me, than they have by me shewed unto them: my desire therefore to be loved of my equals in nature as much as possible may be, imposeth upon me a natural duty of bearing to them-ward fully the like affection; from which relation of equality between ourselves and them that are as ourselves, what several rules and canons natural reason hath drawn, for direction of life, no man is ignorant, Eccl. Pol. Lib. 1.

Sect. 6. But though this be a state of liberty, yet it is not a state of licence: though man in that state have an uncontroulable liberty to dispose of his person or possessions, yet he has not liberty to destroy himself, or so much as any creature in his possession, but where some nobler use than its bare preservation calls for it. The state of nature has a law of nature to govern it, which obliges every one: and reason, which is that law, teaches all mankind, who will but consult it, that being all equal and independent, no one ought to harm another in his life, health, liberty, or possessions: for men being all the workmanship of one omnipotent, and infinitely wise maker; all the servants of one sovereign master, sent into the world by his order, and about his business;

they are his property, whose workmanship they are, made to last during his, not one another's pleasure: and being furnished with like faculties, sharing all in one community of nature, there cannot be supposed any such subordination among us, that may authorize us to destroy one another, as if we were made for one another's uses, as the inferior ranks of creatures are for our's. Every one, as he is bound to preserve himself, and not to quit his station wilfully, so by the like reason, when his own preservation comes not in competition, ought he, as much as he can, to preserve the rest of mankind, and may not, unless it be to do justice on an offender, take away, or impair the life, or what tends to the preservation of the life, the liberty, health, limb, or goods of another.

Sect. 7. And that all men may be restrained from invading others rights, and from doing hurt to one another, and the law of nature be observed, which willeth the peace and preservation of all mankind, the execution of the law of nature is, in that state, put into every man's hands, whereby every one has a right to punish the transgressors of that law to such a degree, as may hinder its violation: for the law of nature would, as all other laws that concern men in this world 'be in vain, if there were no body that in the state of nature had a power to execute that law, and thereby preserve the innocent and restrain offenders. And if any one in the state of nature may punish another for any evil he has done, every one may do so: for in that state of perfect equality, where naturally there is no superiority or jurisdiction of one over another, what any may do in prosecution of that law, every one must needs have a right to do.

Sect. 8. And thus, in the state of nature, one man comes by a power over another; but yet no absolute or arbitrary power, to use a criminal, when he has got him in his hands, according to the passionate heats, or boundless extravagancy of his own will; but only to retribute to him, so far as calm reason and conscience dictate, what is proportionate to his transgression, which is so much as may serve for reparation and restraint: for these two are the only reasons, why one man may lawfully do harm to another, which is that we call punishment. In transgressing the law of nature, the offender declares himself to live by another rule than that of reason and common equity, which is that measure God has set to the actions of men, for their mutual security; and so he becomes dangerous to mankind, the tye, which is to secure them from injury and violence, being slighted and broken by him. Which being a trespass against the whole species, and the peace and safety of it, provided for by the law of nature, every man upon this score, by the right he hath to preserve mankind in general, may restrain, or where it is necessary, destroy things noxious to them, and so may bring such evil on any one, who hath transgressed that law, as may make him repent the doing of it, and thereby deter him, and by his example others, from doing the like mischief. And in the case, and upon this ground, EVERY MAN HATH A RIGHT TO PUNISH THE OFFENDER, AND BE EXECUTIONER OF THE LAW OF NATURE.

Sect. 9. I doubt not but this will seem a very strange doctrine to some men: but before they condemn it, I desire them to resolve me, by what right any prince or state can put to death, or punish an alien, for any crime he commits in their country. It is certain their laws, by virtue of any sanction they receive from the promulgated will of the legislative, reach not a stranger: they speak not to him, nor, if they did, is he bound to hearken to them. The legislative authority, by which they are in force over the subjects of that commonwealth, hath no power over him. Those who have the supreme power of making laws in England, France or Holland, are to an Indian, but like the rest of the world, men without authority: and therefore, if by the law of nature every man hath not a power to punish offences against it, as he soberly judges the case to require, I see not how the magistrates of any community can punish an alien of another country; since, in reference to him, they can have no more power than what every man naturally may have over another.

Sect, 10. Besides the crime which consists in violating the law, and varying from the right rule of reason, whereby a man so far becomes degenerate, and declares himself to quit the principles of human nature, and to be a noxious creature, there is commonly injury done to some person or other, and some other man receives damage by his transgression: in which case he who hath received any damage, has, besides the right of punishment common to him with other men, a particular right to seek reparation from him that has done it: and any other person, who finds it just, may also join with him that is injured, and assist him in recovering from the offender so much as may make satisfaction for the harm he has suffered.

Sect. 11. From these two distinct rights, the one of punishing the crime for restraint, and preventing the like offence, which right of punishing is in every body; the other of taking reparation, which belongs only to the injured party, comes it to pass that the magistrate, who by being magistrate hath the common right of punishing put into his hands, can often, where the public good demands not the execution of the law, remit the punishment of criminal offences by his own authority, but yet cannot remit the satisfaction due to any private man for the damage he has received. That, he who has suffered the damage has a right to demand in his own name, and he alone can remit: the damnified person has this power of appropriating to himself the goods or service of the offender, by right of self-preservation, as every man has a power to punish the crime, to prevent its being committed again, by the right he has of preserving all mankind, and doing all reasonable things he can in order to that end: and thus it is, that every man, in the state of nature, has a power to kill a murderer, both to deter others from doing the like injury, which no reparation can compensate, by the example of the punishment that attends it from every body, and also to secure men from the attempts of a criminal, who having renounced reason, the common rule and measure God hath given to mankind, hath, by the unjust violence and slaughter he hath committed upon one, declared war against all mankind, and therefore may be destroyed as a lion or a tyger, one of those wild savage beasts, with whom men can have no society nor security: and upon this is grounded that great law of nature, Whoso sheddeth man's blood, by man shall his blood be shed. And Cain was so fully convinced, that every one had a right to destroy such a criminal, that after the murder of his brother, he cries out, Every one that findeth me, shall slay me; so plain was it writ in the hearts of all mankind.

Sect. 12. By the same reason may a man in the state of nature punish the lesser breaches of that law. It will perhaps be demanded, with death? I answer, each transgression may be punished to that degree, and with so much severity, as will suffice to make it an ill bargain to the offender, give him cause to repent, and terrify others from doing the like. Every offence, that can be committed in the state of nature, may in the state of nature be also punished equally, and as far forth as it may, in a commonwealth: for though it would be besides my present purpose, to enter here into the particulars of the law of nature, or its measures of punishment; yet, it is certain there is such a law, and that too, as intelligible and plain to a rational creature, and a studier of that law, as the positive laws of commonwealths; nay, possibly plainer; as much as reason is easier to be understood, than the fancies and intricate contrivances of men, following contrary and hidden interests put into words; for so truly are a great part of the municipal laws of countries, which are only so far right, as they are founded on the law of nature, by which they are to be regulated and interpreted.

Sect. 13. To this strange doctrine, viz. That in the state of nature every one has the executive power of the law of nature, I doubt not but it will be objected, that it is unreasonable for men to be judges in their own cases, that self-love will make men partial to themselves and their friends: and on the other side, that ill nature, passion and revenge will carry them too far in punishing others; and hence nothing but confusion and disorder will follow, and that therefore God hath certainly appointed government to restrain the partiality and violence of men. I easily grant, that civil government is the proper remedy for the inconveniencies of the state of nature, which must certainly be great, where men may be judges in their own case, since it is easy to be imagined, that he who was so unjust as to do his brother an injury, will scarce be so just as to condemn himself for it: but I shall desire those who make this objection, to remember, that absolute monarchs are but men; and if government is to be the remedy of those evils, which necessarily follow from men's being judges in their own cases, and the state of nature is therefore not to be endured, I desire to know what kind of government that is, and how much better it is than the state of nature, where one man, commanding a multitude, has the liberty to be judge in his own case, and may do to all his subjects whatever he pleases, without the least liberty to any one to question or controul those who execute his pleasure? and in whatsoever he doth, whether led by reason, mistake or passion, must be submitted to? much better it is in the state of nature, wherein men are not bound to submit to the unjust will of another: and if he that judges, judges amiss in his own, or any other case, he is answerable for it to the rest of mankind.

Sect. 14. It is often asked as a mighty objection, where are, or ever were there any men in such a state of nature? To which it may suffice as an answer at present, that since all princes and rulers of independent governments all through the world, are in a state of nature, it is plain the world never was, nor ever will be, without numbers of men in that state. I have named all governors of independent communities, whether they are, or are not, in league with others: for it is not every compact that puts an end to the state of nature between men, but only this one of agreeing together mutually to enter into one community, and make one body politic; other promises, and compacts, men may make one with another, and yet still be in the state of nature. The promises and bargains for truck, &c. between the two men in the desert island, mentioned by Garcilasso de la Vega, in his history of Peru; or between a Swiss and an Indian, in the woods of

America, are binding to them, though they are perfectly in a state of nature, in reference to one another: for truth and keeping of faith belongs to men, as men, and not as members of society.

Sect. 15. To those that say, there were never any men in the state of nature, I will not only oppose the authority of the judicious Hooker, Eccl. Pol. lib. i. sect. 10, where he says,

The laws which have been hitherto mentioned, i.e. the laws of nature, do bind men absolutely, even as they are men, although they have never any settled fellowship, never any solemn agreement amongst themselves what to do, or not to do: but forasmuch as we are not by ourselves sufficient to furnish ourselves with competent store of things, needful for such a life as our nature doth desire, a life fit for the dignity of man; therefore to supply those defects and imperfections which are in us, as living single and solely by ourselves, we are naturally induced to seek communion and fellowship with others: this was the cause of men's uniting themselves at first in politic societies.

But I moreover affirm, that all men are naturally in that state, and remain so, till by their own consents they make themselves members of some politic society; and I doubt not in the sequel of this discourse, to make it very clear.

CHAPTER. V: OF PROPERTY

Sect. 25. Whether we consider natural reason, which tells us, that men, being once born, have a right to their preservation, and consequently to meat and drink, and such other things as nature affords for their subsistence: or revelation, which gives us an account of those grants God made of the world to Adam, and to Noah, and his sons, it is very clear, that God, as king David says, Psal. cxv. 16. has given the earth to the children of men; given it to mankind in common. But this being supposed, it seems to some a very great difficulty, how any one should ever come to have a property in any thing: I will not content myself to answer, that if it be difficult to make out property, upon a supposition that God gave the world to Adam, and his posterity in common, it is impossible that any man, but one universal monarch, should have any property upon a supposition, that God gave the world to Adam, and his heirs in succession, exclusive of all the rest of his posterity. But I shall endeavour to shew, how men might come to have a property in several parts of that which God gave to mankind in common, and that without any express compact of all the commoners.

Sect. 26. God, who hath given the world to men in common, hath also given them reason to make use of it to the best advantage of life, and convenience. The earth, and all that is therein, is given to men for the support and comfort of their being. And tho' all the fruits it naturally produces, and beasts it feeds, belong to mankind in common, as they are produced by the spontaneous hand of nature; and no body has originally a private dominion, exclusive of the rest of mankind, in any of them, as they are thus in their natural state: yet being given for the use of men, there must of necessity be a means to appropriate them some way or other, before they can be of any use, or at all beneficial to any particular man. The fruit, or venison, which nourishes the wild Indian, who knows no enclosure, and is still a tenant in common, must be his, and so his, i.e. a part of him, that another can no longer have any right to it, before it can do him any good for the support of his life.

Sect. 27. Though the earth, and all inferior creatures, be common to all men, yet every man has a property in his own person: this no body has any right to but himself. The labour of his body, and the work of his hands, we may say, are properly his. Whatsoever then he removes out of the state that nature hath provided, and left it in, he hath mixed his labour with, and joined to it something that is his own, and thereby makes it his property. It being by him removed from the common state nature hath placed it in, it hath by this labour something annexed to it, that excludes the common right of other men: for this labour being the unquestionable property of the labourer, no man but he can have a right to what that is once joined to, at least where there is enough, and as good, left in common for others.

Sect. 28. He that is nourished by the acorns he picked up under an oak, or the apples he gathered from the trees in the wood, has certainly appropriated them to himself. No body can deny but the nourishment is his. I ask then, when did they begin to be his? when he digested? or when he eat? or when he boiled? or when he brought them home? or when he picked them up? and it is plain, if the first gathering made them not his, nothing else could. That labour put a distinction between them and common: that added something to them more than nature, the common mother of all, had done; and so they became his private right. And will any one say, he had no right to those acorns or apples, he thus appropriated, because he had not the consent of all mankind to make them his? Was it a robbery thus to assume to himself what belonged to all in common? If such a consent as that was necessary, man had starved, notwithstanding the plenty God had given him. We see in commons, which remain so by compact, that it is the taking any part of what is common, and removing it out of the state nature leaves it in, which begins the property; without which the common is of no use. And the taking of this or that part, does not depend on the express consent of all the commoners. Thus the grass my horse has bit; the turfs my servant has cut; and the ore I have digged in any place, where I have a right to them in common with others, become my property, without the assignation or consent of any body. The labour that was mine, removing them out of that common state they were in, hath fixed my property in them.

Sect. 29. By making an explicit consent of every commoner, necessary to any one's appropriating to himself any part of what is given in common, children or servants could not cut the meat, which their father or master had provided for them in common, without assigning to every one his peculiar part. Though the water running in the fountain be every one's, yet who can doubt, but that in the pitcher is his only who drew it out? His labour hath taken it out of the hands of nature, where it was common, and belonged equally to all her children, and hath thereby appropriated it to himself.

Sect. 30. Thus this law of reason makes the deer that Indian's who hath killed it; it is allowed to be his goods, who hath bestowed his labour upon it, though before it was the common right of every one. And amongst those who are counted the civilized part of mankind, who have made and multiplied positive laws to determine property, this original law of nature, for the beginning of property, in what was before common, still takes place; and by virtue thereof, what fish any one catches in the ocean, that great and still remaining common of mankind; or what amber-grise any one takes up here, is by the labour that removes it out of that common state nature left it in, made his property, who takes that pains about it. And even amongst us, the hare that any one is hunting, is thought his who pursues her during the chase: for being a beast that is still looked upon as common, and no man's private possession; whoever has employed so much labour about any of that kind, as to find and pursue her, has thereby removed her from the state of nature, wherein she was common, and hath begun a property.

Sect. 31. It will perhaps be objected to this, that if gathering the acorns, or other fruits of the earth, &c. makes a right to them, then any one may ingross as much as he will. To which I answer, Not so. The same law of nature, that does by this means give us property, does also bound that property too. God has given us all things richly, 1 Tim. vi. 12. is the voice of reason confirmed by inspiration. But how far has he given it us? To enjoy. As much as any one can make use of to any advantage of life before it spoils, so much he may by his Tabour fix a property in: whatever is beyond this, is more than his share, and belongs to others. Nothing was made by God for man to spoil or destroy. And thus, considering the plenty of natural provisions there was a long time in the world, and the few spenders; and to how small a part of that provision the industry of one man could extend itself, and ingross it to the prejudice of others; especially keeping within the bounds, set by reason, of what might serve for his use; there could be then little room for quarrels or contentions about property so established.

Sect. 32. But the chief matter of property being now not the fruits of the earth, and the beasts that subsist on it, but the earth itself; as that which takes in and carries with it all the rest; I think it is plain, that property in that too is acquired as the former. As much land as a man tills, plants, improves, cultivates, and can use the product of, so much is his property. He by his labour does, as it were, inclose it from the common. Nor will it invalidate his right, to say every body else has an equal title to it; and therefore he cannot appropriate, he cannot inclose, without the consent of all his fellow-commoners, all mankind. God, when he gave the world in common to all mankind, commanded man also to labour, and the penury of his condition required it of him. God and his reason commanded him to subdue the earth, i.e. improve it for the benefit of life, and therein lay out something upon it that was his own, his labour. He that in obedience to this command of God, subdued, tilled and sowed any part of it, thereby annexed to it something that was his property, which another had no title to, nor could without injury take from him.

Sect. 33. Nor was this appropriation of any parcel of land, by improving it, any prejudice to any other man, since there was still enough, and as good left; and more than the yet unprovided could use. So that, in effect, there was never the less left for others because of his enclosure for himself: for he that leaves as much as another can make use of, does as good as take nothing at all. No body could think himself injured by the drinking of another man, though he took a good draught, who had a whole river of the same water left him to quench his thirst: and the case of land and water, where there is enough of both, is perfectly the same.

Sect. 34. God gave the world to men in common; but since he gave it them for their benefit, and the greatest conveniencies of life they were capable to draw from it, it cannot be supposed he meant it should always remain common and uncultivated. He gave it to the use of the industrious and rational, (and labour was to be his title to it;) not to the fancy or covetousness of the quarrelsome and contentious. He that had as good left for his improvement, as was already taken up, needed not complain, ought not to meddle with what was already improved by another's labour: if he did, it is plain he desired the benefit of another's pains, which he had no right to, and not the ground which God had given him in common with others to labour on, and whereof there was as good left, as that already possessed, and more than he knew what to do with, or his industry could reach to.

Sect. 35. It is true, in land that is common in England, or any other country, where there is plenty of people under government, who have money and commerce, no one can inclose or appropriate any part, without the consent of all his fellow-commoners; because this is left common by compact, i.e. by the law of the land, which is not to be violated. And though it be common, in respect of some men, it is not so to all mankind; but is the joint property of this country, or this parish. Besides, the remainder, after such enclosure, would not be as good to the rest of the commoners, as the whole was when they could all make use of the whole; whereas in the beginning and first peopling of the great common of the world, it was quite otherwise. The law man was under, was rather for appropriating. God commanded, and his wants forced him to labour. That was his property which could not be taken from him where-ever he had fixed it. And hence subduing or cultivating the earth, and having dominion, we see are joined together. The one gave title to the other. So that God, by commanding to subdue, gave authority so far to appropriate: and the condition of human life, which requires labour and materials to work on, necessarily introduces private possessions.

Sect. 36. The measure of property nature has well set by the extent of men's labour and the conveniencies of life: no man's labour could subdue, or appropriate all; nor could his enjoyment consume more than a small part; so that it was impossible for any man, this way, to intrench upon the right of another, or acquire to himself a property, to the prejudice of his neighbour, who would still have room for as good, and as large a possession (after the other had taken out his) as before it was appropriated. This measure did confine every man's possession to a very moderate proportion, and such as he might appropriate to himself, without injury to any body, in the first ages of the world, when men were more in danger to be lost, by wandering from their company, in the then vast wilderness of the earth, than to be straitened for want of room to plant in. And the same measure may be allowed still without prejudice to any body, as full as the world seems: for supposing a man, or family, in the state they were at first peopling of the world by the children of Adam, or Noah; let him plant in some inland, vacant places of America, we shall find that the possessions he could make himself, upon the measures we have given, would not be very large, nor, even to this day, prejudice the rest of mankind, or give them reason to complain, or think themselves injured by this man's incroachment, though the race of men have now spread themselves to all the corners of the world, and do infinitely exceed the small number was at the beginning. Nay, the extent of ground is of so little value, without labour, that I have heard it affirmed, that in Spain itself a man may be permitted to plough, sow and reap, without being disturbed, upon land he has no other title to, but only his making use of it. But, on the contrary, the inhabitants think themselves beholden to him, who, by his industry on neglected, and consequently waste land, has increased the stock of corn, which they wanted. But be this as it will, which I lay no stress on; this I dare boldly affirm, that the same rule of propriety, (viz.) that every man should have as much as he could make use of, would hold still in the world, without straitening any body; since there is land enough in the world to suffice double the inhabitants, had not the invention of money, and the tacit agreement of men to put a value on it, introduced (by consent) larger possessions, and a right to them; which, how it has done, I shall by and by shew more at large.

Sect. 37. This is certain, that in the beginning, before the desire of having more than man needed had altered the intrinsic value of things, which depends only on their usefulness to the life of man; or had agreed, that a little piece of yellow metal, which would keep without wasting or decay, should be worth a great piece of flesh, or a whole heap of corn; though men had a right to appropriate, by their labour, each one of himself, as much of the things of nature, as he could use: yet this could not be much, nor to the prejudice of others, where the same plenty was still left to those who would use the same industry. To which let me add, that he who appropriates land to himself by his labour, does not lessen, but increase the common stock of mankind: for the provisions serving to the support of human life, produced by one acre of inclosed and cultivated land, are (to speak much within compass) ten times more than those which are yielded by an acre of land of an equal richness lying waste in common. And therefore he that incloses land, and has a greater plenty of the conveniencies of life from ten acres, than he could have from an hundred left to nature, may truly be said to give ninety acres to mankind: for his labour now supplies him with provisions out of ten acres, which were but the product of an hundred lying in common. I have here rated the improved land very low, in making its product but as ten to one, when it is much nearer an hundred to one: for I ask, whether in the wild woods and uncultivated waste of America, left to nature, without any improvement, tillage or husbandry, a thousand acres yield the needy and wretched inhabitants as many conveniencies of life, as ten acres of equally fertile land do in Devonshire, where they are well cultivated?

Before the appropriation of land, he who gathered as much of the wild fruit, killed, caught, or tamed, as many of the beasts, as he could; he that so imployed his pains about any of the spontaneous products of nature, as any way to alter them from the state which nature put them in, by placing any of his labour on them, did thereby acquire a propriety in them: but if they perished, in his possession, without their due use; if the fruits rotted, or the venison putrified, before he could spend it, he offended against the common law of nature, and was liable to be punished; he invaded his neighbour's share, for he had no right, farther than his use called for any of them, and they might serve to afford him conveniencies of life.

Sect. 38. The same measures governed the possession of land too: whatsoever he tilled and reaped, laid up and made use of, before it spoiled, that was his peculiar right; whatsoever he enclosed, and could feed, and make use of, the cattle and product was also his. But if either the grass of his enclosure rotted on the ground, or the fruit of his planting perished without gathering, and laying up, this part of the earth, notwithstanding his enclosure, was still to be looked on as waste, and might be the possession of any other. Thus, at the beginning, Cain might take as much ground as he could till, and make it his own land, and yet leave enough to Abel's sheep to feed on; a few acres would serve for both their possessions. But as families increased, and industry inlarged their stocks, their possessions inlarged with the need of them; but yet it was commonly without any fixed property in the ground they made use of, till they incorporated, settled themselves together, and built cities; and then, by consent, they came in time, to set out the bounds of their distinct territories, and agree on limits between them and their neighbours; and by laws within themselves, settled the properties of those of the same society: for we see, that in that part of the world which was first inhabited, and therefore like to be best peopled, even as low down as Abraham's time, they wandered with their flocks, and their herds, which was their substance, freely up and down; and this Abraham did, in a country where he was a stranger. Whence it is plain, that at least a great part of the land lay in common; that the inhabitants valued it not, nor claimed property in any more than they made use of. But when there was not room enough in the same place, for their herds to feed together, they by consent, as Abraham and Lot did, Gen. xiii. 5. separated and inlarged their pasture, where it best liked them. And for the same reason Esau went from his father, and his brother, and planted in mount Seir, Gen. xxxvi. 6.

Sect. 39. And thus, without supposing any private dominion, and property in Adam, over all the world, exclusive of all other men, which can no way be proved, nor any one's property be made out from it; but supposing the world given, as it was, to the children of men in common, we see how labour could make men distinct titles to several parcels of it, for their private uses; wherein there could be no doubt of right, no room for quarrel.

Sect. 40. Nor is it so strange, as perhaps before consideration it may appear, that the property of labour should be able to over-balance the community of land: for it is labour indeed that puts the difference of value on every thing; and let any one consider what the difference is between an acre of land planted with tobacco or sugar, sown with wheat or barley, and an acre of the same land lying in common, without any husbandry upon it, and he will find, that the improvement of labour makes the far greater part of the value. I think it will be but a very modest computation to say, that of the products of the earth useful to the life of man nine tenths are the effects of labour: nay, if we will rightly estimate things as they come to our use, and cast up the several expences about them, what in them is purely owing to nature, and what to labour, we shall find, that in most of them ninety-nine hundredths are wholly to be put on the account of labour.

Sect. 41. There cannot be a clearer demonstration of any thing, than several nations of the Americans are of this, who are rich in land, and poor in all the comforts of life; whom nature having furnished as liberally as any other people, with the materials of plenty, i.e. a fruitful soil, apt to produce in abundance, what might serve for food, raiment, and delight; yet for want of improving it by labour, have not one hundredth part of the conveniencies we enjoy: and a king of a large and fruitful territory there, feeds, lodges, and is clad worse than a day-labourer in England.

Sect. 42. To make this a little clearer, let us but trace some of the ordinary provisions of life, through their several progresses, before they come to our use, and see how much they receive of their value from human industry. Bread, wine and cloth, are things of daily use, and great plenty; yet notwithstanding, acorns, water and leaves, or skins, must be our bread, drink and cloathing, did not labour furnish us with these more useful commodities: for whatever bread is more worth than acorns, wine than water, and cloth or silk, than leaves, skins or moss, that is wholly owing to labour and industry; the one of these being the food and raiment which unassisted nature furnishes us with; the other, provisions which our industry and pains prepare for us, which how much they exceed the other in value, when any one hath computed, he will then see how much labour makes the far greatest part of the value of things we enjoy in this world: and the ground which produces the materials, is scarce to be reckoned in, as any, or at most, but a very small part of it; so little, that even amongst us, land that is left wholly to nature, that hath no improvement of pasturage, tillage, or planting, is called, as indeed it is, waste; and we shall find the benefit of it amount to little more than nothing.

This shews how much numbers of men are to be preferred to largeness of dominions; and that the increase of lands, and the right employing of them, is the great art of government: and that prince, who shall be so wise and godlike, as by established laws of liberty to secure protection and encouragement to the honest industry of mankind, against the oppression of power and narrowness of party, will quickly be too hard for his neighbours: but this by the by.

To return to the argument in hand.

Sect. 43. An acre of land, that bears here twenty bushels of wheat, and another in America, which, with the same husbandry, would do the like, are, without doubt, of the same natural intrinsic value: but yet the benefit mankind receives from the one in a year, is worth 5l. and from the other possibly not worth a penny, if all the profit an Indian received from it were to be valued, and sold here; at least, I may truly say, not one thousandth. It is labour then which puts the greatest part of value upon land, without which it would scarcely be worth any thing: it is to that we owe the greatest part of all its useful products; for all that the straw, bran, bread, of that acre of wheat, is more worth than the product of an acre of as good land, which lies waste, is all the effect of labour: for it is not barely the plough-man's pains, the reaper's and thresher's toil, and the baker's sweat, is to be counted into the bread we eat; the labour of those who broke the oxen, who digged and wrought the iron and stones, who felled and framed the timber employed about the plough, mill, oven, or any other utensils, which are a vast number, requisite to this corn, from its being feed to be sown to its being made bread, must all be charged on the account of labour, and received as an effect of that: nature and the earth furnished only the almost worthless materials, as in themselves. It would be a strange catalogue of things, that industry provided and made use of, about every loaf of bread, before it came to our use, if we could trace them; iron, wood, leather, bark, timber, stone, bricks, coals, lime, cloth, dying drugs, pitch, tar, masts, ropes, and all the materials made use of in the ship, that brought any of the commodities made use of by any of the workmen, to any part of the work; all which it would be almost impossible, at least too long, to reckon up.

Sect. 44. From all which it is evident, that though the things of nature are given in common, yet man, by being master of himself, and proprietor of his own person, and the actions or labour of it, had still in himself the great foundation of property; and that, which made up the great part of what he applied to the support or comfort of his being, when invention and arts had improved the conveniencies of life, was perfectly his own, and did not belong in common to others.

Sect. 45. Thus labour, in the beginning, gave a right of property, wherever any one was pleased to employ it upon what was common, which remained a long while the far greater part, and is yet more than mankind makes use of. Men, at first, for the most part, contented themselves with what unassisted nature offered to their necessities: and though afterwards, in some parts of the world, (where the increase of people and stock, with the use of money, had made land scarce, and so of some value) the several communities settled the bounds of their distinct territories, and by laws within themselves regulated the properties of the private men of their society, and so, by compact and agreement, settled the property which labour and industry began; and the leagues that have been made between several states and kingdoms, either expresly or tacitly disowning all claim and right to the land in the others possession, have, by common consent, given up their pretences to their natural common right, which originally they had to those coun-tries, and so have, by positive agreement, settled a property amongst themselves, in distinct parts and parcels of the earth; yet there are still great tracts of ground to be found, which (the inhabitants thereof not having joined with the rest of mankind, in the consent of the use of their common money) lie waste, and are more than the people who dwell on it do, or can make use of, and so still lie in common; tho' this can scarce happen amongst that part of mankind that have consented to the use of money.

Sect. 46. The greatest part of things really useful to the life of man, and such as the necessity of subsisting made the first commoners of the world look after, as it doth the Americans now, are generally things of short duration; such as, if they are not consumed by use, will decay and perish of themselves: gold, silver and diamonds, are things that fancy or agreement hath put the value on, more than real use, and the necessary support of life. Now of those good things which nature hath provided in common, every one had a right (as hath been said) to as much as he could use, and property in all that he could effect with his labour; all that his industry could extend to, to alter from the state nature had put it in, was his. He that gathered a hundred bushels of acorns or apples, had thereby a property in them, they were his goods as soon as gathered. He was only to look, that he used them before they spoiled, else he took more than his share, and robbed others. And indeed it was a foolish thing, as well as dishonest, to hoard up more than he could make use of. If he gave away a part to any body else, so that it perished not uselesly in his possession, these he also made use of. And if he also bartered away plums, that would have rotted in a week, for nuts that would last good for his eating a whole year, he did no injury; he wasted not the common stock; destroyed no part of the portion of goods that belonged to others, so long as nothing perished uselessly in his hands. Again, if he would give his nuts for a piece of metal, pleased with its colour; or exchange his sheep for shells, or wool for a sparkling pebble or a diamond, and keep those by him all his life he invaded not the right of others, he might heap up as much of these durable things as he pleased; the exceeding of the bounds of his just property not lying in the largeness of his possession, but the perishing of any thing uselesly in it.

Sect. 47. And thus came in the use of money, some lasting thing that men might keep without spoiling, and that by mutual consent men would take in exchange for the truly useful, but perishable supports of life.

Sect. 48. And as different degrees of industry were apt to give men possessions in different proportions, so this invention of money gave them the opportunity to continue and enlarge them: for supposing an island, separate from all possible commerce with the rest of the world, wherein there were but an hundred families, but there were sheep, horses and cows, with other useful animals, wholsome fruits, and land enough for corn for a hundred thousand times as many, but nothing in the island, either because of its commonness, or perishableness, fit to supply the place of money; what reason could any one have there to enlarge his possessions beyond the use of his family, and a plentiful supply to its consumption, either in what their own industry produced, or they could barter for like perishable, useful commodities, with others? Where there is not some thing, both lasting and scarce, and so valuable to be hoarded up, there men will not be apt to enlarge their possessions of land, were it never so rich, never so free for them to take: for I ask, what would a man value ten thousand, or an hundred thousand acres of excellent land, ready cultivated, and well stocked too with cattle, in the middle of the inland parts of America, where he had no hopes of commerce with other parts of the world, to draw money to him by the sale of the product? It would not be worth the enclosing, and we should see him give up again to the wild common of nature, whatever was more than would supply the conveniencies of life to be had there for him and his family.

Sect. 49. Thus in the beginning all the world was America, and more so than that is now; for no such thing as money was any where known. Find out something that hath the use and value of money amongst his neighbours, you shall see the same man will begin presently to enlarge his possessions.

Sect. 50. But since gold and silver, being little useful to the life of man in proportion to food, raiment, and carriage, has its value only from the consent of men, whereof labour yet makes, in great part, the measure, it is plain, that men have agreed to a disproportionate and unequal possession of the earth, they having, by a tacit and voluntary consent, found out, a way how a man may fairly possess more land than he himself can use the product of, by receiving in exchange for the overplus gold and silver, which may be hoarded up without injury to any one; these metals not spoiling or decaying in the hands of the possessor. This partage of things in an inequality of private possessions, men have made practicable out of the bounds of society, and without compact, only by putting a value on gold and silver, and tacitly agreeing in the use of money: for in governments, the laws regulate the right of property, and the possession of land is determined by positive constitutions.

Sect. 51. And thus, I think, it is very easy to conceive, without any difficulty, how labour could at first begin a title of property in the common things of nature, and how the spending it upon our uses bounded it. So that there could then be no reason of quarrelling about title, nor any doubt about the largeness of possession it gave. Right and conveniency went together; for as a man had a right to all he could employ his labour upon, so he had no temptation to labour for more than he could make use of. This left no room for controversy about the title, nor for encroachment on the right of others; what portion a man carved to himself, was easily seen; and it was useless, as well as dishonest, to carve himself too much, or take more than he needed.

CHAPTER 9

Mary Wollstonecraft

The Degradation of Women

A S A PHILOSOPHER and intellectual in eighteenth-century England, Mary Wollstonecraft (1759–1797) made major contributions to political philosophy and to the study of modern society, where she concentrated on the place of women in a world dominated by men. In this way, her contributions to what is today a vibrant philosophical tradition of feminist thought can be matched by very few.

Wollstonecraft is one of a handful of women to have made important and lasting contributions to philosophical debates in the modern era. In fact, one of the great virtues of Wollstonecraft's now-classic *Vindication of the Rights of Women*, from which we have an excerpt, is that she carefully explores and identifies the manifold reasons why so few women of her time would make contributions to scholarly and intellectual debates. Her argument may, at first glance, seem a little harsh: Women for the most part do not have sufficient virtue to be able to make such contributions. But, the argument's brashness is matched only by its complex subtlety. Wollstonecraft is interested in why women find themselves in this situation. In the selection that follows, Wollstonecraft explains the social, political, economic, psychological, and cultural reasons why women are generally subjugated to a degraded station in life.

Important Concepts: Virtue; freedom; splendid cage; oppression

At the beginning of the selection, Wollstonecraft asks about the status of women in her time: "Ah! Why do women, I write with affectionate solicitude, condescend to receive a degree of attention and respect from strangers, different from that reciprocation of civility which the dictates of humanity and the politeness of civilization authorise between man and man?" (127) One can hear the frustration in her voice. The difference between how men and women are treated shields women from any of the challenges in life that build character, develop virtue, and offer instruction in a life of liberty. She continues: "Confined then in cages like the feathered race, they have nothing to do but to plume themselves, and stalk with mock majesty from perch to perch." (128) Women are revered for their splendor, cherished like beautiful birds in a cage, and provided with a comfortable life, but, Wollstonecraft observes, "health, liberty, and virtue, are given in exchange." (128) A woman may well be provided for, but the price is degradation; the price is acquiescence to the *splendid cage*.

Why tolerate this degradation? Partly, she argues, from a lack of education—society simply does not furnish women with the intellectual resources required to question the status quo. Partly, it's due to a certain kind of education—women are taught to behave a certain way and to expect certain behavior from men. It's also partly due to comfort—women are in some ways happy to be cared for by men, despite the condescension and degradation. Wollstonecraft seems to suggest that this last reason is also a symptom of the problem; that is, women would not be so comfortable in their state of degradation were they properly equipped through education and socialization to expect the appropriate level of respect. "The grand source of female folly and vice has ever appeared to me to arise from narrowness of mind," Wollstonecraft writes, "the very constitution of civil governments has put almost insuperable obstacles in the way to prevent the cultivation of the female understanding ... yet virtue can be built on no other foundation!" (127) The issue, then, is at least two-fold: (a) Women are beset with a narrowness of mind that precludes their intellectual and moral development, and (b) this is due not to women themselves, but rather to social obstacles that stand in the way of the cultivation of the female character. The solution, then, is to decipher these obstacles and systematically remove them.

Wollstonecraft was deeply influenced by the political philosophy of John Locke, and it is perhaps easy to see her attraction. Recall from the last chapter that Locke takes freedom to be a basic, primordial condition we all have. In the state of nature, we are all free, and it is the actions of people that create obstacles to the practice and enjoyment of our natural-born freedom. Wollstonecraft posits that the central problem facing women in her time is that there are several obstacles (which she identifies as social, political, cultural, psychological, and economic in nature) that interfere with a woman's ability to enjoy her own freedom. In this sense, Wollstonecraft seems to agree with Locke that the path to freedom consists in removing obstacles to freedom and allowing women to simply be what they are by nature.

It is interesting to notice that Wollstonecraft also seems to understand freedom as Hobbes does, as a problem to be solved, as something society needs to carefully cultivate. Left to itself, the social order does women no favors. The freedom of women is a problem that society needs to pay particular attention to in order to solve. It is not just a matter of removing obstacles to freedom since women in her time tend to, as Wollstonecraft puts it, "despise the freedom which they have not sufficient virtue to struggle to attain...." (127) One of the deeper philosophical points that Wollstonecraft makes is, then, a deeply Hobbesian one; namely, that freedom is something that needs to be cultivated. People who are accustomed to oppression do not see that oppression and, even worse, *do not know how to be free* when obstacles to freedom are removed. The problem Wollstonecraft identifies is one of determining the social structures that will guarantee that all members are given an equal shot at freedom and virtue.

Observations on the State of Degradation to Which Woman Is Reduced by Various Causes

Mary Wollstonecraft

That woman is naturally weak, or degraded by a concurrence of circumstances, is, I think, clear. But this position I shall simply contrast with a conclusion, which I have frequently heard fall from sensible men in favour of an aristocracy: that the mass of mankind cannot be anything, or the obsequious slaves, who patiently allow themselves to be driven forward, would feel their own consequence, and spurn their chains. Men, they further observe, submit every where to oppression, when they have only to lift up their heads to throw off the yoke; yet, instead of asserting their birthright, they quietly lick the dust, and say, let us eat and drink, for tomorrow we die.[1] Women, I argue from analogy, are degraded by the same propensity to enjoy the present moment; and, at last, despise the freedom which they have not sufficient virtue to struggle to attain....

I shall not go back to the remote annals of antiquity to trace the history of woman; it is sufficient to allow that she has always been either a slave, or a despot, and to remark, that each of these situations equally retards the progress of reason. The grand source of female folly and vice has ever appeared to me to arise from narrowness of mind; and the very constitution of civil governments has put almost insuperable obstacles in the way to prevent the cultivation of the female understanding:—yet virtue can be built on no other foundation! The same obstacles are thrown in the way of the rich, and the same consequences ensue.

... Happy is it when people have the cares of life to struggle with; for these struggles prevent their becoming a prey to enervating vices, merely from idleness! ...

Pleasure is the business of woman's life, according to the present modification of society, and while it continues to be so, little can be expected from such weak beings....

Ah! why do women, I write with affectionate solicitude, condescend to receive a degree of attention and respect from strangers, different from that reciprocation of civility which the dictates of humanity and the politeness of civilization authorise between man and man? And, why do they not discover, when "in the noon of beauty's power,"[2] that they are treated like queens only to be deluded by hollow respect, till they are led to resign, or not assume, their

---

1 "Birthright … tomorrow we die": a series of well-known Biblical maxims, including Hebrews 12:16, "Esau, who for one morsel of meat sold his birthright"; Psalms 72:9, "And his enemies shall lick the dust"; and 1 Corinthians 15:32, "Let us eat and drink; for tomorrow we die."

2 "In the noon of beauty's power": a quote from Wollstonecraft's own review of a translation of Christoph Martin Wieland's novel *Henrietta of Gerstenfeld* (1787-1788), in Johnson's *Analytical Review* (June 1788, article xxxvi). Wollstonecraft used the phrase to summarize that novel's longer description of a woman's beauty at its peak.

natural prerogatives? Confined then in cages like the feathered race, they have nothing to do but to plume themselves, and stalk with mock majesty from perch to perch. It is true they are provided with food and raiment, for which they neither toil nor spin;[3] but health, liberty, and virtue, are given in exchange. But, where, amongst mankind, has been found sufficient strength of mind to enable a being to resign these adventitious prerogatives; one who, rising with the calm dignity of reason above opinion, dared to be proud of the privileges inherent in man? And it is vain to expect it whilst hereditary power chokes the affections and nips reason in the bud.

Lewis the XIVth, in particular,[4] spread factitious manners, and caught, in a specious way, the whole nation in his toils; for, establishing an artful chain of despotism, he made it the interest of the people at large, individually to respect his station and support his power. And women, whom he flattered by a puerile attention to the whole sex, obtained in his reign that prince-like distinction so fatal to reason and virtue.

A king is always a king—and a woman always a woman: his authority and her sex, ever stand between them and rational converse....

I lament that women are systematically degraded by receiving the trivial attentions, which men think it manly to pay to the sex, when, in fact, they are insultingly supporting their own superiority. It is not condescension to bow to an inferior. So ludicrous, in fact, do these ceremonies appear to me, that I scarcely am able to govern my muscles, when I see a man start with eager, and serious solicitude, to lift a handkerchief, or shut a door, when the *lady* could have done it herself, had she only moved a pace or two.

A wild wish has just flown from my heart to my head, and I will not stifle it though it may excite a horse-laugh.—I do earnestly wish to see the distinction of sex confounded in society, unless where love animates the behaviour....

...Women, commonly called Ladies, are not to be contradicted in company, are not allowed to exert any manual strength; and from them the negative virtues only are expected, when any virtues are expected, patience, docility, good-humour, and flexibility; virtues incompatible with any vigorous exertion of intellect. Besides, by living more with each other, and being seldom absolutely alone, they are more under the influence of sentiments than passions. Solitude and reflection are necessary to give to wishes the force of passions, and to enable the imagination to enlarge the object, and make it the most desirable. The same may be said of the rich; they do not sufficiently deal in general ideas, collected by impassioned

---

3   "Neither toil nor spin": Matthew 6:28, "Consider the lilies of the field, how they grow; they toil not, neither do they spin." Luke 12:27 gives another version of the saying.

4   "Lewis, the XIVth, in particular": Louis XIV (1638–1715), the "Sun King" who first built the spectacular Palace of Versailles, represents the highest point of European absolute monarchy and thus is frequently invoked in Enlightenment debates about the corruption of the Old Regime and courtly excesses. The notoriously corrupt Cardinal Guillaume Dubois previously mentioned (see Chapter I, note 19) was a favorite of Louis XIV. English writers of the period often spelled the name "Lewis," partly to match their pronunciation of what in French is closer to "Louie."

thinking, or calm investigation, to acquire that strength of character on which great resolves are built....

In the middle rank of life[5] ... men, in their youth, are prepared for professions, and marriage is not considered as the grand feature in their lives; whilst women, on the contrary, have no other scheme to sharpen their faculties. It is not business, extensive plans, or any of the excursive flights of ambition, that engross their attention; no, their thoughts are not employed in rearing such noble structures. To rise in the world, and have the liberty of running from pleasure to pleasure, they must marry advantageously, and to this object their time is sacrificed, and their persons often legally prostituted. A man when he enters any profession has his eye steadily fixed on some future advantage (and the mind gains great strength by having all its efforts directed to one point), and, full of his business, pleasure is considered as mere relaxation; whilst women seek for pleasure as the main purpose of existence. In fact, from the education, which they receive from society, the love of pleasure may be said to govern them all; but does this prove that there is a sex in souls? It would be just as rational to declare that the courtiers in France, when a destructive system of despotism had formed their character, were not men, because liberty, virtue, and humanity, were sacrificed to pleasure and vanity.—Fatal passions, which have ever domineered over the *whole* race!

The same love of pleasure, fostered by the whole tendency of their education, gives a trifling turn to the conduct of women in most circumstances: for instance, they are ever anxious about secondary things; and on the watch for adventures, instead of being occupied by duties.

A man, when he undertakes a journey, has, in general, the end in view; a woman thinks more of the incidental occurrences, the strange things that may possibly occur on the road; the impression that she may make on her fellow-travellers; and, above all, she is anxiously intent on the care of the finery that she carries with her, which is more than ever a part of herself, when going to figure on a new scene; when, to use an apt French turn of expression, she is going to produce a sensation.—Can dignity of mind exist with such trivial cares?

In short, women, in general, as well as the rich of both sexes, have acquired all the follies and vices of civilization, and missed the useful fruit.... Civilized women are, therefore, so weakened by false refinement, that, respecting morals, their condition is much below what it would be were they left in a state nearer to nature. Ever restless and anxious, their over exercised sensibility not only renders them uncomfortable themselves, but troublesome, to use a soft phrase, to others. All their thoughts turn on things calculated to excite emotion; and feeling, when they should reason, their conduct is unstable, and their opinions are wavering—not the wavering produced by deliberation or progressive views, but by contradictory emotions. By fits and starts they are warm in many pursuits; yet this warmth, never concentrated into perseverance, soon exhausts itself; exhaled by its own heat, or meeting with some other fleeting passion, to which reason

---

5   "Middle rank of life": as she promised earlier (see Introduction, note 13), Wollstonecraft is primarily concerned with the mores of the commercial and professional classes who are concerned "to rise in the world"; those whose social standing, prospects, and norms are improving most rapidly during the Enlightenment and revolutionary era.

has never given any specific gravity, neutrality ensues. Miserable, indeed, must be that being whose cultivation of mind has only tended to inflame its passions! A distinction should be made between inflaming and strengthening them. The passions thus pampered, whilst the judgment is left unformed, what can be expected to ensue?—Undoubtedly, a mixture of madness and folly!

Novels, music, poetry, and gallantry, all tend to make women the creatures of sensation, and their character is thus formed in the mould of folly during the time they are acquiring accomplishments, the only improvement they are excited, by their station in society, to acquire. This overstretched sensibility naturally relaxes the other powers of the mind, and prevents intellect from attaining that sovereignty which it ought to attain to render a rational creature useful to others, and content with its own station: for the exercise of the understanding, as life advances, is the only method pointed out by nature to calm the passions.

And will moralists pretend to assert, that this is the condition in which one half of the human race should be encouraged to remain with listless inactivity and stupid acquiescence? Kind instructors! what were we created for? To remain, it may be said, innocent; they mean in a state of childhood.—We might as well never have been born, unless it were necessary that we should be created to enable man to acquire the noble privilege of reason, the power of discerning good from evil, whilst we lie down in the dust from whence we were taken, never to rise again.—

Fragile in every sense of the word, they are obliged to look up to man for every comfort. In the most trifling dangers they cling to their support, with parasitical tenacity, piteously demanding succour; and their *natural* protector extends his arm, or lifts up his voice, to guard the lovely trembler—from what? Perhaps the frown of an old cow, or the jump of a mouse; a rat, would be a serious danger. In the name of reason, and even common sense, what can save such beings from contempt; even though they be soft and fair?

I am fully persuaded that we should hear of none of these infantine airs, if girls were allowed to take sufficient exercise, and not confined in close rooms till their muscles are relaxed, and their powers of digestion destroyed. To carry the remark still further, if fear in girls, instead of being cherished, perhaps, created, were treated in the same manner as cowardice in boys, we should quickly see women with more dignified aspects. It is true, they could not then with equal propriety be termed the sweet flowers that smile in the walk of man; but they would be more respectable members of society, and discharge the important duties of life by the light of their own reason. 'Educate women like men,' says Rousseau, 'and the more they resemble our sex the less power will they have over us.'[6] This is the very point I aim at. I do not wish them to have power over men; but over themselves.

In the same strain have I heard men argue against instructing the poor; for many are the forms that aristocracy assumes. "Teach them to read and write," say they, "and you take them out of the station assigned them by nature." An eloquent Frenchman has answered them, I will borrow his sentiments. But they know not, when they make man a brute, that they may expect

6 "Educate women … over us": from *Emile, or On Education.* The full passage reads: "Educate them, if you think proper, like the men; we shall readily consent to it. The more they resemble our sex, the less power they will have over us; and when they once become like ourselves, we shall then be truly their masters."

every instant to see him transformed into a ferocious beast.[7] Without knowledge there can be no morality!

When I treat of the peculiar duties of women, as I should treat of the peculiar duties of a citizen or father, it will be found that I do not mean to insinuate that they should be taken out of their families....

In the regulation of a family, in the education of children, understanding, in an unsophisticated sense, is particularly required: strength both of body and mind; yet the men who, by their writings, have most earnestly laboured to domesticate women, have endeavoured, by arguments dictated by a gross appetite, which satiety had rendered fastidious, to weaken their bodies and cramp their minds. But, if even by these sinister methods they really *persuaded* women, by working on their feelings, to stay at home, and fulfil the duties of a mother and mistress of a family, I should cautiously oppose opinions that led women to right conduct, by prevailing on them to make the discharge of such important duties the main business of life, though reason were insulted. Yet, and I appeal to experience, if by neglecting the understanding they be as much, nay, more detached from these domestic employments, than they could be by the most serious intellectual pursuit, though it may be observed, that the mass of mankind will never vigorously pursue an intellectual object. I may be allowed to infer that reason is absolutely necessary to enable a woman to perform any duty properly, and I must again repeat, that sensibility is not reason.

The comparison with the rich still occurs to me; for, when men neglect the duties of humanity, women will follow their example; a common stream hurries them both along with thoughtless celerity. Riches and honours prevent a man from enlarging his understanding, and enervate all his powers by reversing the order of nature, which has ever made true pleasure the reward of labour. Pleasure—enervating pleasure is, likewise, within women's reach without earning it. But, till hereditary possessions are spread abroad, how can we expect men to be proud of virtue? And, till they are, women will govern them by the most direct means, neglecting their dull domestic duties to catch the pleasure that sits lightly on the wing of time.

I am, indeed, persuaded that the heart, as well as the understanding, is opened by cultivation; and by, which may not appear so clear, strengthening the organs; I am not now talking of momentary flashes of sensibility, but of affections. And, perhaps, in the education of both sexes, the most difficult task is so to adjust instruction as not to narrow the understanding, whilst the heart is warmed by the generous juices of spring, just raised by the electric fermentation of the season; nor to dry up the feelings by employing the mind in investigations remote from life.

---

7   "Teach them ... ferocious beast": sources for the quote and paraphrase in this paragraph are not known. The paraphrase refers to the idea that it is primarily poor social conditions of prior oppression and inequality that encourage mass violence. The idea is widespread, but some scholars argue that Wollstonecraft draws it from Mirabeau (Honoré Gabriel Riqueti, Count of Mirabeau; 1749–1791), who said in the French revolutionary assembly, "You have loosed the bull—do you not expect it to use its horns?" Had the French lower classes been treated more generously and equitably, that is, they would not have unleashed their resentment so violently.

Mankind seem to agree that children should be left under the management of women during their childhood. Now, from all the observation that I have been able to make, women of sensibility are the most unfit for this task, because they will infallibly, carried away by their feelings, spoil a child's temper. The management of the temper, the first, and most important branch of education, requires the sober steady eye of reason; a plan of conduct equally distant from tyranny and indulgence: yet these are the extremes that people of sensibility alternately fall into; always shooting beyond the mark....

The female understanding has often been spoken of with contempt, as arriving sooner at maturity than the male....

It has also been asserted, by some naturalists, that men do not attain their full growth and strength till thirty; but that women arrive at maturity by twenty.[8] I apprehend that they reason on false ground, led astray by the male prejudice, which deems beauty the perfection of woman—mere beauty of features and complexion, the vulgar acceptation of the word, whilst male beauty is allowed to have some connection with the mind. Strength of body, and that character of countenance, which the French term a *physionomie*, women do not acquire before thirty, any more than men. The little artless tricks of children, it is true, are particularly pleasing and attractive; yet, when the pretty freshness of youth is worn off, these artless graces become studied airs, and disgust every person of taste. In the countenance of girls we only look for vivacity and bashful modesty; but, the spring-tide of life over, we look for soberer sense in the face, and for traces of passion, instead of the dimples of animal spirits; expecting to see individuality of character, the only fastener of the affections. We then wish to converse, not to fondle; to give scope to our imaginations as well as to the sensations of our hearts.

At twenty the beauty of both sexes is equal; but the libertinism of man leads him to make the distinction, and superannuated coquettes are commonly of the same opinion; for, when they can no longer inspire love, they pay for the vigour and vivacity of youth. The French, who admit more of mind into their notions of beauty, give the preference to women of thirty. I mean to say that they allow women to be in their most perfect state, when vivacity gives place to reason, and to that majestic seriousness of character, which marks maturity;—or, the resting point. In youth, till twenty, the body shoots out, till thirty the solids are attaining a degree of density; and the flexible muscles, growing daily more rigid, give character to the countenance; that is, they trace the operations of the mind with the iron pen of fate, and tell us not only what powers are within, but how they have been employed.

It is proper to observe, that animals who arrive slowly at maturity, are the longest lived, and of the noblest species. Men cannot, however, claim any natural superiority from the grandeur of longevity; for in this respect nature has not distinguished the male.

---

8   "Maturity by twenty": Buffon (Georges-Louis Leclerc, Count of Buffon; 1707–1788), the best-known naturalist of the century, wrote in his *Natural History* that "a woman at twenty years is as perfectly formed as a man at thirty."

CHAPTER 10

Immanuel Kant

The Age of Enlightenment

I MMANUEL KANT (1724–1804) is arguably the most widely read and influential philosopher to have written in the modern era. It is difficult if not impossible to get a degree in philosophy without encountering Kant, and no history of philosophy is complete without a significant chapter devoted to his thinking. There is today a vibrant academic industry that revolves almost entirely around the study of Kant's extensive work. Many people devote their entire lives to understanding Kant, and universities devote many resources to support such efforts. Kant's philosophy is deeply complex in how it weaves together questions of knowledge, morality, politics, beauty, creativity, man's relationship with nature, human destiny, and the nature of humankind. The answers he proposes are just as interesting as the questions themselves. Nothing in philosophy remained untouched by Kant's original and penetrating arguments about human experience, morality, beauty, and the vocation of humankind.

Kant lived in a small city in northern Prussia called Königsburg, (now called Kaliningrad, now in Russia). He is famous for living his entire life in this small isolated city. Indeed, he rarely left. It is not that he was not ambitious or that he never had the chance to move to a more vibrant metropolis and a larger university. It's that he seemed to prefer a quiet, academic life where he was free to teach his courses, write his books, and maintain a lively social life. Kant became quite famous and people would frequently make the long journey to visit him, and he corresponded regularly with Europe's most important intellectual figures. He was far from isolated.

Important Concepts: Copernican revolution; Enlightenment; dogmatism; immaturity; Sapere Aude!

Kant has the designation of having set in motion a complete revolution in philosophy, in how philosophers understood what they were doing and in what the legitimate domain of philosophy actually is. Known as his "Copernican revolution," it challenged some of the most basic assumptions about the relationship between the human mind and the world. Just as Copernicus (1473–1543) had challenged the idea that the earth was the center of the universe and proposed that is was instead the sun, Kant challenged the idea that world furnishes us with all our ideas and instead proposed that the human mind arranges and organizes information received through the senses in order to constitute meaningful human experience. The mind, by analogy with our solar system, is like the sun—everything is illuminated by it, and nothing can be what it is without it.

Kant lived during a period in modern European history known as the Enlightenment. Not to be confused with today's use of the term to refer to a kind of spiritual awakening, the Enlightenment names a period in intellectual history in which rationality, freedom from external authority, the rejection of dogmatism, and the celebration of the individual use of reason were celebrated and systematically developed by philosophers. Kant's answer to the question, "What is Enlightenment?" is a classic statement of Enlightenment ideals.

"Enlightenment," Kant writes in the first sentence, "is mankind's exit from his self-incurred immaturity." It's not that we do not have the ability to become enlightened. We do this to ourselves—we rely on the judgment of others, we don't think before we act, we accept what other people tell us, we don't think for ourselves, we are lazy. This is our self-incurred immaturity. And, just as Kant thought that the human mind is the organizing source of a meaningful world, human understanding has the capacity to think for itself, arrive at its own conclusions. To become enlightened is to become free from this state of immaturity, of not being able to think and speak for yourself. It is not an intellectual error, or a natural lack of ability; it's a moral error, an error of our will. The cure? *Sapere Aude!* Dare to use your own understanding. Enlightenment is thus a kind of personal moral obligation, but it is also a collective process that we engage in as a people through the public use of reason. And all we need is freedom and the courage to use it.

What Is Enlightenment?

Immanuel Kant

Enlightenment is man's emergence from his self-imposed nonage. Nonage is the inability to use one's own understanding without another's guidance. This nonage is self-imposed if its cause lies not in lack of understanding but in indecision and lack of courage to use one's own mind without another's guidance. Dare to know! (*Sapere aude*) "Have the courage to use your own understanding," is therefore the motto of the enlightenment.

Laziness and cowardice are the reasons why such a large part of mankind gladly remain minors all their lives, long after nature has freed them from external guidance. They are the reasons why it is so easy for others to set themselves up as guardians. It is so comfortable to be a minor. If I have a book that thinks for me, a pastor who acts as my conscience, a physician who prescribes my diet, and so on—then I have no need to exert myself. I have no need to think, if only I can pay; others will take care of that disagreeable business for me. Those guardians who have kindly taken supervision upon themselves see to it that the overwhelming majority of mankind—among them the entire fair sex—should consider the step to maturity, not only as hard, but as extremely dangerous. First, these guardians make their domestic cattle stupid and carefully prevent the docile creatures from taking a single step without the leading-strings to which they have fastened them. Then they show them the danger that would threaten them if they should try to walk by themselves. Now this danger is really not very great; after stumbling

Immanuel Kant, "What is Enlightenment?" trans. Mary C. Smith, 1784.

a few times they would, at last, learn to walk. However, examples of such failures intimidate and generally discourage all further attempts.

Thus it is very difficult for the individual to work himself out of the nonage which has become almost second nature to him. He has even grown to like it, and is at first really incapable of using his own understanding because he has never been permitted to try it. Dogmas and formulas, these mechanical tools designed for reasonable use—or rather—abuse of his natural gifts, are the fetters of an everlasting nonage. The man who casts them off would make an uncertain leap over the narrowest ditch, because he is not used to such free movement. That is why there are only a few men who walk firmly, and who have emerged from nonage by cultivating their own minds.

It is more nearly possible, however, for the public to enlighten itself; indeed, if it is only given freedom, enlightenment is almost inevitable. There will always be a few independent thinkers, even among the self-appointed guardians of the multitude. Once such men have thrown off the yoke of nonage, they will spread about them the spirit of a reasonable appreciation of man's value and of his duty to think for himself. It is especially to be noted that the public which was earlier brought under the yoke by these men afterwards forces these very guardians to remain in submission, if it is so incited by some of its guardians who are themselves incapable of any enlightenment. That shows how pernicious it is to implant prejudices: they will eventually revenge themselves upon their authors or their authors' descendants. Therefore, a public can achieve enlightenment only slowly. A revolution may bring about the end of a personal despotism or of avaricious tyrannical oppression, but never a true reform of modes of thought. New prejudices will serve, in place of the old, as guide lines for the unthinking multitude.

This enlightenment requires nothing but freedom—and the most innocent of all that may be called "freedom": freedom to make public use of one's reason in all matters. Now I hear the cry from all sides: "Do not argue!" The officer says: "Do not argue—drill!" The tax collector: "Do not argue—pay!" The pastor: "Do not argue—believe!" Only one ruler in the world says: "Argue as much as you please, but obey!" We find restrictions on freedom everywhere. But which restriction is harmful to enlightenment? Which restriction is innocent, and which advances enlightenment? I reply: the public use of one's reason must be free at all times, and this alone can bring enlightenment to mankind.

On the other hand, the private use of reason may frequently be narrowly restricted without especially hindering the progress of enlightenment. By "public use of one's reason" I mean that use which a man, as scholar, makes of it before the reading public. I call "private use" that use which a man makes of his reason in a civic post that has been entrusted to him. In some affairs affecting the interest of the community a certain [governmental] mechanism is necessary in which some members of the community remain passive. This creates an artificial unanimity which will serve the fulfillment of public objectives, or at least keep these objectives from being destroyed. Here arguing is not permitted: one must obey. Insofar as a part of this machine considers himself at the same time a member of a universal community—a world society of citizens—(let us say that he thinks of himself as a scholar rationally addressing his public through his writings) he may indeed argue, and the affairs with which he is associated in part as a passive member will not suffer. Thus it would be very unfortunate if an officer on duty and under orders from his superiors should want to criticize the appropriateness or utility of his orders. He must obey. But as a scholar he could not rightfully be prevented from taking notice of the mistakes in the military service and from submitting his views to his public for its judgment. The citizen cannot refuse to pay the taxes levied upon him; indeed, impertinent censure of such taxes could be punished as a scandal that might cause general disobedience. Nevertheless, this man does not violate the duties of a citizen if, as a scholar, he publicly expresses his objections to the impropriety or possible injustice of such levies. A pastor, too, is bound to preach to his congregation in accord with the doctrines of the church which he serves, for he was ordained on that condition. But as a scholar he has full freedom, indeed the obligation, to communicate to his public all his carefully examined and constructive thoughts concerning errors in that doctrine and his proposals concerning improvement of religious dogma and church institutions. This is nothing that could burden his conscience. For what he teaches in pursuance of his office as representative of the church, he represents as something which he is not free to teach as he sees it. He speaks as one who is employed to speak in the name and under the orders of another. He will say: "Our church teaches this or that; these are the proofs which it employs." Thus he will benefit his congregation as much as possible by presenting doctrines to which he may not subscribe with full conviction. He can commit himself to teach them because it is not completely impossible that they may contain hidden truth. In any event, he has found nothing in the doctrines that contradicts the heart of religion. For if he believed that such contradictions existed he would not be able to administer his office with a clear conscience. He would have to resign it. Therefore the use which a scholar makes of his reason before the congregation that employs him is only a private use, for no matter how sizable, this is only a domestic audience. In view of this he, as preacher, is not free and ought not to be free, since he is carrying out the orders of others. On the other hand, as the scholar who speaks to his own public (the world) through his writings, the minister in the public use of his reason enjoys unlimited freedom to use his own reason and to speak for himself. That the spiritual guardians of the people should themselves be treated as minors is an absurdity which would result in perpetuating absurdities.

But should a society of ministers, say a Church Council, ... have the right to commit itself by oath to a certain unalterable doctrine, in order to secure perpetual guardianship over all its members and through them over the people? I say that this is quite impossible. Such a contract, concluded to keep all further enlightenment from humanity, is simply null and void even if it should be confirmed by the sovereign power, by parliaments, and the most solemn treaties. An epoch cannot conclude a pact that will commit succeeding ages, prevent them from increasing their significant insights, purging themselves of errors, and generally progressing in enlightenment. That would be a crime against human nature whose proper destiny lies precisely in such progress. Therefore, succeeding ages are fully entitled to repudiate such decisions as unauthorized and outrageous. The touchstone of all those decisions that may be made into law for a people lies in this question: Could a people impose such a law upon itself? Now it might be possible to introduce a certain order for a definite short period of time in expectation of better order. But, while this provisional order continues, each citizen (above all, each pastor acting as a scholar) should be left free to publish his criticisms of the faults of existing institutions. This should continue until public understanding of these matters has gone so far that, by uniting the voices of many (although not necessarily all) scholars, reform proposals could be brought before the sovereign to protect those congregations which had decided according to their best lights upon an altered religious order, without, however, hindering those who want to remain true to the old institutions. But to agree to a perpetual religious constitution which is not publicly questioned by anyone would be, as it were, to annihilate a period of time in the progress of man's improvement. This must be absolutely forbidden.

A man may postpone his own enlightenment, but only for a limited period of time. And to give up enlightenment altogether, either for oneself or one's descendants, is to violate and to trample upon the sacred rights of man. What a people may not decide for itself may even less be decided for it by a monarch, for his reputation as a ruler consists precisely in the way in which he unites the will of the whole people within his own. If he only sees to it that all true or supposed [religious] improvement remains in step with the civic order, he can for the rest leave his subjects alone to do what they find necessary for the salvation of their souls. Salvation is none of his business; it is his business to prevent one man from forcibly keeping another from determining and promoting his salvation to the best of his ability. Indeed, it would be prejudicial to his majesty if he meddled in these matters and supervised the writings in which his subjects seek to bring their [religious] views into the open, even when he does this from his own highest insight, because then he exposes himself to the reproach: Caesar *non est supra grammaticos*. 2 It is worse when he debases his sovereign power so far as to support the spiritual despotism of a few tyrants in his state over the rest of his subjects.

When we ask, Are we now living in an enlightened age? the answer is, No, but we live in an age of enlightenment. As matters now stand it is still far from true that men are already capable of using their own reason in religious matters confidently and correctly without external guidance. Still, we have some obvious indications that the field of working toward the goal [of religious truth] is now opened. What is more, the hindrances against general enlightenment or the emergence from self-imposed nonage are gradually diminishing. In this respect this is the age of the enlightenment and the century of Frederick [the Great].

A prince ought not to deem it beneath his dignity to state that he considers it his duty not to dictate anything to his subjects in religious matters, but to leave them complete freedom. If he repudiates the arrogant word "tolerant", he is himself enlightened; he deserves to be praised by a grateful world and posterity as that man who was the first to liberate mankind from dependence, at least on the government, and let everybody use his own reason in matters of conscience. Under his reign, honorable pastors, acting as scholars and regardless of the duties of their office, can freely and openly publish their ideas to the world for inspection, although they deviate here and there from accepted doctrine. This is even more true of every person not restrained by any oath of office. This spirit of freedom is spreading beyond the boundaries [of

Prussia] even where it has to struggle against the external hindrances established by a government that fails to grasp its true interest. [Frederick's Prussia] is a shining example that freedom need not cause the least worry concerning public order or the unity of the community. When one does not deliberately attempt to keep men in barbarism, they will gradually work out of that condition by themselves.

I have emphasized the main point of the enlightenment—man's emergence from his self-imposed nonage—primarily in religious matters, because our rulers have no interest in playing the guardian to their subjects in the arts and sciences. Above all, nonage in religion is not only the most harmful but the most dishonorable. But the disposition of a sovereign ruler who favors freedom in the arts and sciences goes even further: he knows that there is no danger in permitting his subjects to make public use of their reason and to publish their ideas concerning a better constitution, as well as candid criticism of existing basic laws. We already have a striking example [of such freedom], and no monarch can match the one whom we venerate.

But only the man who is himself enlightened, who is not afraid of shadows, and who commands at the same time a well disciplined and numerous army as guarantor of public peace—only he can say what [the sovereign of] a free state cannot dare to say: "Argue as much as you like, and about what you like, but obey!" Thus we observe here as elsewhere in human affairs, in which almost everything is paradoxical, a surprising and unexpected course of events: a large degree of civic freedom appears to be of advantage to the intellectual freedom of the people, yet at the same time it establishes insurmountable barriers. A lesser degree of civic freedom, however, creates room to let that free spirit expand to the limits of its capacity. Nature, then, has carefully cultivated the seed within the hard core—namely the urge for and the vocation of free thought. And this free thought gradually reacts back on the modes of thought of the people, and men become more and more capable of acting in freedom. At last free thought acts even on the fundamentals of government and the state finds it agreeable to treat man, who is now more than a machine, in accord with his dignity.

PART THREE

Late-Modern and Postmodern Philosophy

W E ENDED OUR section on modern philosophy with Kant, but Kant really represents a transition to something new. We will recall that Kant's Copernican revolution in philosophy consisted in the argument that the human mind arranges and organizes information received through the senses in order to constitute meaningful human experience. There are two things that make this revolution important to subsequent developments in philosophy. First, it locates the center of meaning in ourselves, in the human mind, and not in the universe, not in God, not anywhere else but us. Second, since the human mind is responsible for organizing our experience in a meaningful way, what the world is beyond human experience is simply unknowable. You can see how these two results of the Kantian philosophy are two sides of the same coin—we give the universe meaning, and so what the universe *in-itself* is unknowable.

The idea that we cannot know the world as it is *in-itself* caused all sorts of controversy in Kant's time, and philosophers still debate it today. Many people simply cannot accept Kant's view since it seems impossible to accept that the world itself is simply off limits to our knowledge, that we can only know the world according to a human way of knowing. Yet, the other side of this idea, that individual human beings are sources of meaning, was extremely compelling in Kant's time. Kant published his first major work in 1781, and his philosophy remained central to intellectual life until well after his death in 1804. Also at this time, the *French Revolution* (1789–1799) was in the process of completely changing the face of political organization all over Europe. Kant's picture of individual human reason as paramount (recall his Enlightenment essay), and human beings as sources of meaning was perfectly suited to the evolving political order, which shifted power from the wealthy aristocracy to establish a democracy in which each person has a voice that counts. The individual use of reason becomes paramount in the liberal-democratic order that was emerging in the late eighteenth and early nineteenth century in Europe. As we will see especially in chapters 14 (Hannah Arendt) and 15 (Cornel West), issues of moral responsibility and the democratic order are important themes in philosophy in the twentieth century and today.

Another important part of philosophy in the nineteenth century and beyond is *historicism*, the idea that history is a determining factor in human life and that we cannot understand anything, such as art, science, politics, and even human reason, without seeing how these things are determined by their time and place, by their history. One of the ideas that historicism challenges is the still rather intuitively compelling idea that there is some truth about the world, something that always has been, always will be, and can, at least in principle, be discovered. Historicism challenges this by making truth contingent on history. What is true for a group of people at a given time and place is not true for another group of people at another time and place. G.W.F. Hegel is one of the most important figures here, but Marx and Engels are famous for applying this idea of historicism to the study of economics to explain the rise of the wage labor and concentration of wealth and power in the small minority of people who control capital. For Marx and Engels, the history of the development of differences in class and economic fortune is the history of the development of the material conditions of labor. As workers are subjected to wage labor to a greater and greater degree, they are separated from the actual products of their labor; they are separated, that is, from an important part of themselves that makes them who they are.

There is perhaps no other philosopher who challenged the philosophy's exhalation of truth more vigorously than Friedrich Nietzsche (1844–1900). It might sound almost ridiculous, but Nietzsche (chapter 12) argues that truth is neither something that is simply out there to be discovered, nor something that changes over time. For Nietzsche, truth is just something we've invented. And we invented truth only to feed our own pride. We're so important, we think, that truth is available only to us, and we often claim that very few of us are capable of seeing truth. All of this is just an invention.

In his own way, William James (1842–1910) also challenged philosophy's commitment to the idea of a stable, universal truth, and his challenge is, in its own way, just as radical as Nietzsche's. In chapter 13, we will see that James agrees with Nietzsche that truth is nothing special, but he qualifies himself by arguing that truth is less important than usefulness. If there is no practical difference between two different accounts of the way something is, then the difference is meaningless, idle argument. For instance, an *idealist* might say that the glass of water is partly a construction of the mind; the *realist* might say that the glass of water is an existing thing in the world, regardless of whatever I happen to think about it. The *realist* and *idealist* can go on and on arguing their respective sides, but when they get thirsty, they will both do the same thing. The difference between *idealism* and *realism* is, in this way, just a meaningless, idle dispute that makes no practical difference. James points out that arguments of this sort about the truth of the glass of water are meaningless disputes because they make no real difference to anyone. James wants to hold philosophy itself up to this standard: Philosophy must be meaningfully relevant to everyone in a practical way.

Philosophy in late- and postmodernity is an extremely diverse discipline with almost nothing to unify it as a single movement. If nothing else, philosophers over the past one hundred to two hundred years have been occupied with challenging the philosophical cannon in one way or another. But, the ways in which philosophers have broken from the past is not merely negative. People such as Nietzsche and James do not want to dispense with the notion of truth as much as they want to redefine that concept, help us understand our past, and make it relevant for us today. Arendt does not just want to get rid of the idea of human nature; she wants to rethink human nature *as the human condition*, where the things that condition our existence come to us partly from nature and partly from conditions we have created for ourselves. And Cornel West wants to turn our attention toward the old idea of democracy to help us think through what it actually requires of us. Philosophy today remains a vibrant tradition precisely because great thinkers continue to develop new concepts as well as interrogate old concepts so that we have the conceptual and intellectual resources to be able to understand our own time, its problems, its achievements, its history, and its way forward.

CHAPTER 11

Marx and Engels

Manifesto of the Communist Party

Y OU HAVE PROBABLY heard of Karl Marx, or at least of his name that generally gets attached to any idea with a whiff of socialism. People often use the term "Marxism" as an insult, which is unfortunate since such people often have very little knowledge of what Marx actually said or what Marx and Engels understood socialism to actually be. The fact is that whether you have sympathies for socialism or not, whether you support capitalism or not, Marx's work with Friedrich Engels is one of the most important historical sources for the critique of capitalism as an economic and social model. Still today, the arguments that Marx and Engels formulate are highly relevant and enlightening. The reading, here, is a selection from one of their most famous works, written as a kind of call to arms for those working class people (what Marx and Engels call "the proletariat") who work as wage-laborers and whose economic share of the products and the capital they help to produce is becoming smaller and smaller. It is revolutionary in tone and captures the sense of class struggle that so defines Marx and Engels' work and that continues to animate discussions of social justice today.

Important Concepts: Bourgeoisie; proletariat; capital; wage-labor; material conditions

Marx and Engels tell us a story about the development of what they call "the bourgeoisie," the class of people who own the means of production. Marx and Engels are famous for this story; it's a compelling one that uses the method of *historical materialism* to explain how historical changes in the material conditions of life facilitated the socio-economic organization we know today. Marx explains this method at the beginning of his famous analysis of the French Revolution, *the Eighteenth Brumaire of Louis Bonaparte*:

> *Men make their own history, but they do not make it just as they please; they do not make it under circumstance chosen just by themselves, but under circumstances directly encountered, given and transmitted from the past.*[1]

Marx and Engels are trying, then, to explain the conditions that produced the bourgeois and the proletariat classes. They examine the breakdown of traditional means of production and the

---

1   Karl Marx, *Eighteenth Brumaire of Louis Bonaparte* (New York: International Publishers, 1998), 15.

transition to new ways of organizing the production and distribution of goods. As the story goes, as populations grew, the demand for material products increased, and the old feudal guilds simply could not keep up with the demand. This material condition is what gave rise to large-scale, centralized industrial production. When the demand for products is so high, it becomes very difficult for small produces or cooperatives of producers to meet demand. Because of this, an opportunity is created for large-scale production to change the means by which things are produced. At first, Marx and Engel explain, this was organized by a middle class of industrial managers, who understood production methods and could facilitate a large-scale distribution network. But, as demand increased and the industrial infrastructure got larger, these industrial managers became millionaires. This is the birth of the modern bourgeoisie.

The bourgeoisie played a highly revolutionary role in society. Indeed, even today we tend to value precisely the things the bourgeoisie made possible. The bourgeoisie systematically eliminated all the systems put in place to bind people to superior power. When you're a millionaire, influence can be bought and sold, and the older feudal system of power through which power is controlled by a small group of feudal lords becomes less and less relevant to real power. And, with the rise of the bourgeoisie, corresponding political advances occurred, ostensibly for all, but really only for the incipient bourgeoisie.

This is where the ostensible praise ends. While the bourgeoisie have, as Marx and Engels put it, "pitilessly torn asunder the motley feudal ties that bound man to his 'natural superiors,'" the bourgeoisie have also "left remaining no other nexus between man and man than naked self-interest, than callous 'cash payment' [...] It has resolved personal worth into exchange value and, in place of the numberless indefeasible chartered freedoms, has set up that single unconscionable freedom—free trade." (147) People were free from oppression by religious and feudal authority, but they were thereby reduced to a cash value to be bought and sold. Freedom to pursue self-interest, then, comes at a steep price. Marx and Engels wrote things such as *the Manifesto* in order to make this oppression clear to the proletariat and to unite the working class into an international movement. This is a task that some may think is still in process today.

One of the most powerful arguments from the reading revolves around the claim that capital, the quantity of wealth and purchasing power created by companies who buy and sell products and services, should be understood as *social property*. The idea is that capital cannot be created by a single person, or even by a small group of people. Creating capital requires the labor of many people and some sophisticated social organization. From this point of view, the problem with capitalism is simply that it is dishonest about the source of capital, the source of wealth. When all the benefits of economic activity are funneled up to the highest levels, to the bourgeoisie, the real contribution of everyone involved in the creation of capital is denied. This is capitalism's dishonesty, and the source of its fundamental injustice. Capitalism relies on socialism, but pretends it does not.

This criticism is strikingly relevant still today. Nobody likes to pay taxes, but everyone wants nicely paved roads, strong social services, and abundant government incentives. A growing majority of the population in modern industrial economies is stuck in precarious employment (creating a class of people that today we call, in an homage to Marx and Engels, the "precariat") where companies makes no commitments to their wage laborers beyond compensation for piece work—all profits are funneled to the top, where a shrinking number of wealthy and powerful individuals enjoy the majority of the benefits of economic growth. Do the reading and see if you agree.

Manifesto of the Communist Party

Karl Marx

A spectre is haunting Europe—the spectre of communism. All the powers of old Europe have entered into a holy alliance to exorcise this spectre: Pope and Tsar, Metternich and Guizot, French Radicals and German police-spies.

Where is the party in opposition that has not been decried as communistic by its opponents in power? Where is the opposition that has not hurled back the branding reproach of communism, against the more advanced opposition parties, as well as against its reactionary adversaries?

Two things result from this fact:

I. Communism is already acknowledged by all European powers to be itself a power.

II. It is high time that Communists should openly, in the face of the whole world, publish their views, their aims, their tendencies, and meet this nursery tale of the Spectre of Communism with a manifesto of the party itself.

To this end, Communists of various nationalities have assembled in London and sketched the following manifesto, to be published in the English, French, German, Italian, Flemish and Danish languages.

I. Bourgeois and Proletarians[2]

The history of all hitherto existing society[3] is the history of class struggles.

---

2   By bourgeoisie is meant the class of modern capitalists, owners of the means of social production and employers of wage labour. By proletariat, the class of modern wage labourers who, having no means of production of their own, are reduced to selling their labour power in order to live. [Engels, 1888 English edition]

3   That is, all written history. In 1847, the pre-history of society, the social organisation existing previous to recorded history, all but unknown. Since then, August von Haxthausen (1792–1866) discovered common ownership of land in Russia, Georg Ludwig von Maurer proved it to be the social foundation from which all Teutonic races started in history, and, by and by, village communities were found to be, or to have been, the primitive form of society everywhere from India to Ireland. The inner organisation of this primitive communistic society was laid bare, in its typical form, by Lewis Henry Morgan's (1818–1861) crowning discovery of the true nature of the gens and its relation to the tribe. With the dissolution of the primeval communities, society begins to be differentiated into separate and finally antagonistic classes. I have attempted to retrace this dissolution in The Origin of the Family, Private Property, and the State, second edition, Stuttgart, 1886. [Engels, 1888 English Edition and 1890 German Edition (with the last sentence omitted)]

Karl Marx and Frederick Engels, Selection from *Manifesto of the Communist Party*, trans. Samuel Moore, 1888.

Freeman and slave, patrician and plebeian, lord and serf, guild-master[4] and journeyman, in a word, oppressor and oppressed, stood in constant opposition to one another, carried on an uninterrupted, now hidden, now open fight, a fight that each time ended, either in a revolutionary reconstitution of society at large, or in the common ruin of the contending classes.

In the earlier epochs of history, we find almost everywhere a complicated arrangement of society into various orders, a manifold gradation of social rank. In ancient Rome we have patricians, knights, plebeians, slaves; in the Middle Ages, feudal lords, vassals, guild-masters, journeymen, apprentices, serfs; in almost all of these classes, again, subordinate gradations.

The modern bourgeois society that has sprouted from the ruins of feudal society has not done away with class antagonisms. It has but established new classes, new conditions of oppression, new forms of struggle in place of the old ones.

Our epoch, the epoch of the bourgeoisie, possesses, however, this distinct feature: it has simplified class antagonisms. Society as a whole is more and more splitting up into two great hostile camps, into two great classes directly facing each other—Bourgeoisie and Proletariat.

From the serfs of the Middle Ages sprang the chartered burghers of the earliest towns. From these burgesses the first elements of the bourgeoisie were developed.

The discovery of America, the rounding of the Cape, opened up fresh ground for the rising bourgeoisie. The East-Indian and Chinese markets, the colonisation of America, trade with the colonies, the increase in the means of exchange and in commodities generally, gave to commerce, to navigation, to industry, an impulse never before known, and thereby, to the revolutionary element in the tottering feudal society, a rapid development.

The feudal system of industry, in which industrial production was monopolised by closed guilds, now no longer sufficed for the growing wants of the new markets. The manufacturing system took its place. The guild-masters were pushed on one side by the manufacturing middle class; division of labour between the different corporate guilds vanished in the face of division of labour in each single workshop.

Meantime the markets kept ever growing, the demand ever rising. Even manufacturer no longer sufficed. Thereupon, steam and machinery revolutionised industrial production. The place of manufacture was taken by the giant, Modern Industry; the place of the industrial middle class by industrial millionaires, the leaders of the whole industrial armies, the modern bourgeois.

Modern industry has established the world market, for which the discovery of America paved the way. This market has given an immense development to commerce, to navigation, to communication by land. This development has, in its turn, reacted on the extension of industry; and in proportion as industry, commerce, navigation, railways extended, in the same proportion the bourgeoisie developed, increased its capital, and pushed into the background every class handed down from the Middle Ages.

---

4 Guild-master, that is, a full member of a guild, a master within, not a head of a guild. [Engels, 1888 English Edition]

We see, therefore, how the modern bourgeoisie is itself the product of a long course of development, of a series of revolutions in the modes of production and of exchange.

Each step in the development of the bourgeoisie was accompanied by a corresponding political advance of that class. An oppressed class under the sway of the feudal nobility, an armed and self-governing association in the medieval commune[5]: here independent urban republic (as in Italy and Germany); there taxable "third estate" of the monarchy (as in France); afterwards, in the period of manufacturing proper, serving either the semi-feudal or the absolute monarchy as a counterpoise against the nobility, and, in fact, cornerstone of the great monarchies in general, the bourgeoisie has at last, since the establishment of Modern Industry and of the world market, conquered for itself, in the modern representative State, exclusive political sway. The executive of the modern state is but a committee for managing the common affairs of the whole bourgeoisie.

The bourgeoisie, historically, has played a most revolutionary part.

The bourgeoisie, wherever it has got the upper hand, has put an end to all feudal, patriarchal, idyllic relations. It has pitilessly torn asunder the motley feudal ties that bound man to his "natural superiors", and has left remaining no other nexus between man and man than naked self-interest, than callous "cash payment". It has drowned the most heavenly ecstasies of religious fervour, of chivalrous enthusiasm, of philistine sentimentalism, in the icy water of egotistical calculation. It has resolved personal worth into exchange value, and in place of the numberless indefeasible chartered freedoms, has set up that single, unconscionable freedom—Free Trade. In one word, for exploitation, veiled by religious and political illusions, it has substituted naked, shameless, direct, brutal exploitation.

The bourgeoisie has stripped of its halo every occupation hitherto honoured and looked up to with reverent awe. It has converted the physician, the lawyer, the priest, the poet, the man of science, into its paid wage labourers.

The bourgeoisie has torn away from the family its sentimental veil, and has reduced the family relation to a mere money relation.

The bourgeoisie has disclosed how it came to pass that the brutal display of vigour in the Middle Ages, which reactionaries so much admire, found its fitting complement in the most slothful indolence. It has been the first to show what man's activity can bring about. It has accomplished wonders far surpassing Egyptian pyramids, Roman aqueducts, and Gothic cathedrals; it has conducted expeditions that put in the shade all former Exoduses of nations and crusades.

---

5   This was the name given their urban communities by the townsmen of Italy and France, after they had purchased or conquered their initial rights of self-government from their feudal lords. [Engels, 1890 German edition] "Commune" was the name taken in France by the nascent towns even before they had conquered from their feudal lords and masters local self-government and political rights as the "Third Estate." Generally speaking, for the economical development of the bourgeoisie, England is here taken as the typical country, for its political development, France. [Engels, 1888 English Edition]

The bourgeoisie cannot exist without constantly revolutionising the instruments of production, and thereby the relations of production, and with them the whole relations of society. Conservation of the old modes of production in unaltered form, was, on the contrary, the first condition of existence for all earlier industrial classes. Constant revolutionising of production, uninterrupted disturbance of all social conditions, everlasting uncertainty and agitation distinguish the bourgeois epoch from all earlier ones. All fixed, fast-frozen relations, with their train of ancient and venerable prejudices and opinions, are swept away, all new-formed ones become antiquated before they can ossify. All that is solid melts into air, all that is holy is profaned, and man is at last compelled to face with sober senses his real conditions of life, and his relations with his kind.

The need of a constantly expanding market for its products chases the bourgeoisie over the entire surface of the globe. It must nestle everywhere, settle everywhere, establish connexions everywhere.

The bourgeoisie has through its exploitation of the world market given a cosmopolitan character to production and consumption in every country. To the great chagrin of Reactionists, it has drawn from under the feet of industry the national ground on which it stood. All old-established national industries have been destroyed or are daily being destroyed. They are dislodged by new industries, whose introduction becomes a life and death question for all civilised nations, by industries that no longer work up indigenous raw material, but raw material drawn from the remotest zones; industries whose products are consumed, not only at home, but in every quarter of the globe. In place of the old wants, satisfied by the production of the country, we find new wants, requiring for their satisfaction the products of distant lands and climes. In place of the old local and national seclusion and self-sufficiency, we have intercourse in every direction, universal interdependence of nations. And as in material, so also in intellectual production. The intellectual creations of individual nations become common property. National one-sidedness and narrow-mindedness become more and more impossible, and from the numerous national and local literatures, there arises a world literature.

The bourgeoisie, by the rapid improvement of all instruments of production, by the immensely facilitated means of communication, draws all, even the most barbarian, nations into civilisation. The cheap prices of commodities are the heavy artillery with which it batters down all Chinese walls, with which it forces the barbarians' intensely obstinate hatred of foreigners to capitulate. It compels all nations, on pain of extinction, to adopt the bourgeois mode of production; it compels them to introduce what it calls civilisation into their midst, i.e., to become bourgeois themselves. In one word, it creates a world after its own image.

The bourgeoisie has subjected the country to the rule of the towns. It has created enormous cities, has greatly increased the urban population as compared with the rural, and has thus rescued a considerable part of the population from the idiocy of rural life. Just as it has made the country dependent on the towns, so it has made barbarian and semi-barbarian countries dependent on the civilised ones, nations of peasants on nations of bourgeois, the East on the West.

The bourgeoisie keeps more and more doing away with the scattered state of the population, of the means of production, and of property. It has agglomerated population, centralised the means of production, and has concentrated property in a few hands. The necessary consequence of this was political centralisation. Independent, or but loosely connected provinces, with separate interests, laws, governments, and systems of taxation, became lumped together into one nation, with one government, one code of laws, one national class-interest, one frontier, and one customs-tariff.

The bourgeoisie, during its rule of scarce one hundred years, has created more massive and more colossal productive forces than have all preceding generations together. Subjection of Nature's forces to man, machinery, application of chemistry to industry and agriculture, steam-navigation, railways, electric telegraphs, clearing of whole continents for cultivation, canalisation of rivers, whole populations conjured out of the ground—what earlier century had even a presentiment that such productive forces slumbered in the lap of social labour?

We see then: the means of production and of exchange, on whose foundation the bourgeoisie built itself up, were generated in feudal society. At a certain stage in the development of these means of production and of exchange, the conditions under which feudal society produced and exchanged, the feudal organisation of agriculture and manufacturing industry, in one word, the feudal relations of property became no longer compatible with the already developed productive forces; they became so many fetters. They had to be burst asunder; they were burst asunder.

Into their place stepped free competition, accompanied by a social and political constitution adapted in it, and the economic and political sway of the bourgeois class.

A similar movement is going on before our own eyes. Modern bourgeois society, with its relations of production, of exchange and of property, a society that has conjured up such gigantic means of production and of exchange, is like the sorcerer who is no longer able to control the powers of the nether world whom he has called up by his spells. For many a decade past the history of industry and commerce is but the history of the revolt of modern productive forces against modern conditions of production, against the property relations that are the conditions for the existence of the bourgeois and of its rule. It is enough to mention the commercial crises that by their periodical return put the existence of the entire bourgeois society on its trial, each time more threateningly. In these crises, a great part not only of the existing products, but also of the previously created productive forces, are periodically destroyed. In these crises, there breaks out an epidemic that, in all earlier epochs, would have seemed an absurdity—the epidemic of over-production. Society suddenly finds itself put back into a state of momentary barbarism; it appears as if a famine, a universal war of devastation, had cut off the supply of every means of subsistence; industry and commerce seem to be destroyed; and why? Because there is too much civilisation, too much means of subsistence, too much industry, too much commerce. The productive forces at the disposal of society no longer tend to further the development of the conditions of bourgeois property; on the contrary, they have become too powerful for these conditions, by which they are fettered, and so soon as they overcome these fetters, they bring disorder into the whole of bourgeois society, endanger the existence of bourgeois property. The conditions of bourgeois society are too narrow to comprise the wealth created by them. And how does the bourgeoisie get over these crises? On the one hand by enforced destruction of a mass of productive forces; on the other, by the conquest of new markets, and by the more thorough exploitation of the old ones. That is to say, by paving the way for more extensive and more destructive crises, and by diminishing the means whereby crises are prevented.

The weapons with which the bourgeoisie felled feudalism to the ground are now turned against the bourgeoisie itself.

But not only has the bourgeoisie forged the weapons that bring death to itself; it has also called into existence the men who are to wield those weapons—the modern working class— the proletarians.

In proportion as the bourgeoisie, i.e., capital, is developed, in the same proportion is the proletariat, the modern working class, developed—a class of labourers, who live only so long as they find work, and who find work only so long as their labour increases capital. These labourers, who must sell themselves piecemeal, are a commodity, like every other article of commerce, and are consequently exposed to all the vicissitudes of competition, to all the fluctuations of the market.

Owing to the extensive use of machinery, and to the division of labour, the work of the proletarians has lost all individual character, and, consequently, all charm for the workman. He becomes an appendage of the machine, and it is only the most simple, most monotonous, and most easily acquired knack, that is required of him. Hence, the cost of production of a workman is restricted, almost entirely, to the means of subsistence that he requires for maintenance, and for the propagation of his race. But the price of a commodity, and therefore also of labour, is equal to its cost of production. In proportion, therefore, as the repulsiveness of the work increases, the wage decreases. Nay more, in proportion as the use of machinery and division of labour increases, in the same proportion the burden of toil also increases, whether by prolongation of the working hours, by the increase of the work exacted in a given time or by increased speed of machinery, etc.

Modern Industry has converted the little workshop of the patriarchal master into the great factory of the industrial capitalist. Masses of labourers, crowded into the factory, are organised like soldiers. As privates of the industrial army they are placed under the command of a perfect hierarchy of officers and sergeants. Not only are they slaves of the bourgeois class, and of the bourgeois State; they are daily and hourly enslaved by the machine, by the overlooker, and, above all, by the individual bourgeois manufacturer himself. The more openly this despotism proclaims gain to be its end and aim, the more petty, the more hateful and the more embittering it is.

The less the skill and exertion of strength implied in manual labour, in other words, the more modern industry becomes developed, the more is the labour of men superseded by that of women. Differences of age and sex have no longer any distinctive social validity for the working class. All are instruments of labour, more or less expensive to use, according to their age and sex.

No sooner is the exploitation of the labourer by the manufacturer, so far, at an end, that he receives his wages in cash, than he is set upon by the other portions of the bourgeoisie, the landlord, the shopkeeper, the pawnbroker, etc.

The lower strata of the middle class—the small tradespeople, shopkeepers, and retired tradesmen generally, the handicraftsmen and peasants—all these sink gradually into the proletariat, partly because their diminutive capital does not suffice for the scale on which Modern Industry is carried on, and is swamped in the competition with the large capitalists, partly because their specialised skill is rendered worthless by new methods of production. Thus the proletariat is recruited from all classes of the population.

The proletariat goes through various stages of development. With its birth begins its struggle with the bourgeoisie. At first the contest is carried on by individual labourers, then by the workpeople of a factory, then by the operative of one trade, in one locality, against the individual bourgeois who directly exploits them. They direct their attacks not against the bourgeois conditions of production, but against the instruments of production themselves; they destroy imported wares that compete with their labour, they smash to pieces machinery, they set factories ablaze, they seek to restore by force the vanished status of the workman of the Middle Ages.

At this stage, the labourers still form an incoherent mass scattered over the whole country, and broken up by their mutual competition. If anywhere they unite to form more compact bodies, this is not yet the consequence of their own active union, but of the union of the bourgeoisie, which class, in order to attain its own political ends, is compelled to set the whole proletariat in motion, and is moreover yet, for a time, able to do so. At this stage, therefore, the proletarians do not fight their enemies, but the enemies of their enemies, the remnants of absolute monarchy, the landowners, the non-industrial bourgeois, the petty bourgeois. Thus, the whole historical movement is concentrated in the hands of the bourgeoisie; every victory so obtained is a victory for the bourgeoisie.

But with the development of industry, the proletariat not only increases in number; it becomes concentrated in greater masses, its strength grows, and it feels that strength more. The various interests and conditions of life within the ranks of the proletariat are more and more equalised, in proportion as machinery obliterates all distinctions of labour, and nearly everywhere reduces wages to the same low level. The growing competition among the bourgeois, and the resulting commercial crises, make the wages of the workers ever more fluctuating. The increasing improvement of machinery, ever more rapidly developing, makes their livelihood more and more precarious; the collisions between individual workmen and individual bourgeois take more and more the character of collisions between two classes. Thereupon, the workers begin to form combinations (Trades' Unions) against the bourgeois; they club together in order to keep up the rate of wages; they found permanent associations in order to make provision beforehand for these occasional revolts. Here and there, the contest breaks out into riots.

Now and then the workers are victorious, but only for a time. The real fruit of their battles lies, not in the immediate result, but in the ever expanding union of the workers. This union is helped on by the improved means of communication that are created by modern industry, and that place the workers of different localities in contact with one another. It was just this contact that was needed to centralise the numerous local struggles, all of the same character, into one national struggle between classes. But every class struggle is a political struggle. And that union, to attain which the burghers of the Middle Ages, with their miserable highways, required centuries, the modern proletarian, thanks to railways, achieve in a few years.

This organisation of the proletarians into a class, and, consequently into a political party, is continually being upset again by the competition between the workers themselves. But it ever rises up again, stronger, firmer, mightier. It compels legislative recognition of particular interests of the workers, by taking advantage of the divisions among the bourgeoisie itself. Thus, the ten-hours' bill in England was carried.

Altogether collisions between the classes of the old society further, in many ways, the course of development of the proletariat. The bourgeoisie finds itself involved in a constant battle. At first with the aristocracy; later on, with those portions of the bourgeoisie itself, whose interests have become antagonistic to the progress of industry; at all time with the bourgeoisie of foreign countries. In all these battles, it sees itself compelled to appeal to the proletariat, to ask for help, and thus, to drag it into the political arena. The bourgeoisie itself, therefore, supplies the proletariat with its own elements of political and general education, in other words, it furnishes the proletariat with weapons for fighting the bourgeoisie.

Further, as we have already seen, entire sections of the ruling class are, by the advance of industry, precipitated into the proletariat, or are at least threatened in their conditions of existence. These also supply the proletariat with fresh elements of enlightenment and progress.

Finally, in times when the class struggle nears the decisive hour, the progress of dissolution going on within the ruling class, in fact within the whole range of old society, assumes such a violent, glaring character, that a small section of the ruling class cuts itself adrift, and joins the revolutionary class, the class that holds the future in its hands. Just as, therefore, at an earlier period, a section of the nobility went over to the bourgeoisie, so now a portion of the bourgeoisie goes over to the proletariat, and in particular, a portion of the bourgeois ideologists, who have raised themselves to the level of comprehending theoretically the historical movement as a whole.

Of all the classes that stand face to face with the bourgeoisie today, the proletariat alone is a really revolutionary class. The other classes decay and finally disappear in the face of Modern Industry; the proletariat is its special and essential product.

The lower middle class, the small manufacturer, the shopkeeper, the artisan, the peasant, all these fight against the bourgeoisie, to save from extinction their existence as fractions of the middle class. They are therefore not revolutionary, but conservative. Nay more, they are reactionary, for they try to roll back the wheel of history. If by chance, they are revolutionary, they are only so in view of their impending transfer into the proletariat; they thus defend not their present, but their future interests, they desert their own standpoint to place themselves at that of the proletariat.

The "dangerous class", [*lumpenproletariat*] the social scum, that passively rotting mass thrown off by the lowest layers of the old society, may, here and there, be swept into the movement by a proletarian revolution; its conditions of life, however, prepare it far more for the part of a bribed tool of reactionary intrigue.

In the condition of the proletariat, those of old society at large are already virtually swamped. The proletarian is without property; his relation to his wife and children has no longer anything in common with the bourgeois family relations; modern industry labour, modern subjection to capital, the same in England as in France, in America as in Germany, has stripped him of every trace of national character. Law, morality, religion, are to him so many bourgeois prejudices, behind which lurk in ambush just as many bourgeois interests.

All the preceding classes that got the upper hand sought to fortify their already acquired status by subjecting society at large to their conditions of appropriation. The proletarians cannot become masters of the productive forces of society, except by abolishing their own previous mode of appropriation, and thereby also every other previous mode of appropriation. They have nothing of their own to secure and to fortify; their mission is to destroy all previous securities for, and insurances of, individual property.

All previous historical movements were movements of minorities, or in the interest of minorities. The proletarian movement is the self-conscious, independent movement of the immense majority, in the interest of the immense majority. The proletariat, the lowest stratum of our present society, cannot stir, cannot raise itself up, without the whole superincumbent strata of official society being sprung into the air.

Though not in substance, yet in form, the struggle of the proletariat with the bourgeoisie is at first a national struggle. The proletariat of each country must, of course, first of all settle matters with its own bourgeoisie.

In depicting the most general phases of the development of the proletariat, we traced the more or less veiled civil war, raging within existing society, up to the point where that war breaks out into open revolution, and where the violent overthrow of the bourgeoisie lays the foundation for the sway of the proletariat.

Hitherto, every form of society has been based, as we have already seen, on the antagonism of oppressing and oppressed classes. But in order to oppress a class, certain conditions must be assured to it under which it can, at least, continue its slavish existence. The serf, in the period of serfdom, raised himself to membership in the commune, just as the petty bourgeois, under the yoke of the feudal absolutism, managed to develop into a bourgeois. The modern labourer, on the contrary, instead of rising with the process of industry, sinks deeper and deeper below the conditions of existence of his own class. He becomes a pauper, and pauperism develops more rapidly than population and wealth. And here it becomes evident, that the bourgeoisie is unfit any longer to be the ruling class in society, and to impose its conditions of existence upon society as an over-riding law. It is unfit to rule because it is incompetent to assure an existence to its slave within his slavery, because it cannot help letting him sink into such a state, that it has to feed him, instead of being fed by him. Society can no longer live under this bourgeoisie, in other words, its existence is no longer compatible with society.

The essential conditions for the existence and for the sway of the bourgeois class is the formation and augmentation of capital; the condition for capital is wage-labour. Wage-labour rests exclusively on competition between the labourers. The advance of industry, whose involuntary promoter is the bourgeoisie, replaces the isolation of the labourers, due to competition, by the revolutionary combination, due to association. The development of Modern Industry, therefore, cuts from under its feet the very foundation on which the bourgeoisie produces and appropriates products. What the bourgeoisie therefore produces, above all, are its own grave-diggers. Its fall and the victory of the proletariat are equally inevitable.

II. Proletarians and Communists

In what relation do the Communists stand to the proletarians as a whole?

The Communists do not form a separate party opposed to the other working-class parties.

They have no interests separate and apart from those of the proletariat as a whole.

They do not set up any sectarian principles of their own, by which to shape and mould the proletarian movement.

The Communists are distinguished from the other working-class parties by this only:

1. In the national struggles of the proletarians of the different countries, they point out and bring to the front the common interests of the entire proletariat, independently of all nationality. 2. In the various stages of development which the struggle of the working class against the bourgeoisie has to pass through, they always and everywhere represent the interests of the movement as a whole.

The Communists, therefore, are on the one hand, practically, the most advanced and resolute section of the working-class parties of every country, that section which pushes forward all others; on the other hand, theoretically, they have over the great mass of the proletariat the advantage of clearly understanding the line of march, the conditions, and the ultimate general results of the proletarian movement.

The immediate aim of the Communists is the same as that of all other proletarian parties: formation of the proletariat into a class, overthrow of the bourgeois supremacy, conquest of political power by the proletariat.

The theoretical conclusions of the Communists are in no way based on ideas or principles that have been invented, or discovered, by this or that would-be universal reformer.

They merely express, in general terms, actual relations springing from an existing class struggle, from a historical movement going on under our very eyes. The abolition of existing property relations is not at all a distinctive feature of communism.

All property relations in the past have continually been subject to historical change consequent upon the change in historical conditions.

The French Revolution, for example, abolished feudal property in favour of bourgeois property.

The distinguishing feature of Communism is not the abolition of property generally, but the abolition of bourgeois property. But modern bourgeois private property is the final and most complete expression of the system of producing and appropriating products, that is based on class antagonisms, on the exploitation of the many by the few.

In this sense, the theory of the Communists may be summed up in the single sentence: Abolition of private property.

We Communists have been reproached with the desire of abolishing the right of personally acquiring property as the fruit of a man's own labour, which property is alleged to be the groundwork of all personal freedom, activity and independence.

Hard-won, self-acquired, self-earned property! Do you mean the property of petty artisan and of the small peasant, a form of property that preceded the bourgeois form? There is no need to abolish that; the development of industry has to a great extent already destroyed it, and is still destroying it daily.

Or do you mean the modern bourgeois private property?

But does wage-labour create any property for the labourer? Not a bit. It creates capital, *i.e.*, that kind of property which exploits wage-labour, and which cannot increase except upon condition of begetting a new supply of wage-labour for fresh exploitation. Property, in its present form, is based on the antagonism of capital and wage labour. Let us examine both sides of this antagonism.

To be a capitalist, is to have not only a purely personal, but a social *status* in production. Capital is a collective product, and only by the united action of many members, nay, in the last resort, only by the united action of all members of society, can it be set in motion.

Capital is therefore not only personal; it is a social power.

When, therefore, capital is converted into common property, into the property of all members of society, personal property is not thereby transformed into social property. It is only the social character of the property that is changed. It loses its class character.

Let us now take wage-labour.

The average price of wage-labour is the minimum wage, *i.e.*, that quantum of the means of subsistence which is absolutely requisite to keep the labourer in bare existence as a labourer. What, therefore, the wage-labourer appropriates by means of his labour, merely suffices to prolong and reproduce a bare existence. We by no means intend to abolish this personal appropriation of the products of labour, an appropriation that is made for the maintenance and reproduction of human life, and that leaves no surplus wherewith to command the labour of others. All that we want to do away with is the miserable character of this appropriation, under which the labourer lives merely to increase capital, and is allowed to live only in so far as the interest of the ruling class requires it.

In bourgeois society, living labour is but a means to increase accumulated labour. In Communist society, accumulated labour is but a means to widen, to enrich, to promote the existence of the labourer.

In bourgeois society, therefore, the past dominates the present; in Communist society, the present dominates the past. In bourgeois society capital is independent and has individuality, while the living person is dependent and has no individuality.

And the abolition of this state of things is called by the bourgeois, abolition of individuality and freedom! And rightly so. The abolition of bourgeois individuality, bourgeois independence, and bourgeois freedom is undoubtedly aimed at.

By freedom is meant, under the present bourgeois conditions of production, free trade, free selling and buying.

But if selling and buying disappears, free selling and buying disappears also. This talk about free selling and buying, and all the other "brave words" of our bourgeois about freedom in general, have a meaning, if any, only in contrast with restricted selling and buying, with the fettered traders of the Middle Ages, but have no meaning when opposed to the Communistic abolition of buying and selling, of the bourgeois conditions of production, and of the bourgeoisie itself.

You are horrified at our intending to do away with private property. But in your existing society, private property is already done away with for nine-tenths of the population; its existence for the few is solely due to its non-existence in the hands of those nine-tenths. You reproach us, therefore, with intending to do away with a form of property, the necessary condition for whose existence is the non-existence of any property for the immense majority of society.

In one word, you reproach us with intending to do away with your property. Precisely so; that is just what we intend.

From the moment when labour can no longer be converted into capital, money, or rent, into a social power capable of being monopolised, *i.e.*, from the moment when individual property can no longer be transformed into bourgeois property, into capital, from that moment, you say, individuality vanishes.

You must, therefore, confess that by "individual" you mean no other person than the bourgeois, than the middle-class owner of property. This person must, indeed, be swept out of the way, and made impossible.

Communism deprives no man of the power to appropriate the products of society; all that it does is to deprive him of the power to subjugate the labour of others by means of such appropriations.

It has been objected that upon the abolition of private property, all work will cease, and universal laziness will overtake us.

According to this, bourgeois society ought long ago to have gone to the dogs through sheer idleness; for those of its members who work, acquire nothing, and those who acquire anything do not work. The whole of this objection is but another expression of the tautology: that there can no longer be any wage-labour when there is no longer any capital.

All objections urged against the Communistic mode of producing and appropriating material products, have, in the same way, been urged against the Communistic mode of producing and appropriating intellectual products. Just as, to the bourgeois, the disappearance of class property is the disappearance of production itself, so the disappearance of class culture is to him identical with the disappearance of all culture.

That culture, the loss of which he laments, is, for the enormous majority, a mere training to act as a machine.

But don't wrangle with us so long as you apply, to our intended abolition of bourgeois property, the standard of your bourgeois notions of freedom, culture, law, &c. Your very ideas are but the outgrowth of the conditions of your bourgeois production and bourgeois property, just as your jurisprudence is but the will of your class made into a law for all, a will whose essential character and direction are determined by the economical conditions of existence of your class.

The selfish misconception that induces you to transform into eternal laws of nature and of reason, the social forms springing from your present mode of production and form of property—historical relations that rise and disappear in the progress of production—this misconception you share with every ruling class that has preceded you. What you see clearly in the case of ancient property, what you admit in the case of feudal property, you are of course forbidden to admit in the case of your own bourgeois form of property.

Abolition [*Aufhebung*] of the family! Even the most radical flare up at this infamous proposal of the Communists.

On what foundation is the present family, the bourgeois family, based? On capital, on private gain. In its completely developed form, this family exists only among the bourgeoisie. But this state of things finds its complement in the practical absence of the family among the proletarians, and in public prostitution.

The bourgeois family will vanish as a matter of course when its complement vanishes, and both will vanish with the vanishing of capital.

Do you charge us with wanting to stop the exploitation of children by their parents? To this crime we plead guilty.

But, you say, we destroy the most hallowed of relations, when we replace home education by social.

And your education! Is not that also social, and determined by the social conditions under which you educate, by the intervention direct or indirect, of society, by means of schools, &c.? The Communists have not invented the intervention of society in education; they do but seek to alter the character of that intervention, and to rescue education from the influence of the ruling class.

The bourgeois clap-trap about the family and education, about the hallowed co-relation of parents and child, becomes all the more disgusting, the more, by the action of Modern Industry, all the family ties among the proletarians are torn asunder, and their children transformed into simple articles of commerce and instruments of labour.

But you Communists would introduce community of women, screams the bourgeoisie in chorus.

The bourgeois sees his wife a mere instrument of production. He hears that the instruments of production are to be exploited in common, and, naturally, can come to no other conclusion that the lot of being common to all will likewise fall to the women.

He has not even a suspicion that the real point aimed at is to do away with the status of women as mere instruments of production.

For the rest, nothing is more ridiculous than the virtuous indignation of our bourgeois at the community of women which, they pretend, is to be openly and officially established by the Communists. The Communists have no need to introduce community of women; it has existed almost from time immemorial.

Our bourgeois, not content with having wives and daughters of their proletarians at their disposal, not to speak of common prostitutes, take the greatest pleasure in seducing each other's wives.

Bourgeois marriage is, in reality, a system of wives in common and thus, at the most, what the Communists might possibly be reproached with is that they desire to introduce, in substitution for a hypocritically concealed, an openly legalised community of women. For the rest, it is self-evident that the abolition of the present system of production must bring with it the abolition of the community of women springing from that system, i.e., of prostitution both public and private.

The Communists are further reproached with desiring to abolish countries and nationality.

The working men have no country. We cannot take from them what they have not got. Since the proletariat must first of all acquire political supremacy, must rise to be the leading class of the nation, must constitute itself the nation, it is so far, itself national, though not in the bourgeois sense of the word.

National differences and antagonism between peoples are daily more and more vanishing, owing to the development of the bourgeoisie, to freedom of commerce, to the world market, to uniformity in the mode of production and in the conditions of life corresponding thereto.

The supremacy of the proletariat will cause them to vanish still faster. United action, of the leading civilised countries at least, is one of the first conditions for the emancipation of the proletariat.

In proportion as the exploitation of one individual by another will also be put an end to, the exploitation of one nation by another will also be put an end to. In proportion as the antagonism between classes within the nation vanishes, the hostility of one nation to another will come to an end.

The charges against Communism made from a religious, a philosophical and, generally, from an ideological standpoint, are not deserving of serious examination.

Does it require deep intuition to comprehend that man's ideas, views, and conception, in one word, man's consciousness, changes with every change in the conditions of his material existence, in his social relations and in his social life?

What else does the history of ideas prove, than that intellectual production changes its character in proportion as material production is changed? The ruling ideas of each age have ever been the ideas of its ruling class.

When people speak of the ideas that revolutionise society, they do but express that fact that within the old society the elements of a new one have been created, and that the dissolution of the old ideas keeps even pace with the dissolution of the old conditions of existence.

When the ancient world was in its last throes, the ancient religions were overcome by Christianity. When Christian ideas succumbed in the 18th century to rationalist ideas, feudal society fought its death battle with the then revolutionary bourgeoisie. The ideas of religious liberty and freedom of conscience merely gave expression to the sway of free competition within the domain of knowledge.

"Undoubtedly," it will be said, "religious, moral, philosophical, and juridical ideas have been modified in the course of historical development. But religion, morality, philosophy, political science, and law, constantly survived this change."

"There are, besides, eternal truths, such as Freedom, Justice, etc., that are common to all states of society. But Communism abolishes eternal truths, it abolishes all religion, and all morality, instead of constituting them on a new basis; it therefore acts in contradiction to all past historical experience."

What does this accusation reduce itself to? The history of all past society has consisted in the development of class antagonisms, antagonisms that assumed different forms at different epochs.

But whatever form they may have taken, one fact is common to all past ages, *viz.*, the exploitation of one part of society by the other. No wonder, then, that the social consciousness of past ages, despite all the multiplicity and variety it displays, moves within certain common forms, or general ideas, which cannot completely vanish except with the total disappearance of class antagonisms.

The Communist revolution is the most radical rupture with traditional property relations; no wonder that its development involved the most radical rupture with traditional ideas.

But let us have done with the bourgeois objections to Communism.

We have seen above, that the first step in the revolution by the working class is to raise the proletariat to the position of ruling class to win the battle of democracy.

The proletariat will use its political supremacy to wrest, by degree, all capital from the bourgeoisie, to centralise all instruments of production in the hands of the State, *i.e.*, of the proletariat organised as the ruling class; and to increase the total productive forces as rapidly as possible.

Of course, in the beginning, this cannot be effected except by means of despotic inroads on the rights of property, and on the conditions of bourgeois production; by means of measures, therefore, which appear economically insufficient and untenable, but which, in the course of the movement, outstrip themselves, necessitate further inroads upon the old social order, and are unavoidable as a means of entirely revolutionising the mode of production.

These measures will, of course, be different in different countries.

Nevertheless, in most advanced countries, the following will be pretty generally applicable.

1. Abolition of property in land and application of all rents of land to public purposes.
2. A heavy progressive or graduated income tax.
3. Abolition of all rights of inheritance.
4. Confiscation of the property of all emigrants and rebels.
5. Centralisation of credit in the hands of the state, by means of a national bank with State capital and an exclusive monopoly.
6. Centralisation of the means of communication and transport in the hands of the State.
7. Extension of factories and instruments of production owned by the State; the bringing into cultivation of waste-lands, and the improvement of the soil generally in accordance with a common plan.
8. Equal liability of all to work. Establishment of industrial armies, especially for agriculture.
9. Combination of agriculture with manufacturing industries; gradual abolition of all the distinction between town and country by a more equable distribution of the populace over the country.
10. Free education for all children in public schools. Abolition of children's factory labour in its present form. Combination of education with industrial production, &c, &c.

When, in the course of development, class distinctions have disappeared, and all production has been concentrated in the hands of a vast association of the whole nation, the public power will lose its political character. Political power, properly so called, is merely the organised power of one class for oppressing another. If the proletariat during its contest with the bourgeoisie is compelled, by the force of circumstances, to organise itself as a class, if, by means of a revolution, it makes itself the ruling class, and, as such, sweeps away by force the old conditions of production, then it will, along with these conditions, have swept away the conditions for the existence of class antagonisms and of classes generally, and will thereby have abolished its own supremacy as a class.

In place of the old bourgeois society, with its classes and class antagonisms, we shall have an association, in which the free development of each is the condition for the free development of all.

CHAPTER 12

Nietzsche

What Is Truth?

F RIEDRICH NIETZSCHE (1844–1900) is perhaps the most infamous philosopher to have ever lived. If you've heard of any philosopher at all, there is a good chance it's Nietzsche. He was such a powerful and influential critic of everything that came before him that it's hard to imagine philosophy today without Nietzsche.

Nietzsche's genius was discovered early, at age fourteen or so, when he was sent to the famous Schulpforta, a school for gifted children. Nietzsche received a rigorous and excellent education. He showed an early strength for languages and religion. He remained at the Schulpforta until he was twenty, at which point he moved with his professor to Leipzig to study philology.

In 1869, at the very young age of twenty-four, Nietzsche became a professor of philology in Basel. He is still one of the youngest professors to teach at the university. Despite this early success, Nietzsche pursued a more or less independent academic career. His first book, *The Birth of Tragedy*, was an interpretation of Greek tragic drama that challenged prevailing views at the time. The book was not very well received; indeed, it was very harshly criticized in an early review. Nietzsche's works were rarely well received. He wrote a lot, published several books, often at his own expense, and he rereleased his older works with new introductions to put his work in a new light.

Nietzsche suffered a mental breakdown in Turin in 1889 at the age of fifty-six. No one really knows what happened, but at some point after his breakdown, Nietzsche sent numerous letters to his friends, who became so worried about his mental health that they went to get him from Turin and bring him back to Germany. Nietzsche spent some time in a mental institution but was eventually released to his sister's care and lived out his final years in Weimar, Germany. Some use this fact that Nietzsche suffered a breakdown to preemptively discredit his thinking as that of a madman. Like all great geniuses, Nietzsche's writing is so unique that he surely did have a touch of madness. When reading Nietzsche, I always feel like I need to underline everything, like every word is leaden with a kind of strung-out majesty. Reading him can be intoxicating and addictive, but his musings are not those of a madman. Nietzsche was a highly disciplined individual with superlative academic credentials and a remarkable talent for historical analysis and subtle argument. For those with patience and the right disposition, reading Nietzsche can be life-changing.

Important Concepts: Truth; knowing; intellect; invention versus discovery; metaphor

As a thinker, Nietzsche was restless and aggressive. He wanted to disrupt some of the most obvious and conventional truths—he wanted to show us that the things we take to be absolute and unshakeable are contingent on a long process of development, on choices made and actions taken, for which we are ultimately responsible. In one of his earliest essays, *On Truth and Falsity in their Ultramoral Sense,* reproduced in full here, Nietzsche invites us to see knowledge from the perspective of the universe. "[H]ow aimless and arbitrary the human intellect looks within nature," Nietzsche remarks, "[t]here were centuries during which it did not exist." (163) Far from being a lamp light of truth, the human intellect is portrayed as a meaningless blip on the cosmic radar. Indeed, the parable suggests that the human intellect has no impact on anything at all because its reach does not extend beyond the human. Knowledge makes a difference, but only to us. Beyond the human, knowledge is nothing more than a spur to a puffed-up ego. Nietzsche writes, "There is nothing so reprehensible and unimportant in nature that it would not immediately swell up like a balloon at the slightest puff of this power of knowing." (163)

Notice the characterization of "knowing" in the opening paragraph. Nietzsche calls its invention (notice the word here: "invention," not "discovery"—Nietzsche is making a play on the German words *erfinden* and *finden* invention and discovery) the "most arrogant and mendacious minute of world history." (163) It's amazing, Nietzsche thinks, that the pride and self-importance that characterizes humanity can be traced back to the intellect. But what does the intellect do for us? With it, our eyes "glance only over the surface of things and see 'forms.'" (163–164) The intellect never comes close to revealing anything completely. Indeed, it is the intellect that confines us in such a limited sphere of abstraction and illusion. We are capable of so much more than the intellect, yet the whole history of philosophy has celebrated the intellect so powerfully that it seems so obvious to us today that the intellect is the only way we can really get at the truth of things.

So where, Nietzsche goes on to ask, does the idea of truth come from? Truth is one of those ideas that Nietzsche wants to trace back to its contingencies. The idea of truth is just an idea, just like the idea of knowledge, just like the idea of an intellect. So, what is truth contingent upon? From a desire for peace, for communication, a relief from boredom. The truth is simply an agreed-upon designation, (compare this to William James's pragmatic conception of truth, which we will explore in the next chapter), invented to help us get along, live in peace. "Truths," Nietzsche states in an unforgettable quip, "are illusions which we have forgotten are illusions." (166)

On Truth and Falsity in their Ultramoral Sense

Friedrich Nietzsche

1.

In some remote corner of the universe, effused into innumerable solar-systems, there was once a star upon which clever animals invented cognition. It was the haughtiest, most mendacious moment in the history of this world, but yet only a moment. After Nature had taken breath awhile the star congealed and the clever animals had to die.—Someone might write a fable after this style, and yet he would not have illustrated sufficiently, how wretched,; shadow-like, transitory, purposeless and fanciful the human intellect appears in Nature. There were eternities during which this intellect did not exist, and when it has once more passed away there will be nothing to show that it has existed. For this intellect is not concerned with any further mission transcending the sphere of human life. No, it is purely human and none but its owner and pro-creator regards it so pathetically as to suppose that the world revolves around it. If, however, we and the gnat could understand each other we should learn that even the gnat swims through the air with the same pathos, and feels within itself the flying centre of the world. Nothing in Nature is so bad or so insignificant that it will not, at the smallest puff of that force cognition, immediately swell up like a balloon, and just as a mere porter wants to have his admirer, so the very proudest man, the philosopher, imagines he sees from all sides the eyes of the universe telescopically directed upon his actions and thoughts.

It is remarkable that this is accomplished by the intellect, which after all has been given to the most unfortunate, the most delicate, the most transient beings only as an expedient, in order to detain them for a moment in existence, from which without that extra-gift they would have every cause to flee as swiftly as Lessing's son.[1] That haughtiness connected with cognition and sensation, spreading blinding fogs before the eyes and over the senses of men, deceives itself therefore as to the value of existence owing to the fact that it bears within itself the most flattering evaluation of cognition. Its most general effect is deception; but even its most particular effects have something of deception in their nature.

The intellect, as a means for the preservation of the individual, develops its chief power in dissimulation; for it is by dissimulation that the feebler, and less robust individuals preserve themselves, since it has been denied them to fight the battle of existence with horns or the sharp teeth of beasts of prey. In man this art of dissimulation reaches its acme of perfection: in him deception, flattery, falsehood and fraud, slander, display, pretentiousness, disguise, cloaking convention, and acting to others and to himself in short, the continual fluttering to and fro around the one flame—Vanity: all these things are so much the rule, and the law, that few things are more incomprehensible than the way in which an honest and pure impulse to truth could have arisen among men. They are deeply immersed in illusions and dream-fancies; their eyes

Friedrich Nietzsche, "On Truth and Falsity in their Ultramoral Sense," *Early Greek Philosophy and Other Essays*, ed. Oscar Levy, 1911.

glance only over the surface of things and see "forms"; their sensation nowhere leads to truth, but contents itself with receiving stimuli and, so to say, with playing hide-and-seek on the back of things. In addition to that, at night man allows his dreams to lie to him a whole life-time long, without his moral sense ever trying to prevent them; whereas men are said to exist who by the exercise of a strong will have overcome the habit of snoring. What indeed does man know about himself? Oh! that he could but once see himself complete, placed as it were in an illuminated glass-case! Does not nature keep secret from him most things, even about his body, e.g., the convolutions of the intestines, the quick flow of the blood-currents, the intricate vibrations of the fibres, so as to banish and lock him up in proud, delusive knowledge? Nature threw away the key; and woe co the fateful curiosity which might be able for a moment to look out and down through a crevice in the chamber of consciousness, and discover that man, indifferent to his own ignorance, is resting on the pitiless, the greedy, the insatiable, the murderous, and, as it were, hanging in dreams on the back of a tiger. Whence, in the wide world, with this state of affairs, arises the impulse to truth?

As far as the individual tries to preserve himself against other individuals, in the natural state of things he uses the intellect in most cases only for dissimulation; since, however, man both from necessity and boredom wants to exist socially and gregariously, he must needs make peace and at least endeavour to cause the greatest *bellum omnium contra omnes* to disappear from his world. This first conclusion of peace brings with it a something which looks like the first step towards the attainment of that enigmatical bent for truth. For that which henceforth is to be "truth" is now fixed; that is to say, a uniformly valid and binding designation of things is invented and the legislature of language also gives the first laws of truth: since here, for the first time, originates the contrast between truth and falsity. The liar uses the valid designations, the words, in order to make the unreal appear as real; e.g., he says, "I am rich," whereas the right designation for his state would be "poor." He abuses the fixed conventions by convenient substitution or even inversion of terms. If he does this in a selfish and moreover harmful fashion, society will no longer trust him but will even exclude him. In this way men avoid not so much being defrauded, but being injured by fraud. At bottom, at this juncture too, they hate not deception, but the evil, hostile consequences of certain species of deception. And it is in a similarly limited sense only that man desires truth: he covets the agreeable, life-preserving consequences of truth; he is indifferent towards pure, ineffective knowledge; he is even inimical towards truths which possibly might prove harmful or destroying. And, moreover, what after all are those conventions op language? Are they possibly products of knowledge, of the love of truth; do the designations and the things coincide? Is language the adequate expression of all realities?

Only by means of forgetfulness can man ever arrive at imagining that he possesses "truth" in that degree just indicated. If he does not mean to content himself with truth in the shape of tautology, that is, with empty husks, he will always obtain illusions instead of truth. What is a word? The expression of a nerve-stimulus in sounds. But to infer a cause outside us from the nerve-stimulus is already the result of a wrong and unjustifiable application of the proposition of causality. How should we dare, if truth with the genesis of language, if the point of view of certainty with the designations had alone been decisive; how indeed should we dare to say: the stone is hard; as if "hard" was known to us otherwise; and not merely as an entirely subjective stimulus! We divide things according to genders; we designate the tree as masculine,[2] the plant as feminine:[3] what arbitrary metaphors! How far flown beyond the canon of certainty! We speak of a "serpent";[4] the designation fits nothing but the sinuosity, and could therefore also appertain to the worm. What arbitrary demarcations! what one-sided preferences given sometimes to this, sometimes to that quality of a thing! The different languages placed side by side show that with words truth or adequate expression matters little: for otherwise there would not be so many languages. The "Thing-in-itself" (it is just this which would be the pure ineffective truth) is also quite incomprehensible to the creator of language and not worth making any great endeavour to obtain. He designates only the relations of things to men and for their expression he calls to his help the most daring metaphors. A nerve-stimulus, first transformed into a percept! First metaphor! The percept again copied into a sound! Second metaphor! And each time he leaps completely out of one sphere right into the midst of an entirely different one. One can imagine a man who is quite deaf and has never had a sensation of tone and of music; just as this man will possibly marvel at Chladni's sound figures in the sand, will discover their cause in the vibrations of the string, and will then proclaim that now he knows what man calls "tone"; even so does it happen to us all with language. When we talk about trees, colours, snow and flowers, we believe we know something about the things themselves, and yet we only possess metaphors of the things, and these metaphors do not in the least correspond to the original essentials. Just as the sound shows itself as a sand-figure, in the same way the enigmatical x of the Thing-in-itself is seen first as nerve-stimulus, then as percept, and finally as sound. At any rate the genesis of language did not therefore proceed on logical lines, and the whole material in which and with which the man of truth, the investigator, the philosopher works and builds, originates, if not from Nephelococcygia, cloud-land, at any rate not from the essence of things.

Let us especially think about the formation of ideas. Every word becomes at once an idea not by having, as one might presume, to serve as a reminder for the original experience happening but once and absolutely individualised, to which experience such word owes its origin, no, but by having simultaneously to fit innumerable, more or less similar (which really means never equal, therefore altogether unequal) cases. Every idea originates through equating the unequal. As certainly as no one leaf is exactly similar to any other, so certain is it that the idea "leaf" has been formed through an arbitrary omission of these individual differences, through a forgetting of the differentiating qualities, and this idea now awakens the notion that in nature there is, besides the leaves, a something called the "leaf," perhaps a primal form according to which all leaves were woven, drawn, accurately measured, coloured, crinkled, painted, but by unskilled hands, so that no copy had turned out correct and trustworthy as a true copy of the primal form. We call a man "honest"; we ask, why has he acted so honestly to-day? Our customary answer runs, "On account of his honesty." The Honesty! That means again: the "leaf" is the cause of the leaves. We really and truly do not know anything at all about an essential quality which might be called the honesty, but we do know about numerous individualised, and therefore unequal actions, which we equate by omission of the unequal, and now designate as honest actions; finally out of them we formulate a qualitas occulta with the name "Honesty." The disregarding of the individual and real furnishes us with the idea, as it likewise also gives us the form; whereas nature knows of no forms and ideas, and therefore knows no species but only an x, to us inaccessible and indefinable. For our antithesis of individual and species is anthropomorphic too and does not come from the essence of things, although on the other hand we do not dare to say that it does not correspond to it; for that would be a dogmatic assertion and as such just as undemonstrable as its contrary.

What therefore is truth? A mobile army of metaphors, metonymies, anthropomorphisms: in short a sum of human relations which became poetically and rhetorically intensified, metamorphosed, adorned, and after long usage seem to a nation fixed, canonic and binding; truths are illusions of which one has forgotten that they are illusions; worn-out metaphors which have become powerless to affect the senses; coins which have their obverse effaced and now are no longer of account as coins but merely as metal.

Still we do not yet know whence the impulse to truth comes, for up to now we have heard only about the obligation which society imposes in order to exist: to be truthful, that is, to use the usual metaphors, therefore expressed morally: we have heard only about the obligation to lie according to a fixed convention, to lie gregariously in a style binding for all. Now man of course forgets that matters are going thus with him; he therefore lies in that fashion pointed out unconsciously and according to habits of centuries' standing—and by this very unconsciousness, by this very forgetting, he arrives at a sense for truth. Through this feeling of being obliged to designate one thing as "red," another as "cold," a third one as "dumb," awakes a moral emotion relating to truth. Out of the antithesis "liar" whom nobody trusts, whom all exclude, man demonstrates to himself the venerableness, reliability, usefulness of truth. Now as a "rational" being he submits his actions to the sway of abstractions; he no longer suffers himself to be carried away by sudden impressions, by sensations, he first generalises all these impressions into paler, cooler ideas, in order to attach to them the ship of his life and actions. Everything which makes man stand out in bold relief against the animal depends on this faculty of volatilising the concrete metaphors into a schema, and therefore resolving a perception into an idea. For within the range of those schemata a something becomes possible that never could succeed under the first perceptual impressions: to build up a pyramidal order with castes and grades, to create a new world of laws, privileges, sub-orders, delimitations, which now stands opposite the other perceptual world of first impressions and assumes the appearance of being the more fixed, general, known, human of the two and therefore the regulating and imperative one. Whereas every metaphor of perception is individual and without its equal and therefore knows how to escape all attempts to classify it, the great "edifice of ideas shows the rigid regularity of a Roman Columbarium and in logic breathes forth the sternness and coolness which we find in mathematics. He who has been breathed upon by this coolness will scarcely believe, that the idea too, bony and hexa-hedral, and permutable as a die, remains however only as the residuum of a metaphor, and that the illusion of the artistic metamorphosis of a nerve-stimulus into percepts is, if not the mother, then the grand-mother of every idea. Now in this game of dice, "Truth" means to use every die as it is designated, to count its points carefully, to form exact classifications, and never lo violate the order of castes and the sequences of rank. Just as the Romans and Etruscans for their benefit cut up the sky by means of strong mathematical lines and banned a god as it were into a templum, into a space limited in this fashion, so every nation has above its head such a sky of ideas divided up mathematically, and it understands the demand for truth to mean that every conceptual god is to be looked for only in his own sphere. One may here well admire man, who succeeded in piling up an infinitely complex dome of ideas on a movable foundation and as it were on running water, as a powerful genius of architecture. Of course in order to obtain hold on such a foundation it must be as an edifice piled up out of cobwebs, so fragile, as to be carried away by the waves: so firm, as not to be blown asunder by every wind. In this way man as an architectural genius rises high above the bee; she builds with wax, which she brings together out of nature; he with the much more delicate material of ideas, which he must first manufacture within himself. He is very much to be admired here—but not on account of his impulse for truth, his bent for pure cognition of things. If somebody hides a thing behind a bush, seeks it again and finds it in the self-same place, then there is not much to boast of, respecting this seeking and finding; thus, however, matters stand with the seeking and finding of "truth" within the realm of reason. If I make the definition of the mammal and then declare after inspecting a camel, "Behold a mammal," then no doubt a truth is brought to light thereby, but it is of very limited value, I mean it is anthropomorphic through and through, and does not contain one single point which is "true-in-itself," real and universally valid, apart from man. The seeker after such truths seeks at the bottom only the metamorphosis of the world in man, he strives for an understanding of the world as a human-like thing and by his battling gains at best the feeling of an assimilation. Similarly, as the astrologer contemplated the stars in the service of man and in connection with their happiness and unhappiness, such a seeker contemplates the whole world as related to man, as the infinitely protracted echo of an original sound: man; as the multiplied copy of the one arch-type: man. His procedure is to apply man as the measure of all things, whereby he starts from the error of believing that he has these things immediately before him as pure objects. He therefore forgets that the original metaphors of perception are metaphors, and takes them for the things themselves.

Only by forgetting that primitive world of metaphors, only by the congelation and coagulation of an original mass of similes and percepts pouring forth as a fiery liquid out of the primal faculty of human fancy, only by the invincible faith, that this sun, this window, this table is a truth in itself: in short only by the fact that man forgets himself as subject, and what is more as an artistically creating subject: only by all this does he live with some repose, safety and consequence. If he were able to get out of the prison walls of this faith, even for an instant only, his "self-consciousness would be destroyed at once. Already it costs him some trouble to admit to himself that the insect and the bird perceive a world different from his own, and that the question, which of the two world-perceptions is more accurate, is quite a senseless one, since to decide this question it would be necessary to apply the standard of right perception, i.e., to apply a standard which does not exist. On the whole it seems to me that the "right perception"—which would mean the adequate expression of an object in the subject—is a nonentity full of contradictions: for between two utterly different spheres, as between subject and object, there is no causality, no accuracy, no expression, but at the utmost an aesthetical relation, I mean a suggestive metamorphosis, a stammering translation into quite a distinct foreign language, for which purpose however there is needed at any rate an intermediate sphere, an intermediate force, freely composing and freely inventing. The word "phenomenon" contains many seductions, and on that account I avoid it as much as possible, for it is not true that the essence of things appears in the empirical world. A painter who had no hands and wanted to express the picture distinctly present to his mind by the agency of song, would still reveal much more with this permutation of spheres, than the empiric world reveals about the essence of things. The very relation of a nerve-stimulus to the produced percept is in itself no necessary one; but if the same percept has been reproduced millions of times and has been the inheritance of many successive generations of man, and in the end appears each time to all mankind as the result of the same cause, then it attains finally for man the same importance as if it were the unique, necessary percept and as if that relation between the original nerve-stimulus and the percept produced were a close relation of causality: just as a dream eternally repeated, would be perceived and judged as though real. But the congelation and coagulation of a metaphor does not at all guarantee the necessity and exclusive justification of that metaphor.

Surely every human being who is at home with such contemplations has felt a deep distrust against any idealism of that kind, as often as he has distinctly convinced himself of the eternal rigidity, omnipresence, and infallibility of nature's laws: he has arrived at the conclusion that as far as we can penetrate the heights of the telescopic and the depths of the microscopic world, everything is quite secure, complete, infinite, determined, and continuous. Science will have to dig in these shafts eternally and successfully and all things found are sure to have to harmonize and not to contradict one another. How little does this resemble a product of fancy, for if it were one it would necessarily betray somewhere its nature of appearance and unreality. Against this it may be objected in the first place that if each of us had for himself a different sensibility, if we ourselves were only able to perceive sometimes as a bird, sometimes as a worm, sometimes as a plant, or if one of us saw the same stimulus as red, another as blue, if a third person even perceived it as a tone, then nobody would talk of such an orderliness of nature, but would conceive of her only as an extremely subjective structure. Secondly, what is, for us in general, a law of nature? It is not known in itself but only in its effects, that is to say in its relations to other laws of nature, which again are known to us only as sums of relations. Therefore all these relations refer only one to another and are absolutely incomprehensible to us in their essence; only that which we add: time, space, i.e., relations of sequence and numbers, are really known to us in them. Everything wonderful, however, that we marvel at in the laws of nature, everything that demands an explanation and might seduce us into distrusting idealism, lies really and solely in the mathematical rigour and inviolability of the conceptions of time and space. These however we produce within ourselves and throw them forth with that necessity with which the spider spins; since we are compelled to conceive all things under these forms only, then it is no longer wonderful that in all things we actually conceive none but these forms: for they all must bear within themselves the laws of number, and this very idea of number is the most marvellous in all things. All obedience to law which impresses us so forcibly in the orbits of stars and in chemical processes coincides at the bottom with those qualities which we ourselves attach to those things, so that it is we who thereby make the impression upon ourselves. Whence it clearly follows that that artistic formation of metaphors, with which every sensation in us begins, already presupposes those forms, and is therefore only consummated within them; only out of the persistency of these primal forms the possibility explains itself, how afterwards—out of the metaphors themselves a structure of ideas, could again be compiled. For the latter is an imitation of the relations of time, space and number in the realm of metaphors.

[1] The German poet, Lessing, had been married for just a little over one year to Eva König. A son was born and died the same day, and the mother's life was despaired of. In a letter to his friend Eschenburg the poet wrote: "... and I lost him so unwillingly, this son! For he had so much understanding! so much understanding! Do not suppose that the few hours of fatherhood have made me an ape of a father! I know what I say. Was it not understanding, that they had to drag him into the world with a pair of forceps? that he so soon suspected the evil of this world? Was it not understanding, that he seized the first opportunity to get away from it?..."

Eva König died a week later.—TR.

[2] In German the tree—der Baum—is masculine.—TR.

[3] In German the plant—die Pflanze—is feminine—TR.

[4] Cf. the German die Schlange and schlingen, the English serpent from the Latin serpere.—TR.

2.

As we saw, it is language which has worked originally at the construction of ideas; in later times it is science. Just as the bee works at the same time at the cells and fills them with honey, thus science works irresistibly at that great columbarium of ideas, the cemetery of perceptions, builds ever newer and higher storeys; supports, purifies, renews the old cells, and endeavours above all to fill that gigantic framework and to arrange within it the whole of the empiric world, i.e., the anthropomorphic world. And as the man of action binds his life to reason and its ideas, in order to avoid being swept away and losing himself, so the seeker after truth builds his hut close to the towering edifice of science in order to collaborate with it and to find protection. And he needs protection. For there are awful powers which continually press upon him, and which hold out against the "truth" of science "truths" fashioned in quite another way, bearing devices of the most heterogeneous character.

That impulse towards the formation of metaphors, mat fundamental impulse of man, which we cannot reason away for one moment—for thereby we should reason away man himself—is in truth not defeated nor even subdued by the fact that out of its evaporated products, the ideas, a regular and rigid new world has been built as a stronghold for it. This impulse seeks for itself a new realm of action and another river-bed, and finds it in Mythos and more generally in Art. This impulse constantly confuses the rubrics and cells of the ideas, by putting up new figures of speech, metaphors, metonymies; it constantly shows its passionate longing for shaping the existing world of waking man as motley, irregular, inconsequentially incoherent, attractive, and eternally new as the world of dreams is. For indeed, waking man per se is only clear about his being awake through the rigid and orderly woof of ideas, and it is for this very reason that he sometimes comes to believe that he was dreaming when that woof of ideas has for a moment been torn by Art. Pascal is quite right, when he asserts, that if the same dream came to us every night we should be just as much occupied by it as by the things which we see every day; to quote his words, "If an artisan were certain that he would dream every night for fully twelve hours that he was a king, I believe that he would be just as happy as a king who dreams every night for twelve hours that he is an artisan." The wide-awake day of a people mystically excitable, let us say of the earlier Greeks, is in fact through the continually-working wonder, which the mythos presupposes, more akin to the dream than to the day of the thinker sobered by science. If every tree may at some time talk as a nymph, or a god under the disguise of a bull, carry away virgins, if the goddess Athene herself be suddenly seen as, with a beautiful team, she drives, accompanied by Pisistratus, through the markets of Athens—and every honest Athenian did believe this—at any moment, as in a dream, everything is possible; and all nature swarms around man as if she were nothing but the masquerade of the gods, who found it a huge joke to deceive man by assuming all possible forms.

Man himself, however, has an invincible tendency to let himself be deceived, and he is like one enchanted with happiness when the rhapsodist narrates to him epic romances in such a way that they appear real or when the actor on the stage makes the king appear more kingly than reality shows him. Intellect, that master of dissimulation, is free and dismissed from his service as slave, so long as It is able to deceive without injuring, and then It celebrates Its Saturnalia. Never is It richer, prouder, more luxuriant, more skillful and daring; with a creator's delight It throws metaphors into confusion, shifts the boundary-stones of the abstractions, so that for instance It designates the stream as the mobile way which carries man to that place whither he would otherwise go. Now It has thrown off Its shoulders the emblem of servitude. Usually with gloomy officiousness It endeavours to point out the way to a poor individual coveting existence, and It fares forth for plunder and booty like a servant for his master, but now It Itself has become a master and may wipe from Its countenance the expression of indigence. Whatever It now does, compared with Its former doings, bears within itself dissimulation, just as Its former doings bore the character of distortion. It copies human life, but takes it for a good thing and seems to rest quite satisfied with it. That enormous framework and hoarding of ideas, by clinging to which needy man saves himself through life, is to the freed intellect only a scaffolding and a toy for

Its most daring feats, and when It smashes it to pieces, throws it into confusion, and then puts it together ironically, pairing the strangest, separating the nearest items, then It manifests that It has no use for those makeshifts of misery, and that It is now no longer led by ideas but by intuitions. From these intuitions no regular road leads into the land of the spectral schemata, the abstractions; for them the word is not made, when man sees them he is dumb, or speaks in forbidden metaphors and in unheard-of combinations of ideas, in order to correspond creatively with the impression of the powerful present intuition at least by destroying and jeering at the old barriers of ideas.

There are ages, when the rational and the intuitive man stand side by side, the one full of fear of the intuition, the other full of scorn for the abstraction; the latter just as irrational as the former is inartistic. Both desire to rule over life; the one by knowing how to meet the most important needs with foresight, prudence, regularity; the other as an "over-joyous" hero by ignoring those needs and taking that life only as real which simulates appearance and beauty. Wherever intuitive man, as for instance in the earlier history of Greece, brandishes his weapons more powerfully and victoriously than his opponent, there under favourable conditions, a culture can develop and art can establish her rule over life. That dissembling, that denying of neediness, that splendour of metaphorical notions and especially that directness of dissimulation accompany all utterances of such a life. Neither the house of man, nor his way of walking, nor his clothing, nor his earthen jug suggest that necessity invented them; it seems as if they all were intended as the expressions of a sublime happiness, an Olympic cloudlessness, and as it were a playing at seriousness. Whereas the man guided by ideas and abstractions only wards off misfortune by means of them, without even enforcing for himself happiness out of the abstractions; whereas he strives after the greatest possible freedom from pains, the intuitive man dwelling in the midst of culture has from his intuitions a harvest: besides the warding off of evil, he attains a continuous in-pouring of enlightenment, enlivenment and redemption. Of course when he does suffer, he suffers more: and he even suffers more frequently since he cannot learn from experience, but again and again falls into the same ditch into which he has fallen before. In suffering he is just as irrational as in happiness; he cries aloud and finds no consolation. How different matters are in the same misfortune with the Stoic, taught by experience and ruling himself by ideas! He who otherwise only looks for uprightness, truth, freedom from deceptions and shelter from ensnaring and sudden attack, in his misfortune performs the masterpiece of dissimulation, just as the other did in his happiness; he shows no twitching mobile human face but as it were a mask with dignified, harmonious features; he does not cry out and does not even alter his voice; when a heavy thundercloud bursts upon him, he wraps himself up in his cloak and with slow and measured step walks away from beneath it.

CHAPTER 13

William James

Pragmatism

ALTHOUGH WELL KNOWN today as one of the founding figures of the philosophical move-ment pragmatism, William James (1842–1910) was trained as a medical doctor, taught physiology, and was a leading psychologist. It was through his relationship with the philosopher Charles Sanders Peirce, another well-known early pragmatist, that James became involved in philosophical circles.

Pragmatism is a philosophy that lives very much up to its name; that is, it's distinctively prag-matic, and it prefers to handle things in a common sense way, avoiding excessive abstraction and theoretical complexity. Pragmatism focuses not on the truth or falsity of beliefs, but rather on the purpose we use these beliefs for. The meaningfulness of our thoughts does not consist, then, in the extent to which they correctly represent our world, but rather in the extent to which they produce action. Consider how this might change the way we evaluate something such as religious belief and you can get a sense of just how different and radical this way of thinking is. Imagine if we simply forgot about the question of whether God exists and focused instead the kinds of actions that faith compels.

Important Concepts: Pragmatic method; truth; belief.

The selection reproduced here, *What Pragmatism Means,* was originally delivered as the second in a series of eight lectures, grouped under the title *Pragmatism: A New Name for Some Old Ways of Thinking*. James is introducing this idea of philosophical pragmatism to a wide, general audience. James begins with a charming anecdote about philosophical dispute. A man is chasing a squirrel around a tree, but the squirrel continues to run around the tree too, and the man can never get ahead of the squirrel—the squirrel always manages to stay on the other side of the tree. So, a debate arises about whether the man actually goes around the squirrel or not. He of course goes around the tree and the squirrel is on the tree, but he never manages to catch up to the squirrel. James points out that this is an example of an intractable debate, since what side you take depends on what you think "going around" consists of. If you think that going around consists of passing from the north to the south, from the east to the west, then the man does go around the squirrel. But, if you think that going around means going from the front to the back, from right to left, then the man does not go around the squirrel. The significance in James's image is about just how trivial philosophical dispute really is—it's like chasing a squirrel around a tree!

All this debate comes down to is the practical significance one attaches to going around, and all that's needed to resolve the debate is a distinction between the two senses of going around that is understood by the disputants. Practically speaking, there is nothing gained with disputes of this sort, and nothing is to be gained by taking one side over the other.

This anecdote nicely illustrates what James understands as the pragmatic method, primarily a method for settling disputes by paying attention to the practical consequences of one belief or another. James writes, "What difference would it practically make to anyone if this notion rather than that notion were true? If no practical difference whatsoever can be traced, then the alternatives mean practically the same thing, and all dispute is idle." (175) Consider a philosophical debate about the nature of the existence of a chair between an idealist who thinks that the chair is a construct of his mind, and a realist who thinks that the chair has real existence outside of the mind. When it comes to actually sitting down, the dispute between idealism and realism comes to nothing—both parties simply take a seat.

James points out that the word "pragmatism" itself comes from the Greek "praxis," which gives us our words "practice" and "practical." The idea behind such a philosophy is that perfect clarity in one's thinking can be achieved by paying attention to its practical effects. In the case of the dispute about the chair, notice that there is no practical difference between idealism and realism. If we maintain that the chair is ideal, for instance, we cloud our thinking about the chair by focusing on things that make no practical difference whatsoever. This is what is meant by the idea that pragmatism is a way to achieve clarity in our thinking. If an idea has no practical significance, it's senseless.

What Pragmatism Means

William James

Some years ago, being with a camping party in the mountains, I returned from a solitary ramble to find everyone engaged in a ferocious metaphysical dispute. The corpus of the dispute was a squirrel—a live squirrel supposed to be clinging to one side of a tree-trunk; while over against the tree's opposite side a human being was imagined to stand. This human witness tries to get sight of the squirrel by moving rapidly round the tree, but no matter how fast he goes, the squirrel moves as fast in the opposite direction, and always keeps the tree between himself and the man, so that never a glimpse of him is caught. The resultant metaphysical problem now is this: DOES THE MAN GO ROUND THE SQUIRREL OR NOT? He goes round the tree, sure enough, and the squirrel is on the tree; but does he go round the squirrel? In the unlimited leisure of the wilderness, discussion had been worn threadbare. Everyone had taken sides, and was obstinate; and the numbers on both sides were even. Each side, when I appeared, therefore appealed to me to make it a majority. Mindful of the scholastic adage that whenever you meet a contradiction you must make a distinction, I immediately sought and found one, as follows: "Which party

William James, "Lecture II: What Pragmatism Means," *Pragmatism: A New Way for Some Old Ways of Thinking*, 1907.

is right," I said, "depends on what you PRACTICALLY MEAN by 'going round' the squirrel. If you mean passing from the north of him to the east, then to the south, then to the west, and then to the north of him again, obviously the man does go round him, for he occupies these successive positions. But if on the contrary you mean being first in front of him, then on the right of him, then behind him, then on his left, and finally in front again, it is quite as obvious that the man fails to go round him, for by the compensating movements the squirrel makes, he keeps his belly turned towards the man all the time, and his back turned away. Make the distinction, and there is no occasion for any farther dispute. You are both right and both wrong according as you conceive the verb 'to go round' in one practical fashion or the other."

Although one or two of the hotter disputants called my speech a shuffling evasion, saying they wanted no quibbling or scholastic hair-splitting, but meant just plain honest English 'round,' the majority seemed to think that the distinction had assuaged the dispute.

I tell this trivial anecdote because it is a peculiarly simple example of what I wish now to speak of as THE PRAGMATIC METHOD. The pragmatic method is primarily a method of settling metaphysical disputes that otherwise might be interminable. Is the world one or many?—fated or free?—material or spiritual?—here are notions either of which may or may not hold good of the world; and disputes over such notions are unending. The pragmatic method in such cases is to try to interpret each notion by tracing its respective practical consequences. What difference would it practically make to anyone if this notion rather than that notion were true? If no practical difference whatever can be traced, then the alternatives mean practically the same thing, and all dispute is idle. Whenever a dispute is serious, we ought to be able to show some practical difference that must follow from one side or the other's being right.

A glance at the history of the idea will show you still better what pragmatism means. The term is derived from the same Greek word [pi rho alpha gamma mu alpha], meaning action, from which our words 'practice' and 'practical' come. It was first introduced into philosophy by Mr. Charles Peirce in 1878. In an article entitled 'How to Make Our Ideas Clear,' in the 'Popular Science Monthly' for January of that year [Footnote: Translated in the *Revue Philosophique* for January, 1879 (vol. vii).] Mr. Peirce, after pointing out that our beliefs are really rules for action, said that to develop a thought's meaning, we need only determine what conduct it is fitted to produce: that conduct is for us its sole significance. And the tangible fact at the root of all our thought-distinctions, however subtle, is that there is no one of them so fine as to consist in anything but a possible difference of practice. To attain perfect clearness in our thoughts of an object, then, we need only consider what conceivable effects of a practical kind the object may involve—what sensations we are to expect from it, and what reactions we must prepare. Our conception of these effects, whether immediate or remote, is then for us the whole of our conception of the object, so far as that conception has positive significance at all.

This is the principle of Peirce, the principle of pragmatism. It lay entirely unnoticed by anyone for twenty years, until I, in an address before Professor Howison's philosophical union at the University of California, brought it forward again and made a special application of it to religion. By that date (1898) the times seemed ripe for its reception. The word 'pragmatism' spread, and at present it fairly spots the pages of the philosophic journals. On all hands we find the 'pragmatic movement' spoken of, sometimes with respect, sometimes with contumely, seldom with clear understanding. It is evident that the term applies itself conveniently to a number of tendencies that hitherto have lacked a collective name, and that it has 'come to stay.'

To take in the importance of Peirce's principle, one must get accustomed to applying it to concrete cases. I found a few years ago that Ostwald, the illustrious Leipzig chemist, had been making perfectly distinct use of the principle of pragmatism in his lectures on the philosophy of science, though he had not called it by that name.

"All realities influence our practice," he wrote me, "and that influence is their meaning for us. I am accustomed to put questions to my classes in this way: In what respects would the world be different if this alternative or that were true? If I can find nothing that would become different, then the alternative has no sense."

That is, the rival views mean practically the same thing, and meaning, other than practical, there is for us none. Ostwald in a published lecture gives this example of what he means. Chemists have long wrangled over the inner constitution of certain bodies called 'tautomerous.' Their properties seemed equally consistent with the notion that an instable hydrogen atom oscillates inside of them, or that they are instable mixtures of two bodies. Controversy raged; but never was decided. "It would never have begun," says Ostwald, "if the combatants had asked themselves what particular experimental fact could have been made different by one or the other view being correct. For it would then have appeared that no difference of fact could possibly ensue; and the quarrel was as unreal as if, theorizing in primitive times about the raising of dough by yeast, one party should have invoked a 'brownie,' while another insisted on an 'elf' as the true cause of the phenomenon." [Footnote: *'Theorie und Praxis,' Zeitsch. des Oesterreichischen Ingenieur u. Architecten-Vereines*, 1905, Nr. 4 u. 6. I find a still more radical pragmatism than Ostwald's in an address by Professor W. S. Franklin: "I think that the sickliest notion of physics, even if a student gets it, is that it is 'the science of masses, molecules and the ether.' And I think that the healthiest notion, even if a student does not wholly get it, is that physics is the science of the ways of taking hold of bodies and pushing them!" (Science, January 2, 1903.)]

It is astonishing to see how many philosophical disputes collapse into insignificance the moment you subject them to this simple test of tracing a concrete consequence. There can BE no difference any-where that doesn't MAKE a difference elsewhere—no difference in abstract truth that doesn't express itself in a difference in concrete fact and in conduct consequent upon that fact, imposed on somebody, somehow, somewhere and somewhen. The whole function of philosophy ought to be to find out what definite difference it will make to you and me, at definite instants of our life, if this world-formula or that world-formula be the true one.

There is absolutely nothing new in the pragmatic method. Socrates was an adept at it. Aristotle used it methodically. Locke, Berkeley and Hume made momentous contributions to truth by its means. Shadworth Hodgson keeps insisting that realities are only what they are 'known-as.' But these forerunners of pragmatism used it in fragments: they were preluders only. Not until in our time has it generalized itself, become conscious of a universal mission, pretended to a conquering destiny. I believe in that destiny, and I hope I may end by inspiring you with my belief.

Pragmatism represents a perfectly familiar attitude in philosophy, the empiricist attitude, but it represents it, as it seems to me, both in a more radical and in a less objectionable form than it has ever yet assumed. A pragmatist turns his back resolutely and once for all upon a lot of inveterate habits dear to professional philosophers. He turns away from abstraction and insufficiency, from verbal solutions, from bad a priori reasons, from fixed principles, closed systems, and pretended absolutes and origins. He turns towards concreteness and adequacy, towards facts, towards action, and towards power. That means the empiricist temper regnant, and the rationalist temper sincerely given up. It means the open air and possibilities of nature, as against dogma, artificiality and the pretense of finality in truth.

At the same time it does not stand for any special results. It is a method only. But the general triumph of that method would mean an enormous change in what I called in my last lecture the 'temperament' of philosophy. Teachers of the ultra-rationalistic type would be frozen out, much as the courtier type is frozen out in republics, as the ultramontane type of priest is frozen out in protestant lands. Science and metaphysics would come much nearer together, would in fact work absolutely hand in hand.

Metaphysics has usually followed a very primitive kind of quest. You know how men have always hankered after unlawful magic, and you know what a great part, in magic, WORDS have always played. If you have his name, or the formula of incantation that binds him, you can control the spirit, genie, afrite, or whatever the power may be. Solomon knew the names of all the spirits, and having their names, he held them subject to his will. So the universe has always appeared to the natural mind as a kind of enigma, of which the key must be sought in the shape of some illuminating or power-bringing word or name. That word names the universe's PRIN-CIPLE, and to possess it is, after a fashion, to possess the universe itself. 'God,' 'Matter,' 'Reason,' 'the Absolute,' 'Energy,' are so many solving names. You can rest when you have them. You are at the end of your metaphysical quest.

But if you follow the pragmatic method, you cannot look on any such word as closing your quest. You must bring out of each word its practical cash-value, set it at work within the stream of your experience. It appears less as a solution, then, than as a program for more work, and more particularly as an indication of the ways in which existing realities may be CHANGED.

THEORIES THUS BECOME INSTRUMENTS, NOT ANSWERS TO ENIGMAS, IN WHICH WE CAN REST. We don't lie back upon them, we move forward, and, on occasion, make nature over again by their aid. Pragmatism unstiffens all our theories, limbers them up and sets each one at work. Being nothing essentially new, it harmonizes with many ancient philosophic tendencies. It agrees with nominalism for instance, in always appealing to particulars; with utilitarianism in emphasizing practical aspects; with positivism in its disdain for verbal solutions, useless questions, and metaphysical abstractions.

All these, you see, are ANTI-INTELLECTUALIST tendencies. Against rationalism as a pretension and a method, pragmatism is fully armed and militant. But, at the outset, at least, it stands for no particular results. It has no dogmas, and no doctrines save its method. As the young Italian pragmatist Papini has well said, it lies in the midst of our theories, like a corridor in a hotel. Innumerable chambers open out of it. In one you may find a man writing an atheistic volume; in the next someone on his knees praying for faith and strength; in a third a chemist investigating a body's properties. In a fourth a system of idealistic metaphysics is being excogitated; in a fifth the impossibility of metaphysics is being shown. But they all own the corridor, and all must pass through it if they want a practicable way of getting into or out of their respective rooms.

No particular results then, so far, but only an attitude of orientation, is what the pragmatic method means. THE ATTITUDE OF LOOKING AWAY FROM FIRST THINGS, PRINCIPLES, 'CATEGORIES,' SUPPOSED NECESSITIES; AND OF LOOKING TOWARDS LAST THINGS, FRUITS, CONSEQUENCES, FACTS.

So much for the pragmatic method! You may say that I have been praising it rather than explaining it to you, but I shall presently explain it abundantly enough by showing how it works on some familiar problems. Meanwhile the word pragmatism has come to be used in a still wider sense, as meaning also a certain theory of TRUTH. I mean to give a whole lecture to the statement of that theory, after first paving the way, so I can be very brief now. But brevity is hard to follow, so I ask for your redoubled attention for a quarter of an hour. If much remains obscure, I hope to make it clearer in the later lectures.

One of the most successfully cultivated branches of philosophy in our time is what is called inductive logic, the study of the conditions under which our sciences have evolved. Writers on this subject have begun to show a singular unanimity as to what the laws of nature and elements of fact mean, when formulated by mathematicians, physicists and chemists. When the first mathematical, logical and natural uniformities, the first LAWS, were discovered, men were so carried away by the clearness, beauty and simplification that resulted, that they believed themselves to have deciphered authentically the eternal thoughts of the Almighty. His mind also thundered and reverberated in syllogisms. He also thought in conic sections, squares and roots and ratios, and geometrized like Euclid. He made Kepler's laws for the planets to follow; he made velocity increase proportionally to the time in falling bodies; he made the law of the sines for light to obey when refracted; he established the classes, orders, families and genera of plants and animals, and fixed the distances between them. He thought the archetypes of all things, and devised their variations; and when we rediscover any one of these his wondrous institutions, we seize his mind in its very literal intention.

But as the sciences have developed farther, the notion has gained ground that most, perhaps all, of our laws are only approximations. The laws themselves, moreover, have grown so numerous that there is no counting them; and so many rival formulations are proposed in all the branches of science that investigators have become accustomed to the notion that no theory is absolutely a transcript of reality, but that any one of them may from some point of view be useful. Their great use is to summarize old facts and to lead to new ones. They are only a man-made language, a conceptual shorthand, as someone calls them, in which we write our reports of nature; and languages, as is well known, tolerate much choice of expression and many dialects.

Thus human arbitrariness has driven divine necessity from scientific logic. If I mention the names of Sigwart, Mach, Ostwald, Pearson, Milhaud, Poincare, Duhem, Ruyssen, those of you who are students will easily identify the tendency I speak of, and will think of additional names.

Riding now on the front of this wave of scientific logic Messrs. Schiller and Dewey appear with their pragmatistic account of what truth everywhere signifies. Everywhere, these teachers say, 'truth' in our ideas and beliefs means the same thing that it means in science. It means, they say, nothing but this, THAT IDEAS (WHICH THEMSELVES ARE BUT PARTS OF OUR EXPERIENCE) BECOME TRUE JUST IN SO FAR AS THEY HELP US TO GET INTO SATISFACTORY RELATION WITH OTHER PARTS OF OUR EXPERIENCE, to summarize them and get about among them by conceptual short-cuts instead of following the interminable succession of particular phenomena. Any idea upon which we can ride, so to speak; any idea that will carry us prosperously from any one part of our experience to any other part, linking things satisfactorily, working securely, simplifying, saving labor; is true for just so much, true in so far forth, true INSTRUMENTALLY. This is the 'instrumental' view of truth taught so successfully at Chicago, the view that truth in our ideas means their power to 'work,' promulgated so brilliantly at Oxford.

Messrs. Dewey, Schiller and their allies, in reaching this general conception of all truth, have only followed the example of geologists, biologists and philologists. In the establishment of these other sciences, the successful stroke was always to take some simple process actually observable in operation—as denudation by weather, say, or variation from parental type, or change of dialect by incorporation of new words and pronunciations—and then to generalize it, making it apply to all times, and produce great results by summating its effects through the ages.

The observable process which Schiller and Dewey particularly singled out for generalization is the familiar one by which any individual settles into NEW OPINIONS. The process here is always the same. The individual has a stock of old opinions already, but he meets a new experience that puts them to a strain. Somebody contradicts them; or in a reflective moment he discovers that they contradict each other; or he hears of facts with which they are incompatible; or desires arise in him which they cease to satisfy. The result is an inward trouble to which his mind till then had been a stranger, and from which he seeks to escape by modifying his previous mass of opinions. He saves as much of it as he can, for in this matter of belief we are all extreme conservatives. So he tries to change first this opinion, and then that (for they resist change very variously), until at last some new idea comes up which he can graft upon the ancient stock with a minimum of disturbance of the latter, some idea that mediates between the stock and the new experience and runs them into one another most felicitously and expediently.

This new idea is then adopted as the true one. It preserves the older stock of truths with a minimum of modification, stretching them just enough to make them admit the novelty, but conceiving that in ways as familiar as the case leaves possible. An outree explanation, violating all our preconceptions, would never pass for a true account of a novelty. We should scratch round industriously till we found something less eccentric. The most violent revolutions in an individual's beliefs leave most of his old order standing. Time and space, cause and effect, nature and history, and one's own biography remain untouched. New truth is always a go-between, a smoother-over of transitions. It marries old opinion to new fact so as ever to show a minimum of jolt, a maximum of continuity. We hold a theory true just in proportion to its success in solving this 'problem of maxima and minima.' But success in solving this problem is eminently a matter of approximation. We say this theory solves it on the whole more satisfactorily than that theory; but that means more satisfactorily to ourselves, and individuals will emphasize their points of satisfaction differently. To a certain degree, therefore, everything here is plastic.

The point I now urge you to observe particularly is the part played by the older truths. Failure to take account of it is the source of much of the unjust criticism leveled against pragmatism. Their influence is absolutely controlling. Loyalty to them is the first principle—in most cases it is the only principle; for by far the most usual way of handling phenomena so novel that they would make for a serious rearrangement of our preconceptions is to ignore them altogether, or to abuse those who bear witness for them.

You doubtless wish examples of this process of truth's growth, and the only trouble is their superabundance. The simplest case of new truth is of course the mere numerical addition of new kinds of facts, or of new single facts of old kinds, to our experience—an addition that involves no alteration in the old beliefs. Day follows day, and its contents are simply added. The new contents themselves are not true, they simply COME and ARE. Truth is what we say about them, and when we say that they have come, truth is satisfied by the plain additive formula.

But often the day's contents oblige a rearrangement. If I should now utter piercing shrieks and act like a maniac on this platform, it would make many of you revise your ideas as to the probable worth of my philosophy. 'Radium' came the other day as part of the day's content, and seemed for a moment to contradict our ideas of the whole order of nature, that order having come to be identified with what is called the conservation of energy. The mere sight of radium paying heat away indefinitely out of its own pocket seemed to violate that conservation. What to think? If the radiations from it were nothing but an escape of unsuspected 'potential' energy, pre-existent inside of the atoms, the principle of conservation would be saved. The discovery of 'helium' as the radiation's outcome, opened a way to this belief. So Ramsay's view is generally held to be true, because, although it extends our old ideas of energy, it causes a minimum of alteration in their nature.

I need not multiply instances. A new opinion counts as 'true' just in proportion as it gratifies the individual's desire to assimilate the novel in his experience to his beliefs in stock. It must both lean on old truth and grasp new fact; and its success (as I said a moment ago) in doing this, is a matter for the individual's appreciation. When old truth grows, then, by new truth's addition, it is for subjective reasons. We are in the process and obey the reasons. That new idea is truest which performs most felicitously its function of satisfying our double urgency. It makes itself true, gets itself classed as true, by the way it works; grafting itself then upon the ancient body of truth, which thus grows much as a tree grows by the activity of a new layer of cambium.

Now Dewey and Schiller proceed to generalize this observation and to apply it to the most ancient parts of truth. They also once were plastic. They also were called true for human reasons. They also mediated between still earlier truths and what in those days were novel observations. Purely objective truth, truth in whose establishment the function of giving human satisfaction in marrying previous parts of experience with newer parts played no role whatever, is nowhere to be found. The reasons why we call things true is the reason why they ARE true, for 'to be true' MEANS only to perform this marriage-function.

The trail of the human serpent is thus over everything. Truth independent; truth that we FIND merely; truth no longer malleable to human need; truth incorrigible, in a word; such truth exists indeed superabundantly—or is supposed to exist by rationalistically minded thinkers; but then it means only the dead heart of the living tree, and its being there means only that truth also has its paleontology and its 'prescription,' and may grow stiff with years of veteran service and petrified in men's regard by sheer antiquity. But how plastic even the oldest truths nevertheless really are has been vividly shown in our day by the transformation of logical and mathematical ideas, a transformation which seems even to be invading physics. The ancient formulas are reinterpreted as special expressions of much wider principles, principles that our ancestors never got a glimpse of in their present shape and formulation.

Mr. Schiller still gives to all this view of truth the name of 'Humanism,' but, for this doctrine too, the name of pragmatism seems fairly to be in the ascendant, so I will treat it under the name of pragmatism in these lectures.

Such then would be the scope of pragmatism—first, a method; and second, a genetic theory of what is meant by truth. And these two things must be our future topics.

What I have said of the theory of truth will, I am sure, have appeared obscure and unsatisfactory to most of you by reason of us brevity. I shall make amends for that hereafter. In a lecture on 'common sense' I shall try to show what I mean by truths grown petrified by antiquity. In another lecture I shall expatiate on the idea that our thoughts become true in proportion as they successfully exert their go-between function. In a third I shall show how hard it is to discriminate subjective from objective factors in Truth's development. You may not follow me wholly in these lectures; and if you do, you may not wholly agree with me. But you will, I know, regard me at least as serious, and treat my effort with respectful consideration.

You will probably be surprised to learn, then, that Messrs. Schiller's and Dewey's theories have suffered a hailstorm of contempt and ridicule. All rationalism has risen against them. In influential quarters Mr. Schiller, in particular, has been treated like an impudent schoolboy who deserves a spanking. I should not mention this, but for the fact that it throws so much sidelight upon that rationalistic temper to which I have opposed the temper of pragmatism. Pragmatism is uncomfortable away from facts. Rationalism is comfortable only in the presence of abstractions. This pragmatist talk about truths in the plural, about their utility and satisfactoriness, about the success with which they 'work,' etc., suggests to the typical intellectualist mind a sort of coarse lame second-rate makeshift article of truth. Such truths are not real truth. Such tests are merely subjective. As against this, objective truth must be something non-utilitarian, haughty, refined, remote, august, exalted. It must be an absolute correspondence of our thoughts with an equally absolute reality. It must be what we OUGHT to think, unconditionally. The conditioned ways in which we DO think are so much irrelevance and matter for psychology. Down with psychology, up with logic, in all this question!

See the exquisite contrast of the types of mind! The pragmatist clings to facts and concreteness, observes truth at its work in particular cases, and generalizes. Truth, for him, becomes a class-name for all sorts of definite working-values in experience. For the rationalist it remains a pure abstraction, to the bare name of which we must defer. When the pragmatist undertakes to show in detail just WHY we must defer, the rationalist is unable to recognize the concretes from which his own abstraction is taken. He accuses us of DENYING truth; whereas we have only sought to trace exactly why people follow it and always ought to follow it. Your typical ultra-abstractionist fairly shudders at concreteness: other things equal, he positively prefers the pale and spectral. If the two universes were offered, he would always choose the skinny outline rather than the rich thicket of reality. It is so much purer, clearer, nobler.

I hope that as these lectures go on, the concreteness and closeness to facts of the pragmatism which they advocate may be what approves itself to you as its most satisfactory peculiarity. It only follows here the example of the sister-sciences, interpreting the unobserved by the observed. It brings old and new harmoniously together. It converts the absolutely empty notion of a static relation of 'correspondence' (what that may mean we must ask later) between our minds and reality, into that of a rich and active commerce (that anyone may follow in detail and understand) between particular thoughts of ours, and the great universe of other experiences in which they play their parts and have their uses.

But enough of this at present? The justification of what I say must be postponed. I wish now to add a word in further explanation of the claim I made at our last meeting, that pragmatism may be a happy harmonizer of empiricist ways of thinking, with the more religious demands of human beings.

Men who are strongly of the fact-loving temperament, you may remember me to have said, are liable to be kept at a distance by the small sympathy with facts which that philosophy from the present-day fashion of idealism offers them. It is far too intellectualistic. Old fashioned theism was bad enough, with its notion of God as an exalted monarch, made up of a lot of unintelligible or preposterous 'attributes'; but, so long as it held strongly by the argument from design, it kept some touch with concrete realities. Since, however, Darwinism has once for all displaced design from the minds of the 'scientific,' theism has lost that foothold; and some kind of an imminent or pantheistic deity working IN things rather than above them is, if any, the kind recommended to our contemporary imagination. Aspirants to a philosophic religion turn, as a rule, more hopefully nowadays towards idealistic pantheism than towards the older dualistic theism, in spite of the fact that the latter still counts able defenders.

But, as I said in my first lecture, the brand of pantheism offered is hard for them to assimilate if they are lovers of facts, or empirically minded. It is the absolutistic brand, spurning the dust and reared upon pure logic. It keeps no connexion whatever with concreteness. Affirming the Absolute Mind, which is its substitute for God, to be the rational presupposition of all particulars of fact, whatever they may be, it remains supremely indifferent to what the particular facts in our world actually are. Be they what they may, the Absolute will father them. Like the sick lion in Aesop's fable, all footprints lead into his den, but *nulla vestigia retrorsum*. You cannot redescend into the world of particulars by the Absolute's aid, or deduce any necessary consequences of detail important for your life from your idea of his nature. He gives you indeed the assurance that all is well with Him, and for his eternal way of thinking; but thereupon he leaves you to be finitely saved by your own temporal devices.

Far be it from me to deny the majesty of this conception, or its capacity to yield religious comfort to a most respectable class of minds. But from the human point of view, no one can pretend that it doesn't suffer from the faults of remoteness and abstractness. It is eminently a product of what I have ventured to call the rationalistic temper. It disdains empiricism's needs. It substitutes a pallid outline for the real world's richness. It is dapper; it is noble in the bad sense, in the sense in which to be noble is to be inapt for humble service. In this real world of sweat and dirt, it seems to me that when a view of things is 'noble,' that ought to count as a presumption against its truth, and as a philosophic disqualification. The prince of darkness may be a gentleman, as we are told he is, but whatever the God of earth and heaven is, he can surely be no gentleman. His menial services are needed in the dust of our human trials, even more than his dignity is needed in the empyrean.

Now pragmatism, devoted though she be to facts, has no such materialistic bias as ordinary empiricism labors under. Moreover, she has no objection whatever to the realizing of abstractions, so long as you get about among particulars with their aid and they actually carry you somewhere. Interested in no conclusions but those which our minds and our experiences work out together, she has no a priori prejudices against theology. IF THEOLOGICAL IDEAS PROVE TO HAVE A VALUE FOR CONCRETE LIFE, THEY WILL BE TRUE, FOR PRAGMATISM, IN THE SENSE OF BEING GOOD FOR SO MUCH. FOR HOW MUCH MORE THEY ARE TRUE, WILL DEPEND ENTIRELY ON THEIR RELATIONS TO THE OTHER TRUTHS THAT ALSO HAVE TO BE ACKNOWLEDGED.

What I said just now about the Absolute of transcendental idealism is a case in point. First, I called it majestic and said it yielded religious comfort to a class of minds, and then I accused it of remoteness and sterility. But so far as it affords such comfort, it surely is not sterile; it has that amount of value; it performs a concrete function. As a good pragmatist, I myself ought to call the Absolute true 'in so far forth,' then; and I unhesitatingly now do so.

But what does TRUE IN SO FAR FORTH mean in this case? To answer, we need only apply the pragmatic method. What do believers in the Absolute mean by saying that their belief affords them comfort? They mean that since in the Absolute finite evil is 'overruled' already, we may, therefore, whenever we wish, treat the temporal as if it were potentially the eternal, be sure that we can trust its outcome, and, without sin, dismiss our fear and drop the worry of our finite responsibility. In short, they mean that we have a right ever and anon to take a moral holiday, to let the world wag in its own way, feeling that its issues are in better hands than ours and are none of our business.

The universe is a system of which the individual members may relax their anxieties occasionally, in which the don't-care mood is also right for men, and moral holidays in order—that, if I mistake not, is part, at least, of what the Absolute is 'known-as,' that is the great difference in our particular experiences which his being true makes for us, that is part of his cash-value when he is pragmatically interpreted. Farther than that the ordinary lay-reader in philosophy who thinks favorably of absolute idealism does not venture to sharpen his conceptions. He can use the Absolute for so much, and so much is very precious. He is pained at hearing you speak incredulously of the Absolute, therefore, and disregards your criticisms because they deal with aspects of the conception that he fails to follow.

If the Absolute means this, and means no more than this, who can possibly deny the truth of it? To deny it would be to insist that men should never relax, and that holidays are never in order. I am well aware how odd it must seem to some of you to hear me say that an idea is 'true' so long as to believe it is profitable to our lives. That it is GOOD, for as much as it profits, you will gladly admit. If what we do by its aid is good, you will allow the idea itself to be good in so far forth, for we are the better for possessing it. But is it not a strange misuse of the word 'truth,' you will say, to call ideas also 'true' for this reason?

To answer this difficulty fully is impossible at this stage of my account. You touch here upon the very central point of Messrs. Schiller's, Dewey's and my own doctrine of truth, which I cannot discuss with detail until my sixth lecture. Let me now say only this, that truth is ONE SPECIES OF GOOD, and not, as is usually supposed, a category distinct from good, and co-ordinate with it. THE TRUE IS THE NAME OF WHATEVER PROVES ITSELF TO BE GOOD IN THE WAY OF BELIEF, AND GOOD, TOO, FOR DEFINITE, ASSIGNABLE REASONS. Surely you must admit this, that if there were NO good for life in true ideas, or if the knowledge of them were positively disadvantageous and false ideas the only useful ones, then the current notion that truth is divine and precious, and its pursuit a duty, could never have grown up or become a dogma. In a world like that, our duty would be to SHUN truth, rather. But in this world, just as certain foods are not only agreeable to our taste, but good for our teeth, our stomach and our tissues; so certain ideas are not only agreeable to think about, or agreeable as supporting other ideas that we are fond of, but they are also helpful in life's practical struggles. If there be any life that it is really better we should lead, and if there be any idea which, if believed in, would help us to lead that life, then it would be really BETTER FOR US to believe in that idea, UNLESS, INDEED, BELIEF IN IT INCIDENTALLY CLASHED WITH OTHER GREATER VITAL BENEFITS.

'What would be better for us to believe'! This sounds very like a definition of truth. It comes very near to saying 'what we OUGHT to believe': and in THAT definition none of you would find any oddity. Ought we ever not to believe what it is BETTER FOR US to believe? And can we then keep the notion of what is better for us, and what is true for us, permanently apart?

Pragmatism says no, and I fully agree with her. Probably you also agree, so far as the abstract statement goes, but with a suspicion that if we practically did believe everything that made for good in our own personal lives, we should be found indulging all kinds of fancies about this world's affairs, and all kinds of sentimental superstitions about a world hereafter. Your suspicion here is undoubtedly well founded, and it is evident that something happens when you pass from the abstract to the concrete, that complicates the situation.

I said just now that what is better for us to believe is true UNLESS THE BELIEF INCIDENTALLY CLASHES WITH SOME OTHER VITAL BENEFIT. Now in real life what vital benefits is any particular belief of ours most liable to clash with? What indeed except the vital benefits yielded by OTHER BELIEFS when these prove incompatible with the first ones? In other words, the greatest enemy of any one of our truths may be the rest of our truths. Truths have once for all this desperate instinct of self-preservation and of desire to extinguish whatever contradicts them. My belief in the Absolute, based on the good it does me, must run the gauntlet of all my other beliefs. Grant that it may be true in giving me a moral holiday. Nevertheless, as I conceive it,—and let me speak now confidentially, as it were, and merely in my own private person,—it clashes with other truths of mine whose benefits I hate to give up on its account. It happens to be associated with a kind of logic of which I am the enemy, I find that it entangles me in metaphysical paradoxes that are inacceptable, etc., etc.. But as I have enough trouble in life already without adding the trouble of carrying these intellectual inconsistencies, I personally just give up the Absolute. I just TAKE my moral holidays; or else as a professional philosopher, I try to justify them by some other principle.

If I could restrict my notion of the Absolute to its bare holiday-giving value, it wouldn't clash with my other truths. But we cannot easily thus restrict our hypotheses. They carry supernumerary features, and these it is that clash so. My disbelief in the Absolute means then disbelief in those other supernumerary features, for I fully believe in the legitimacy of taking moral holidays.

You see by this what I meant when I called pragmatism a mediator and reconciler and said, borrowing the word from Papini, that he unstiffens our theories. She has in fact no prejudices whatever, no obstructive dogmas, no rigid canons of what shall count as proof. She is completely genial. She will entertain any hypothesis, she will consider any evidence. It follows that in the religious field she is at a great advantage both over positivistic empiricism, with its anti-theological bias, and over religious rationalism, with its exclusive interest in the remote, the noble, the simple, and the abstract in the way of conception.

In short, she widens the field of search for God. Rationalism sticks to logic and the empyrean. Empiricism sticks to the external senses. Pragmatism is willing to take anything, to follow either logic or the senses, and to count the humblest and most personal experiences. She will count mystical experiences if they have practical consequences. She will take a God who lives in the very dirt of private fact-if that should seem a likely place to find him.

Her only test of probable truth is what works best in the way of leading us, what fits every part of life best and combines with the collectivity of experience's demands, nothing being omitted. If theological ideas should do this, if the notion of God, in particular, should prove to do it, how could pragmatism possibly deny God's existence? She could see no meaning in treating as 'not true' a notion that was pragmatically so successful. What other kind of truth could there be, for her, than all this agreement with concrete reality?

In my last lecture I shall return again to the relations of pragmatism with religion. But you see already how democratic she is. Her manners are as various and flexible, her resources as rich and endless, and her conclusions as friendly as those of Mother Nature.

CHAPTER 14

Hannah Arendt

The Human Condition

T̲HE GERMAN-JEWISH PHILOSOPHER Hannah Arendt (1906–1975) was one of the most influential intellectuals of the twentieth century. She was an academically trained philosopher, but her work was influential outside of academia as well. She fled Germany for Paris in 1933 and then left Europe for New York in the early 1940s.

Arendt made important contributions to political philosophy, and she became quite infamous for her controversial claim that the high-ranking Nazi official Adolf Eichmann was not a malicious anti-Semite who wanted to exterminate the Jewish race, but rather just a loyal public servant who was doing his job by following the law of the land and carrying out executive orders. The kind of evil of which Eichmann was guilty was of the *banal* sort; he committed atrocious acts with monstrous efficiency and without any thought about the nature of the act itself—he was a bureaucrat doing his job well. This is perhaps an evil that we are all too familiar with: Families can be separated by immigration officials; people can die for lack of health insurance; and young adults can end up stuck in the prison system all because of a minor offense and a lack of adequate legal representation. These are examples of what Arendt calls "the banality of evil" because those responsible are simply carrying out a role just as they do every day. There is something perversely commonplace about evil being committed by people who have no particular investment in what makes the act so evil.

Important Concepts: Human nature; human condition; *vita activa*; labor; work; action

In the reading excerpted, Arendt explains her concept of the *vita activa*. With this concept, she is trying to name the fundamental conditions under which all human beings live. For Arendt, our lives are made up of *labor, work, and action*. *Labor* names all the basic biological conditions that make life possible, in particular, those that make our bodies. We eat and trillions of bacteria live in our digestive tract and help us extract the nutrients we need, we breathe, blood circulates through our body and feeds our cells, etc. Arendt thinks of *work* as an "unnatural" condition of our existence. *Work* makes our world into an artificial one, as opposed to the natural world. *Work* builds buildings, makes roads, fashions stone tools, and designs the internet. *Action* is a social and political aspect of human existence; as Arendt puts it, it "corresponds to the human condition of plurality, to the fact that men, not Man, live on the earth and inhabit the world." (189) *Action* thus names the fact we don't do anything alone, that we are always, inescapably, among other people. No one creates, discovers, builds, makes, or even conceives of anything alone since everything we do (all human action) is carried out in the context conditioned by others. Everything we do affects others, too. Even if we think we are making decisions that only affect ourselves, our very choices establish that such choices are possible for human life and so set a precedent for others.

It's useful to compare Arendt's notion of *action* to Marx and Engels' idea that capital is a *social* power. Recall that for them, capitalist society is always already socialist insofar as it is the whole of society that creates the conditions that make building capital possible in the first place. Rewarding the few, as is done under capitalism, is, in this way, simply an unjust way to distribute resources since it does not recognize the contributions of the whole of society. Under capitalism, everybody works, but a few reap all the rewards. Arendt is making a similar point and a more general point in that she wants to recognize that nothing can be done without the cooperation of others.

One thing Arendt wants to make clear in her discussion is that what she is calling "the human condition" is not to be confused as a definition of human nature. *Labor, work,* and *action* is not some kind of three-fold definition of human nature: "To avoid misunderstanding," she writes, "the human condition is not the same as human nature, and the sum total of human activities and capabilities which correspond to the human condition does not constitute anything like human nature." (191) In order to answer to the question of human nature, one would have to step outside of one's own humanity to be able to see human nature as a whole, something Arendt likens to stepping over one's own shadow. (191) Such a thing is impossible, which is why, as Arendt points out, definitions of human nature nearly always end up having to conceptualize some kind of deity in order to be able to be able to see human nature in its totality, account for all the conditions of its existence, etc.

But asking about the human condition is not the same thing. In exploring the human condition, Arendt wants to explore the "conditions of human existence." Thus, *labor, work,* and *action* name the conditions under which we exist in this world and on this planet. Notice how different this kind of question is. Humans are always conditioned in some way; that is, there are always conditions under which we exist in the way we do. We are born, we live in a world, we live with other people, and we live on the planet Earth. We can never get to any fundamental core of what it means to be a human being when we ask the question of the human condition since we can never get to a place where humans simply are what they are, without any external conditioning factors.

Thinking about this question in terms of human evolution is illuminating, and paleoanthropological data supports Arendt's thinking, here. Indeed, paleoanthropologists see the remains of the earliest anthropoids among stone tools and they see the beginning of a process of human and technological co-evolution. Humans do not evolve to a point where they are intelligent and resourceful enough to begin using tools and machines. Rather, the evidence suggests that human beings evolve the way we do *because* we use tools. It's intuitively tempting to think that we employ tools to make up for some kind of deficit. But this plays into the myth of some kind of original human nature, perfectly pure and natural, completely unconditioned by the world in which we live. As the French anthropologist André Leroi-Gourhan reflects on paleo-archaeological findings,

> Freedom of the hand almost necessarily implies a technical activity different from that of apes, and a hand that is free during locomotion, together with a short face and the absence of fangs, commands the use of artificial organs, that is, of implements. Erect posture, short face, free hand during locomotion, and possession of movable implements—those are truly the fundamental criteria of humanity.[1]

What it means to be human, then, seems to have more to do with the external conditions of human existence and especially with the capacities human have for engaging and interacting with the world than it does with some fundamental core of human nature. This is why Arendt is more interested in what conditions human existence than she is in any attempt to define human nature.

The Human Condition

Hannah Arendt

1 *VITA ACTIVA* AND THE HUMAN CONDITION

With the term *vita activa*, I propose to designate three fundamental human activities: labor, work, and action. They are fundamental because each corresponds to one of the basic conditions under which life on earth has been given to man.

Labor is the activity which corresponds to the biological process of the human body, whose spontaneous growth, metabolism, and eventual decay are bound to the vital necessities produced and fed into the life process by labor. The human condition of labor is life itself.

Work is the activity which corresponds to the unnaturalness of human existence, which is not imbedded in, and whose mortality is not compensated by, the species' ever-recurring life cycle. Work provides an "artificial" world of things, distinctly different from all natural surroundings. Within its borders each individual life is housed, while this world itself is meant to outlast and transcend them all. The human condition of work is worldliness.

Action, the only activity that goes on directly between men without the intermediary of things or matter, corresponds to the human condition of plurality, to the fact that men, not Man, live on the earth and inhabit the world. While all aspects of the human condition are somehow related to politics, this plurality is specifically *the* condition—not only the *conditio sine qua non*, but the *conditio per quam*—of all political life. Thus the language of the Romans, perhaps the most political people we have known, used the words "to live" and "to be among men" (*inter*

---

1   André Leroi-Gourhan, *Gesture and Speech*, trans. Anna Bostock Berger. (Cambridge, MA: MIT Press, 1993), 19.

homines esse) or "to die" and "to cease to be among men" (*inter homines esse de-si-ne-re*) as synonyms. But in its most elementary form, the human condition of action is implicit even in Genesis ("Male and female created He *them*"), if we understand that this story of man's creation is distinguished in principle from the one according to which God originally created Man (*adam*), "him" and not "them," so that the multitude of human beings becomes the result of multiplication.[2] Action would be an unnecessary luxury, a capricious interference with general laws of behavior, if men were endlessly reproducible repetitions of the same model, whose nature or essence was the same for all and as predictable as the nature or essence of any other thing. Plurality is the condition of human action because we are all the same, that is, human, in such a way that nobody is ever the same as anyone else who ever lived, lives, or will live.

All three activities and their corresponding conditions are intimately connected with the most general condition of human existence: birth and death, natality and mortality. Labor assures not only individual survival, but the life of the species. Work and its product, the human artifact, bestow a measure of permanence and durability upon the futility of mortal life and the fleeting character of human time. Action, in so far as it engages in founding and preserving political bodies, creates the condition for remembrance, that is, for history. Labor and work, as well as action, are also rooted in natality in so far as they have the task to provide and preserve the world for, to foresee and reckon with, the constant influx of newcomers who are born into the world as strangers. However, of the three, action has the closest connection with the human condition of natality; the new beginning inherent in birth can make itself felt in the world only because the newcomer possesses the capacity of beginning something anew, that is, of acting. In this sense of initiative, an element of action, and therefore of natality, is inherent in all human activities. Moreover, since action is the political activity par excellence, natality, and not mortality, may be the central category of political, as distinguished from metaphysical, thought.

The human condition comprehends more than the conditions under which life has been given to man. Men are conditioned beings because everything they come in contact with turns immediately into a condition of their existence. The world in which the *vita activa* spends itself consists of things produced by human activities; but the things that owe their existence

---

2   In the analysis of postclassical political thought, it is often quite illuminating to find out which of the two biblical versions of the creation story is cited. Thus it is highly characteristic of the difference between the teaching of Jesus of Nazareth and of Paul that Jesus, discussing the relationship between man and wife, refers to Genesis 1:27: "Have ye not read, that he which made *them* at the beginning made them male and female" (Matt. 19:4), whereas Paul on a similar occasion insists that the woman was created "of the man" and hence "for the man," even though he then somewhat attenuates the dependence: "neither is the man without the woman, neither the woman without the man" (I Cor. 11:8–12). The difference indicates much more than a different attitude to the role of woman. For Jesus, faith was closely related to action (cf. §33 below); for Paul, faith was primarily related to salvation. Especially interesting in this respect is Augustine (*De civitate Dei* xii. 21), who not only ignores Genesis 1:27 altogether but sees the difference between man and animal in that man was created *unum ac singulum*, whereas all animals were ordered "to come into being several at once" (*plura simul iussit exsistere*). To Augustine, the creation story offers a welcome opportunity to stress the species character of animal life as distinguished from the singularity of human existence.

exclusively to men nevertheless constantly condition their human makers. In addition to the conditions under which life is given to man on earth, and partly out of them, men constantly create their own, self-made conditions, which, their human origin and their variability notwithstanding, possess the same conditioning power as natural things. Whatever touches or enters into a sustained relationship with human life immediately assumes the character of a condition of human existence. This is why men, no matter what they do, are always conditioned beings. Whatever enters the human world of its own accord or is drawn into it by human effort becomes part of the human condition. The impact of the world's reality upon human existence is felt and received as a conditioning force. The objectivity of the world—its object- or thing-character—and the human condition supplement each other; because human existence is conditioned existence, it would be impossible without things, and things would be a heap of unrelated articles, a non-world, if they were not the conditioners of human existence.

To avoid misunderstanding: the human condition is not the same as human nature, and the sum total of human activities and capabilities which correspond to the human condition does not constitute anything like human nature. For neither those we discuss here nor those we leave out, like thought and reason, and not even the most meticulous enumeration of them all, constitute essential characteristics of human existence in the sense that without them this existence would no longer be human. The most radical change in the human condition we can imagine would be an emigration of men from the earth to some other planet. Such an event, no longer totally impossible, would imply that man would have to live under man-made conditions, radically different from those the earth offers him. Neither labor nor work nor action nor, indeed, thought as we know it would then make sense any longer. Yet even these hypothetical wanderers from the earth would still be human; but the only statement we could make regarding their "nature" is that they still are conditioned beings, even though their condition is now self-made to a considerable extent.

The problem of human nature, the Augustinian *quaestio mihi factus sum* ("a question have I become for myself"), seems unanswerable in both its individual psychological sense and its general philosophical sense. It is highly unlikely that we, who can know, determine, and define the natural essences of all things surrounding us, which we are not, should ever be able to do the same for ourselves—this would be like jumping over our own shadows. Moreover, nothing entitles us to assume that man has a nature or essence in the same sense as other things. In other words, if we have a nature or essence, then surely only a god could know and define it, and the first prerequisite would be that he be able to speak about a "who" as though it were a "what."[3] The perplexity is that the modes of human cognition applicable to things with "natural" qualities, including ourselves to the limited extent that we are specimens of the most highly developed

3   Augustine, who is usually credited with having been the first to raise the so-called anthropological question in philosophy, knew this quite well. He distinguishes between the questions of "Who am I?" and "What am I?" the first being directed by man at himself ("And I directed myself at myself and said to me: You, who are you? And I answered: A man"—*tu, quis es?* [*Confessiones* x. 6]) and the second being addressed to God ("What then am I, my God? What is my nature?"—*Quid ergo sum, Deus meus? Quae natura sum?* [x. 17]). For in the "great mystery," the *grande profundum,* which man is (iv. 14), there is "something of man [*aliquid hominis*] which

species of organic life, fail us when we raise the question: And *who* are we? This is why attempts to define human nature almost invariably end with some construction of a deity, that is, with the god of the philosophers, who, since Plato, has revealed himself upon closer inspection to be a kind of Platonic idea of man. Of course, to demask such philosophic concepts of the divine as conceptualizations of human capabilities and qualities is not a demonstration of, hot even an argument for, the non-existence of God; but the fact that attempts to define the nature of man lead so easily into an idea which definitely strikes us as "superhuman" and therefore is identified with the divine may cast suspicion upon the very concept of "human nature."

On the other hand, the conditions of human existence—life itself, natality and mortality, worldliness, plurality, and the earth—can never "explain" what we are or answer the question of who we are for the simple reason that they never condition us absolutely. This has always been the opinion of philosophy, in distinction from the sciences—anthropology, psychology, biology, etc.—which also concern themselves with man. But today we may almost say that we have demonstrated even scientifically that, though we live now, and probably always will, under the earth's conditions, we are not mere earth-bound creatures. Modern natural science owes its great triumphs to having looked upon and treated earth-bound nature from a truly universal viewpoint, that is, from an Archimedean standpoint taken, wilfully and explicitly, outside the earth.

2 THE TERM *VITA ACTIVA*

The term *vita activa* is loaded and overloaded with tradition. It is as old as (but not older than) our tradition of political thought. And this tradition, far from comprehending and conceptualizing all the political experiences of Western mankind, grew out of a specific historical constellation: the trial of Socrates and the conflict between the philosopher and the *polis*. It eliminated many experiences of an earlier past that were irrelevant to its immediate political purposes and proceeded until its end, in the work of Karl Marx, in a highly selective manner. The term itself, in medieval philosophy the standard translation of the Aristotelian *bios politikos*, already occurs in Augustine, where, as *vita negotiosa* or *actuosa*, it still reflects its original meaning: a life devoted to public-political matters.[4]

Aristotle distinguished three ways of life (*bioi*) which men might choose in freedom, that is, in full independence of the necessities of life and the relationships they originated. This prerequisite of freedom ruled out all ways of life chiefly devoted to keeping one's self alive—not

---

the spirit of man which is in him itself knoweth not. But Thou, Lord, who has made him [*fecisti eum*] knowest everything of him [*eius omnia*]" (x. 5). Thus, the most familiar of these phrases which I quoted in the text, the *quaestio mihi factus sum*, is a question raised in the presence of God, "in whose eyes I have become a question for myself" (x. 33). In brief, the answer to the question "Who am I?" is simply: "You are a man—whatever that may be"; and the answer to the question "What am I?" can be given only by God who made man. The question about the nature of man is no less a theological question than the question about the nature of God; both can be settled only within the framework of a divinely revealed answer.

4   See Augustine *De civitate Dei* xix. 2, 19.

only labor, which was the way of life of the slave, who was coerced by the necessity to stay alive and by the rule of his master, but also the working life of the free craftsman and the acquisitive life of the merchant. In short, it excluded everybody who involuntarily or voluntarily, for his whole life or temporarily, had lost the free disposition of his movements and activities.[5] The remaining three ways of life have in common that they were concerned with the "beautiful," that is, with things neither necessary nor merely useful: the life of enjoying bodily pleasures in which the beautiful, as it is given, is consumed; the life devoted to the matters of the *polis*, in which excellence produces beautiful deeds; and the life of the philosopher devoted to inquiry into, and contemplation of, things eternal, whose everlasting beauty can neither be brought about through the producing interference of man nor be changed through his consumption of them.[6]

The chief difference between the Aristotelian and the later medieval use of the term is that the *bios politikos* denoted explicitly only the realm of human affairs, stressing the action, *praxis*, needed to establish and sustain it. Neither labor nor work was considered to possess sufficient dignity to constitute a *bios* at all, an autonomous and authentically human way of life; since they served and produced what was necessary and useful, they could not be free, independent of human needs and wants.[7] That the political way of life escaped this verdict is due to the Greek understanding of *polis* life, which to them denoted a very special and freely chosen form of political organization and by no means just any form of action necessary to keep men together in an orderly fashion. Not that the Greeks or Aristotle were ignorant of the fact that human life always demands some form of political organization and that ruling over subjects might consti- tute a distinct way of life; but the despot's way of life, because it was "merely" a necessity, could not be considered free and had no relationship with the *bios politikos*.[8]

With the disappearance of the ancient city-state—Augustine seems to have been the last to know at least what it once meant to be a citizen—the term *vita activa* lost its specifically

---

5   William L. Westermann ("Between Slavery and Freedom," *American Historical Review,* Vol. L [1945]) holds that the "statement of Aristotle ... that craftsmen live in a condition of limited slavery meant that the artisan, when he made a work contract, disposed of two of the four elements of his free status [viz., of freedom of economic activity and right of unrestricted movement], but by his own volition and for a temporary period"; evidence quoted by Westermann shows that freedom was then understood to consist of "status, personal inviolability, freedom of economic activity, right of unrestricted movement," and slavery consequently "was the lack of these four attributes." Aristotle, in his enumeration of "ways of life" in the *Nicamachean Ethics* (i. 5) and the *Eudemian Ethics* (1215a35 if.), does not even mention a craftsman's way of life; to him it is obvious that a *banausos* is not free (cf. *Politics* 1337b5). He mentions, however, "the life of money-making" and rejects it because it too is "undertaken under compulsion" (*Nic. Eth.* 1096a5). That the criterion is freedom is stressed in the *Eudemian Ethics:* he enumerates only those lives that are chosen *ep' exousian.*
6   For the opposition of the beautiful to the necessary and the useful see *Politics* 1333a30 ff., 1332b32.
7   For the opposition of the free to the necessary and the useful see *ibid.* 1332b2.
8   See *ibid.* 1277b8 for the distinction between despotic rule and politics. For the argument that the life of the despot is not equal to the life of a free man because the former is concerned with "necessary things," see *ibid.* 1325a24.

political meaning and denoted all kinds of active engagement in the things of this world. To be sure, it does not follow that work and labor had risen in the hierarchy of human activities and were now equal in dignity with a life devoted to politics.[9] It was, rather, the other way round: action was now also reckoned among the necessities of earthly life, so that contemplation (the *bios theōrētikos*, translated into the *vita contemplativa*) was left as the only truly free way of life.[10]

However, the enormous superiority of contemplation over activity of any kind, action not excluded, is not Christian in origin. We find it in Plato's political philosophy, where the whole utopian reorganization of *polis* life is not only directed by the superior insight of the philosopher but has no aim other than to make possible the philosopher's way of life. Aristotle's very articulation of the different ways of life, in whose order the life of pleasure plays a minor role, is clearly guided by the ideal of contemplation (*theōria*). To the ancient freedom from the necessities of life and from compulsion by others, the philosophers added freedom and surcease from political activity (*skholē*),[11] so that the later Christian claim to be free from entanglement in worldly affairs, from all the business of this world, was preceded by and originated in the philosophic *apolitia* of late antiquity. What had been demanded only by the few was now considered to be a right of all.

The term *vita activa*, comprehending all human activities and defined from the viewpoint of the absolute quiet of contemplation, therefore corresponds more closely to the Greek *askholia* ("unquiet"), with which Aristotle designated all activity, than to the Greek *bios politikos*. As early as Aristotle the distinction between quiet and unquiet, between an almost breathless abstention from external physical movement and activity of every kind, is more decisive than the distinction between the political and the theoretical way of life, because it can eventually be found within each of the three ways of life. It is like the distinction between war and peace: just as war takes place for the sake of peace, thus every kind of activity, even the processes of mere thought, must culminate in the absolute quiet of contemplation.[12] Every movement, the movements of body and soul as well as of speech and reasoning, must cease before truth. Truth,

---

9 On the widespread opinion that the modern estimate of labor is Christian in origin, see below, § 44.

10 See Aquinas *Summa theologica* ii. 2. 179, esp. art. 2, where the *vita activa* arises out of the *nécessitas vitae praesentis,* and *Expositio in Psahnos* 45.3, where the body politic is assigned the task of finding all that is necessary for life: *in civitate oportet invenire omnia necessaria ad vitam.*

11 The Greek word *skholē,* like the Latin *otium,* means primarily freedom from political activity and not simply leisure time, although both words are also used to indicate freedom from labor and life's necessities. In any event, they always indicate a condition free from worries and cares. An excellent description of the everyday life of an ordinary Athenian citizen, who enjoys full freedom from labor and work, can be found in Fustel de Coulanges, *The Ancient City* (Anchor ed.; 1956), pp. 334–36; it will convince everybody how time-consuming political activity was under the conditions of the city-state. One can easily guess how full of worry this ordinary political life was if one remembers that Athenian law did not permit remaining neutral and punished those who did not want to take sides in factional strife with loss of citizenship.

12 See Aristotle *Politics* 133 3a30-3 3. Aquinas defines contemplation as *quies ab exterioribus motibus* (*Summa theologica* ii. 2. 179. 1).

be it the ancient truth of Being or the Christian truth of the living God, can reveal itself only in complete human stillness.[13]

Traditionally and up to the beginning of the modern age, the term *vita activa* never lost its negative connotation of "un-quiet," *nec-otium, a-skholia*. As such it remained intimately related to the even more fundamental Greek distinction between things that are by themselves whatever they are and things which owe their existence to man, between things that are *physei* and things that are *nomō*. The primacy of contemplation over activity rests on the conviction that no work of human hands can equal in beauty and truth the physical *kosmos*, which swings in itself in changeless eternity without any interference or assistance from outside, from man or god. This eternity discloses itself to mortal eyes only when all human movements and activities are at perfect rest. Compared with this attitude of quiet, all distinctions and articulations within the *vita activa* disappear. Seen from the viewpoint of contemplation, it does not matter what disturbs the necessary quiet, as long as it is disturbed.

Traditionally, therefore, the term *vita activa* receives its meaning from the *vita contemplativa*; its very restricted dignity is bestowed upon it because it serves the needs and wants of contemplation in a living body.[14] Christianity, with its belief in a hereafter whose joys announce themselves in the delights of contemplation,[15] conferred a religious sanction upon the abasement of the *vita activa* to its derivative, secondary position; but the determination of the order itself coincided with the very discovery of contemplation (*theōria*) as a human faculty, distinctly different from thought and reasoning, which occurred in the Socratic school and from then on has ruled metaphysical and political thought throughout our tradition.[16] It seems unnecessary to my present purpose to discuss the reasons for this tradition. Obviously they are deeper than the historical occasion which gave rise to the conflict between the *polis* and the philosopher and thereby, almost incidentally, also led to the discovery of contemplation as the philosopher's way of life. They must lie in an altogether different aspect of the human condition, whose diversity is not exhausted in the various articulations of the *vita activa* and, we may suspect, would not be exhausted even if thought and the movement of reasoning were included in it.

---

13   Aquinas stresses the stillness of the soul and recommends the *vita activa* because it exhausts and therefore "quietens interior passions" and prepares for contemplation (*Summa theologica* ii. 2. 182. 3).

14   Aquinas is quite explicit on the connection between the *vita activa* and the wants and needs of the human body which men and animals have in common (*Summa theologica* ii. 2. 182. 1).

15   Augustine speaks of the "burden" (*sarcina*) of active life imposed by the duty of charity, which would be unbearable without the "sweetness" (*suavitas*) and the "delight of truth" given in contemplation (*De civitate Dei* xix. 19).

16   The time-honored resentment of the philosopher against the human condition of having a body is not identical with the ancient contempt for the necessities of life; to be subject to necessity was only one aspect of bodily existence, and the body, once freed of this necessity, was capable of that pure appearance the Greeks called beauty. The philosophers since Plato added to the resentment of being forced by bodily wants the resentment of movement of any kind. It is because the philosopher lives in complete quiet that it is only his body which, according to Plato, inhabits the city. Here lies also the origin of the early reproach of busy- bodiness (*polypragmosynē*) leveled against those who spent their lives in politics.

If, therefore, the use of the term *vita activa*, as I propose it here, is in manifest contradiction to the tradition, it is because I doubt not the validity of the experience underlying the distinction but rather the hierarchical order inherent in it from its inception. This does not mean that I wish to contest or even to discuss, for that matter, the traditional concept of truth as revelation and therefore something essentially given to man, or that I prefer the modern age's pragmatic assertion that man can know only what he makes himself. My contention is simply that the enormous weight of contemplation in the traditional hierarchy has blurred the distinctions and articulations within the *vita activa* itself and that, appearances notwithstanding, this condition has not been changed essentially by the modern break with the tradition and the eventual reversal of its hierarchical order in Marx and Nietzsche. It lies in the very nature of the famous "turning upside down" of philosophic systems or currently accepted values, that is, in the nature of the operation itself, that the conceptual framework is left more or less intact.

The modern reversal shares with the traditional hierarchy the assumption that the same central human preoccupation must prevail in all activities of men, since without one comprehensive principle no order could be established. This assumption is not a matter of course, and my use of the term *vita activa* presupposes that the concern underlying all its activities is not the same as and is neither superior nor inferior to the central concern of the *vita contemplativa*.

3 ETERNITY VERSUS IMMORTALITY

That the various modes of active engagement in the things of this world, on one side, and pure thought culminating in contemplation, on the other, might correspond to two altogether different central human concerns has in one way or another been manifest ever since "the men of thought and the men of action began to take different paths,"[17] that is, since the rise of political thought in the Socratic school. However, when the philosophers discovered—and it is probable, though unprovable, that this discovery was made by Socrates himself—that the political realm did not as a matter of course provide for all of man's higher activities, they assumed at once, not that they had found something different in addition to what was already known, but that they had found a higher principle to replace the principle that ruled the *polis*. The shortest, albeit somewhat superficial, way to indicate these two different and to an extent even conflicting principles is to recall the distinction between immortality and eternity.

Immortality means endurance in time, deathless life on this earth and in this world as it was given, according to Greek understanding, to nature and the Olympian gods. Against this background of nature's ever-recurring life and the gods' deathless and ageless lives stood mortal men, the only mortals in an immortal but not eternal universe, confronted with the immortal

---

17   See F. M. Cornford, "Plato's Commonwealth," in *Unwritten Philosophy* (1950), p. 54: "The death of Pericles and the Peloponnesian War mark the moment when the men of thought and the men of action began to take different paths, destined to diverge more and more widely till the Stoic sage ceased to be a citizen of his own country and became a citizen of the universe."

lives of their gods but not under the rule of an eternal God. If we trust Herodotus, the difference between the two seems to have been striking to Greek self-understanding prior to the conceptual articulation of the philosophers, and therefore prior to the specifically Greek experiences of the eternal which underlie this articulation. Herodotus, discussing Asiatic forms of worship and beliefs in an invisible God, mentions explicitly that compared with this transcendent God (as we would say today) who is beyond time and life and the universe, the Greek gods are *anthrōpophyeis*, have the same nature, not simply the same shape, as man.[18] The Greeks' concern with immortality grew out of their experience of an immortal nature and immortal gods which together surrounded the individual lives of mortal men. Imbedded in a cosmos where everything was immortal, mortality became the hallmark of human existence. Men are "the mortals," the only mortal things in existence, because unlike animals they do not exist only as members of a species whose immortal life is guaranteed through procreation.[19] The mortality of men lies in the fact that individual life, with a recognizable life-story from birth to death, rises out of biological life. This individual life is distinguished from all other things by the rectilinear course of its movement, which, so to speak, cuts through the circular movement of biological life. This is mortality: to move along a rectilinear line in a universe where everything, if it moves at all, moves in a cyclical order.

The task and potential greatness of mortals lie in their ability to produce things—works and deeds and words[20]—which would deserve to be and, at least to a degree, are at home in everlastingness, so that through them mortals could find their place in a cosmos where everything is immortal except themselves. By their capacity for the immortal deed, by their ability to leave non-perishable traces behind, men, their individual mortality notwithstanding, attain an immortality of their own and prove themselves to be of a "divine" nature. The distinction between man and animal runs right through the human species itself: only the best (*aristoi*), who constantly prove themselves to be the best (*aristeuein*, a verb for which there is no equivalent in any other language) and who "prefer immortal fame to mortal things," are really human; the others, content with whatever pleasures nature will yield them, live and die like animals. This was still

---

18   Herodotus (i. 131), after reporting that the Persians have "no images of the gods, no temples nor altars, but consider these doings to be foolish," goes on to explain that this shows that they "do not believe, as the Greeks do, that the gods are *anthrōpophyeis*, of human nature," or, we may add, that gods and men have the same nature. See also Pindar *Carmina Nemaea* vi.

19   See Ps. Aristotle *Economics* 1343b24: Nature guarantees to the species their being forever through recurrence (*periodos*), but cannot guarantee such being forever to the individual. The same thought, "For living things, life is being," appears in *On the Soul* 415b1 3.

20   The Greek language does not distinguish between "works" and "deeds," but calls both *erga* if they are durable enough to last and great enough to be remembered. It is only when the philosophers, or rather the Sophists, began to draw their "endless distinctions" and to distinguish between making and acting (*poiein* and *prattein*) that the nouns *poiēmata* and *pragmata* received wider currency (see Plato's *Charmides* 163). Homer does not yet know the word *pragmata*, which in Plato (*ta tōn anthrōpōn pragmata*) is best rendered by "human affairs" and has the connotations of trouble and futility. In Herodotus *pragmata* can have the same connotation (cf., for instance, i. 155).

the opinion of Heraclitus,[21] an opinion whose equivalent one will find in hardly any philosopher after Socrates.

In our context it is of no great importance whether Socrates himself or Plato discovered the eternal as the true center of strictly metaphysical thought. It weighs heavily in favor of Socrates that he alone among the great thinkers—unique in this as in many other respects—never cared to write down his thoughts; for it is obvious that, no matter how concerned a thinker may be with eternity, the moment he sits down to write his thoughts he ceases to be concerned primarily with eternity and shifts his attention to leaving some trace of them. He has entered the *vita activa* and chosen its way of permanence and potential immortality. One thing is certain: it is only in Plato that concern with the eternal and the life of the philosopher are seen as inherently contradictory and in conflict with the striving for immortality, the way of life of the citizen, the *bios politikos*.

The philosopher's experience of the eternal, which to Plato was *arrhēton* ("unspeakable"), and to Aristotle *aneu logou* ("without word"), and which later was conceptualized in the paradoxical *nunc stans* ("the standing now"), can occur only outside the realm of human affairs and outside the plurality of men, as we know from the Cave parable in Plato's *Republic,* where the philosopher, having liberated himself from the fetters that bound him to his fellow men, leaves the cave in perfect "singularity," as it were, neither accompanied nor followed by others. Politically speaking, if to die is the same as "to cease to be among men," experience of the eternal is a kind of death, and the only thing that separates it from real death is that it is not final because no living creature can endure it for any length of time. And this is precisely what separates the *vita contemplativa* from the *vita activa* in medieval thought.[22] Yet it is decisive that the experience of the eternal, in contradistinction to that of the immortal, has no correspondence with and cannot be transformed into any activity whatsoever, since even the activity of thought, which goes on within one's self by means of words, is obviously not only inadequate to render it but would interrupt and ruin the experience itself.

Theōria, or "contemplation," is the word given to the experience of the eternal, as distinguished from all other attitudes, which at most may pertain to immortality. It may be that the philosophers' discovery of the eternal was helped by their very justified doubt of the chances of the *polis* for immortality or even permanence, and it may be that the shock of this discovery was so overwhelming that they could not but look down upon all striving for immortality as vanity and vainglory, certainly placing themselves thereby into open opposition to the ancient city-state and the religion which inspired it. However, the eventual victory of the concern with eternity over all kinds of aspirations toward immortality is not due to philosophic thought. The fall of the Roman Empire plainly demonstrated that no work of mortal hands can be immortal, and it was accompanied by the rise of the Christian gospel of an everlasting individual life to its position as the exclusive religion of Western mankind. Both together made any striving for an

---

21   Heraclitus, frag. B29 (Diels, *Fragmente der Vorsokratiker* [4th ed.; 1922]).

22   *In vita activa fixi permanere possumus; in contemplativa autem intenta mente manere nullo modo valemus* (Aquinas *Summa theologica* ii. 2. 181.4).

earthly immortality futile and unnecessary. And they succeeded so well in making the *vita activa* and the *bios politikos* the handmaidens of contemplation that not even the rise of the secular in the modern age and the concomitant reversal of the traditional hierarchy between action and contemplation sufficed to save from oblivion the striving for immortality which originally had been the spring and center of the *vita activa*.

CHAPTER 15

Cornel West

Democratic Responsibility

ORNEL WEST (1953–) is one of the most influential intellectuals living in America today. He has held academic appointments at some of the most prestigious institutions in the world such as Yale, Harvard, Princeton, University of Paris, and the Union Theological Seminary. West is now professor of the practice of public philosophy at Harvard University, where he holds joint appointments in the Department of African American Studies and in the Harvard Divinity School.

This last title is particularly appropriate since West is a *public* philosopher in the best sense of that title. Philosophers are, often fairly, criticized for either (a) working on issues that don't have any relevance outside of the academy, or (b) not making the effort to explain their work to people who would be interested but lack the academic training to be able to understand disciplinary jargon and technical terminology. In my opinion, this is a very serious problem for philosophy. Why would anyone ever want to study philosophy or be a philosopher unless they have a sense of what philosophers do and of what philosophy is about?

West offers us a powerful alternative to that trend in philosophy to remain hermetically sealed in disciplinary jargon, problems, and issues. West speaks to all people willing to listen, and his concerns are relevant for all of us. In addition to the groundbreaking books that launched his career and made him famous, *Race Matters* and *Democracy Matters*, West has a vibrant public speaking career, where he speaks in a manner that is very much free from academic jargon and formality, while remaining challenging, subtle, and sophisticated. West is also an accomplished artist and has released three spoken word albums, collaborated with people such as Prince and KRS-One, and won awards for his music and poetry. His ideas and his style are difficult, but you do not need any particular academic training to read, understand, and learn something from Cornel West. He is truly one of the most unique and challenging voices working in philosophy today.

Important Concepts: Democracy; responsibility; market versus nonmarket value

In the reading that follows, West addresses the question of the kind of responsibilities that citizens in a democracy have in and for that democracy. We have already read a selection from Thomas Hobbes, who offers an argument for why a person would sacrifice some of his or her natural freedom to live in a socially and politically organized state. There, the question is about what a society can do for its citizens, and I think that many people still tend to think in these terms of what a society can do for us—what do I get for my taxes? what does society offer me? But West turns this around and asks about what responsibilities we as citizens have *in and for* democracy and the democratic order. We cannot sit back, pay our taxes, and simply expect that we receive products and services in return. A society is not a business. A government is not running a business. And citizens are not customers! We owe something to our society, and we all need to work to maintain the social order.

West couches his discussion in the context of major issues of social injustice: the erosion of corporate responsibility, alarming increases in poverty, loss of economic stability despite unprecedented wealth and corporate profits. He wants us to understand these issues not as statistics, but rather as existential conditions that affect real people. He takes his lead here from the work of W.E.B. Du Bois, an African American author and equal rights activist from the early-mid twentieth century. Du Bois, West contends, "understood what it meant to be cast as part of a problem people rather than people with problems." (204) According to this analysis, African Americans are seen as a kind of homogeneous block and as a problem for society. For Du Bois and for other existentialist analyses, black people do not themselves have problems; rather, black people, as a people, are a problem for society. This is an indicator of the perverse way in which our society has tended to dehumanize its citizens and reduce people to statistics and problems rather than deal with the problems of people in a caring, nurturing, and loving way. We don't care about people; we try to solve social problems, and we let market forces dictate the extent to which we deal with social problems at all.

Today, we live in what West calls a "decadent" culture: We are living in a culture in decline, where we are experiencing "the relative erosion of system of nurturing and caring, which affects each of us, but which has an especially devastating impact on young people." (206) West makes a distinction between market and non-market value: "The ultimate logic of a market culture is the gangsterization of culture," West writes, "I want power now. I want pleasure now. I want property now. Your property. Give it to me." (206) West is writing this in 2001. Consider how this market culture has developed today, where our own government uses force and aggression to negotiate with other nations, where portions of the population are purposely pitted against one another for political gain, where people cannot access health care for lack of sufficient market value. West continues: "In our own time it is becoming extremely difficult for nonmarket values to gain a foothold. Parenting is a nonmarket value; so much sacrifice and service goes into it without any assurance that the providers will get anything back. Mercy, justice; they are nonmarket. Care, service; nonmarket. Solidarity, fidelity; nonmarket. Sweetness and kindness and gentleness. All nonmarket." (207) What place is left for these values today? What role do they play in policy decisions? West wants to push these kinds of questions. He wants to help us think about the nonmarket values that support and perpetuate the kind of society we want to live in and that we all say we value. Our *democratic responsibility* consists in holding on to these nonmarket values and demanding that they have continuing relevance in our society and to how important decisions are made.

The Moral Obligations of Living in a Democratic Society

Cornel West

One of the fundamental questions of our day is whether the tradition of struggle can be preserved and expanded. I refer to the struggle for decency and dignity, the struggle for freedom and democracy.

In *Tradition and Individual Talent* (1919), T. S. Eliot claims that tradition is not something you inherit—if you want it, you must sacrifice for it. In other words, tradition must be fought for.

We live at the end of a century of unprecedented brutality and barbarity, a period when more than two hundred million fellow human beings have been murdered in the name of some pernicious ideology. Nazism was at the heart of a so-called civilized Europe. Stalinism was at the core of a so-called emancipatory Soviet Union. European colonialism and imperialism in Africa, South America, and Asia have left palpable and lasting scars on fellow human beings. Patriarchal subordination of sisters of all colors and all regions and all countries is evident. The devaluation and degradation of gay brothers and lesbian sisters across race, region, and class, as well as the marginalization of the disabled and physically challenged.

What kind of species are we? What leads us to think that the tradition of struggle for decency and dignity can be preserved into the twenty-first century? Or will it be the case that we shall witness in the twenty-first century the unleashing of new, unnameable and indescribable forms of agony and anguish? At the moment, we are right to fear the emergence of ancient tribalisms that are revitalized under the aegis of an uncontested global capitalism, a movement accompanied by the "gangsterization" of community, nation, and the globe.

What attracts me to the Black-Jewish dialogue is the potential that is inherent to our respective traditions of struggle. It has nothing to do with skin pigmentation *per se,* nor with ethnicity in the abstract. Rather, it is because these two communities have developed a set of responses to combat the fundamental problem of evil.

The problem of evil refers to working out a response to undeserved suffering, unmerited pain, and unjustified harm. It is impossible to talk about Jews or Blacks, symbolically or literally, without discussing the problem of evil because these groups have been consistently devalued and subjugated, if not downright hated and despised. Indeed, the history of that treatment raises very alien dilemmas for America.

Henry James was correct when he declared America to be a "hotel civilization." In fact, this is the reason James left the country; he experienced American society as being too bland and culturally impoverished. At the turn of the twentieth century, America did not want to deal with the problem of evil, let alone the tragic and the comic—it was too preoccupied with the melodramatic and the sentimental.

A hotel—the fusion of a home and a market—is such a wonderful metaphor for America. The warmth, security, and motherhood of the home exists, as does that patriarchal tilt that burdens sisters of all colors, to caretake men who must forage in the marketplace. The men go forth into a heartless world, in a quest for mobility, liquidity, and profit-making. This fusion of home and market has its own distinct ethos: privatistic, individualistic, tribalistic, ethnic-centered, racially subscribed, distrustful of the nation-state, distrustful of bureaucracy, and marginalizing of public interest and the common good.

It is no coincidence then, that the best of the Jewish and Black traditions has consistently infused a sense of the tragic and the comic in order to expand the precious traditions of their struggle. In my own case, I began to struggle with the problem of evil by grappling with the absurd, the absurd in America and the absurd as America. I did not have to read a book by Jean-Paul Sartre or see a play by Samuel Beckett to understand what the absurd was. I had a black body in a civilization deeply shaped by white supremacist perceptions, sensibilities, and institutional practices. When something as irrational and arbitrary as skin pigmentation is the benchmark of measuring one's humanity, then that state of affairs is totally absurd.

What is distinctive about this precious experiment in democracy called America is that it has always been inextricably interwoven with white supremacy and its legacy. Although some scholars call it an irony, I call it a hypocrisy. John J. Chapman described it accurately when he concluded that white supremacy was like a serpent wrapped around the legs of the table upon which the Declaration of Independence was signed by the founding fathers. It haunted America then and nearly 220 years later it still does. The challenge for America today is whether it will continue to deny, evade, and avoid various forms of evil in its midst.

In any discussion about race matters it is vital to situate yourself in a tradition, in a larger narrative that links the past to the present. When we think of Sojourner Truth, Harriet Tubman, Ida Buelle, Wells Barnett, A. Philip Randolph, Marcus Garvey, Ella Baker, James Baldwin, and so many nameless and anonymous ones, we cannot but be moved by their standards of vision and courage. They are wind at one's back.

The recovery of a tradition always begins at the existential level, with the experience of what it is to be human under a specific set of circumstances and conditions. It is very difficult to engage in a candid and frank critical discussion about race by assuming it is going to be a rational exchange. Race must be addressed in a form that can deal with its complexity and irrationality.

Perhaps no one understood the existential dimension of being human and African in America better than W. E. B. Du Bois. He recognized the absurd in American society and realized that being Black in America is to be a problem. Du Bois asserted that race in this country is the fetishization of a problem, black bodies in white space. He understood what it meant to be cast as part of a problem people rather than people with problems. Once the humanity of a people is problematized, they are called into question perennially. Their beauty is attacked: wrong hips, lips, noses, skin texture, skin pigmentation, and hair texture. Black intelligence is always guilty before proven innocent in the court of the life of the mind; *The Bell Curve* is just a manifestation of the cycle. Perhaps the gravest injustice is the image of the welfare queen. Looking at the history of black women in America, on the plantation taking care of white children in white households, how is it possible that they could become the symbol of laziness? All of the foregoing are signs of a humanity that has been problematized.

Du Bois also underscored that to be part of a problem people is to be viewed as part of an undifferentiated blob, a monolithic block. Problem people become indistinguishable and interchangeable, which means that only one of them has to be asked to find out what all the rest of them think.

It is rare in human history, of course, that the notion of individuality and the civic are coupled so that a democratic project is generated. For most of history ordinary people have been viewed as "weeds and rain drops," as part of a mob, a rabble, all of which are ways of constituting them as an undifferentiated mob. Even the Greeks, despite their glorious yet truncated democratic experiment, would only apply the tragic to the elite. Ordinary people were limited to the idyllic and the comic, the assumption being that their lives were less complex and one-dimensional.

A democratic sensibility undeniably cuts against the grain of history. Most of human history is the history of elites, of kings, queens, princes, prelates, magistrates, potentates, knights, earls, and squires, all of whom subordinated and exploited everyday people.

This is why it becomes vital to talk about prevailing forms of oligarchy and plutocracy, and to some degree "pigmentocracy," in America. One percent of the population owns 48 percent of the total net financial wealth. The top 10 percent owns 86 percent of the wealth, while the top 20 percent owns 94 percent of the wealth. Meanwhile, 80 percent of the our population is experiencing stagnating and declining wages.

Corporations speak glibly about downsizing—bureaucratic language that simply means you do not have a job even though we have the highest profits we have had since 1948. And yet 25 percent of all of America's children live in poverty, and 42 percent of young brown brothers and sisters live in poverty, and 51 percent of young black brothers and sisters live in poverty in the richest nation in the history of the world. These sets of conditions are immoral.

When I examine the present state of American democracy, I believe we are living in one of the most terrifying moments in the history of this nation. We are experiencing a lethal and unprecedented linkage of relative economic decline (i.e., working class wage stagnation), cultural decay, and political lethargy. No democracy can survive with a middle class so insecure that it is willing to accept any authoritarian option in order to provide some sense of normalcy and security in their lives. It also opens the door for significant segments of that middle class to scapegoat those who are most vulnerable.

It is past time that we consider in our public discourse the civic responsibilities of corporations. There must be prescribed forms of public accountability for institutions that have a disproportionate amount of wealth, power, and influence. This is not a matter of demonizing corporations, but an issue of democratic survival.

We are all in the same boat, on the same turbulent sea. The boat has a huge leak in it and in the end, we go up and down together. A corporate executive recently said to me, "We are not in the same boat. We're global." His response suggests why it is vital to inquire when corporate commercial interests must be subordinate to the public interest.

Democracy always raises the fundamental question: What is the role of the most disadvantaged in relation to the public interest? It is similar in some ways to the biblical question: What are you to do with the least of these? If we do not want to live in a democracy, we are not obliged to raise that question. In fact, the aristocracy does not address that question at all. Chekhov wrote in a play, "The Czar's police, they don't give a damn about raising that question. That's not the kind of society they are." But within a democratic society that question must be continually raised and pushed.

The conversation matters because the preservation of democracy is threatened by real economic decline. While it is not identical to moral and cultural decay, it is inseparable from it. Even though the pocketbook is important, many Americans are concerned more about the low quality of their lives, the constant fear of violent assault and cruel insult, the mean spiritedness and cold heartedness of social life, and the inability to experience deep levels of intimacy. These are the signs of a culturally decadent civilization.

By "decadent" I mean the relative erosion of systems of nurturing and caring, which affects each of us, but which has an especially devastating impact on young people. Any civilization that is unable to sustain its networks of caring and nurturing will generate enough anger and aggression to make communication near impossible. The result is a society in which we do not even respect each other enough to listen to each other. Dialogue is the lifeblood of democracy and is predicated on certain bonds of trust and respect. At this moment of cultural decay, it is difficult to find places where those ties of sympathy may be nurtured.

The roots of democracy are fundamentally grounded in mutual respect, personal responsibility, and social accountability. Yet democracy is also about giving each person a dignified voice in the decision-making processes in those institutions that guide and regulate their lives. These deeply moral suppositions have a certain spiritual dimension. John Dewey and Josiah Royce, among others, identified a spirituality of genuine questioning and dialogical exchange that allows us to transcend our egocentric predicaments. Spirituality requires an experience of something bigger than our individual selves that binds us to a community. It could be in an authoritarian bind, of course, which is why the kind of spiritual and moral awakening that is necessary for a democracy to function is based on a sense of the public—a sense of what it is to be a citizen among citizens.

Nurturing spirituality is so difficult today because we are bombarded by a market culture that evolves around buying and selling, promoting and advertising. The market tries to convince us that we are really alive only when we are addicted to stimulation and titillation. Given the fact that so much of American culture revolves around sexual foreplay and orgiastic intensity, for many people the good life might mean being hooked up to an orgasm machine and being perennially titillated.

The ultimate logic of a market culture is the gangsterization of culture: I want power now. I want pleasure now. I want property now. Your property. Give it to me.

Young black people call their block a "hood" now. I grew up in a neighborhood; it is a big difference. A neighborhood was a place not only for the nuclear family, but also included aunts and uncles, friends and neighbors, rabbis and priests, deacons and pastors, Little League coaches and dance teachers—all of whom served as a backdrop for socializing young people. This backdrop provided children with a sense of what it is to be human, with all its decency, integrity, and compassion. When those values are practiced, a neighborhood emerges.

Unfortunately, neighborhoods often took shape in my boyhood under patriarchal and homophobic conditions, and that history must be called into question. Still, we must recover its flow of nonmarket values and nonmarket activity.

These days we cannot even talk about love the way James Baldwin and Martin Luther King Jr. did. Nobody wants to hear that syrupy, mushy stuff. James Baldwin, however, said love is the most dangerous discourse in the world. It is daring and difficult because it makes you vulnerable, but if you experience it, it is the peak of human existence.

In our own time it is becoming extremely difficult for nonmarket values to gain a foothold. Parenting is a nonmarket activity; so much sacrifice and service goes into it without any assurance that the providers will get anything back. Mercy, justice; they are nonmarket. Care, service; nonmarket. Solidarity, fidelity; nonmarket. Sweetness and kindness and gentleness. All nonmarket.

Tragically, nonmarket values are relatively scarce, which is one of the reasons why it is so tough to mobilize and organize people in our society around just about any cause. It is hard to convince people that there are alternative options for which they ought to sacrifice. Ultimately, there can be no democratic tradition without nonmarket values.

In the last decade we have witnessed within popular culture wonderful innovation in forms of hip hop and rap. Compare that phenomenon to the 1960s when the Black Panther Party emerged and note the big difference between the two movements. One has to do with sacrifice, paying the price, dealing with the consequences as you bring power and pressure to bear on the prevailing status quo. The other has to do with marketing black rage. One movement had forty-seven local branches across the nation, the other sells millions of albums and CDs. The comparison is not a matter of patronizing this generation. Frankly, it is a critique of each us who has to deal with this market culture and through market mechanisms try to preserve some nonmarket values.

What then are we to do? There is no overnight solution or panacea, of course. We need to begin with something profoundly un-American, namely, recalling a sense of history, a very deep, tragic, and comic sense of history, a historical sensibility linked to empathy. Empathy is not simply a matter of trying to imagine what others are going through, but having the will to muster enough courage to do something about it. In a way, empathy is predicated upon hope.

Hope has nothing to do with optimism. I am in no way optimistic about America, nor am I optimistic about the plight of the human species on this globe. There is simply not enough evidence that allows me to infer that things are going to get better. That has been the perennial state and condition of not simply black people in America, but all self-conscious human beings who are sensitive to the forms of evil around them. We can be prisoners of hope even as we call optimism into question.

To be part of the democratic tradition is to be a prisoner of hope. And you cannot be a prisoner of hope without engaging in a form of struggle in the present moment that keeps the best of the past alive. To engage in that struggle means that one is always willing to acknowledge that there is no triumph around the corner, but that you persist because you believe it is right and just and moral. As T. S. Eliot said, "Ours is in the trying. The rest is not our business."

We are not going to save each other, ourselves, America, or the world. But we certainly can leave it a little bit better. As my grandmother used to say, "If the Kingdom of God is within you, then everywhere you go, you ought to leave a little Heaven behind."

CPSIA information can be obtained
at www.ICGtesting.com
Printed in the USA
LVHW060900020822
724902LV00005B/43